# Liberation in Print

# Liberation in Print

FEMINIST PERIODICALS AND
SOCIAL MOVEMENT IDENTITY

Agatha Beins

The University of Georgia Press

ATHENS

Chapter 4 appeared previously in somewhat different form as "Sisterly Solidarity: Politics and Rhetoric of the Direct Address in U.S. Feminism in the 1970s," in *Women: A Cultural Review* 21 (3) (2010): 293–308. Chapter 5 appeared previously in somewhat different form as "Radical Others: Women of Color and Revolutionary Feminism," in *Feminist Studies* 41 (1) (2015): 150–83.

© 2017 by the University of Georgia Press
Athens, Georgia 30602
www.ugapress.org
All rights reserved
Set in 10/13 Kepler Std by Graphic Composition, Inc.

Most University of Georgia Press titles are
available from popular e-book vendors.

Printed digitally

Library of Congress Cataloging-in-Publication Data

Names: Beins, Agatha, 1976– author.
Title: Liberation in print : feminist periodicals and social movement
    identity / Agatha Beins.
Description: Athens : University of Georgia Press, [2017] | Series: Since
    1970: Histories of contemporary America | Includes bibliographical
    references and index.
Identifiers: LCCN 2016055426 | ISBN 9780820349510 (hardback : alk.
    paper) | ISBN 9780820349534 (pbk. : alk. paper) | ISBN 9780820349527
    (ebook)
Subjects: LCSH: Feminism—United States—History—20th century. |
    Feminism and mass media—United States—History—20th century. |
    Feminism—Press coverage—United States—History—20th century. |
    Women's rights—Press coverage—United States—History—20th
    century. | Women's mass media—United States—History—20th
    century.
Classification: LCC HQ1421 .B445 2017 | DDC 305.420973/0904—dc23
    LC record available at https://lccn.loc.gov/2016055426

# CONTENTS

ILLUSTRATIONS

# ACKNOWLEDGMENTS

It began with a moment I can't precisely remember, but I know that it happened: a friend gave me a zine that her friend had given her. It began with a family that filled our living spaces with books. It began when a teacher encouraged me to write. It began in 1968 with the first issue of *Voice of the Women's Liberation Movement*. It began with the abolitionist newspaper *The Liberator* and with Emma Goldman's *Mother Earth*. It began with a mimeograph machine.

More moments and more people than I can list, remember, count, or even know have carved the path of this book. I wish I had written down the names of all the archivists, student workers, volunteers, and other staff at the libraries and archives I visited. And I wish I could recognize all the people who chronicled 1970s feminism because they mimeographed a page of a newsletter, wrote an article, glued address labels on newspapers for bulk mailing, or supported a periodical with their subscription. How grateful I am as well for those activists who decided to hold onto a piece of paper, a folder, or boxes of ephemera that eventually ended up in an archive. Your imprints texture, strengthen, and haunt this book. It exists because of you.

It is thus with great joy that I can trace a map that locates some of the people and places that enriched this story of U.S. feminism and have allowed me to tell it. First, without the materials of feminism's histories, I could not have pursued the project. In addition to the Lesbian Herstory Archives, where I held my first feminist newspaper from the 1970s, I spent time at the Arthur and Elizabeth Schlesinger Library on the History of Women in America at Radcliffe; the Du Bois Library archives at the University of Massachusetts, Amherst; the Chicano Studies Research Center at UCLA; the University Archives at California State University, Long Beach; the Iowa Women's Archives at the University of Iowa; the Nadine Vorhoff Library and Newcomb College Institute at Tulane University; the Northeastern University Archives; the Southern California Library in Los Angeles; the Sophia Smith Collection at Smith College; the Sallie Bingham Center for Women's History and Culture at Duke University; the Center for the Study of Political Graphics in Los Angeles; the Joseph P. Healey Library archives at the University of Massachusetts, Boston; the New Orleans Public Library; and the Woman's Collection at Texas Woman's University. Generous funding from the Sallie Bingham Center, Schlesinger Library, Sophia Smith Collection, Vorhoff Library, State Historical Society of Iowa, Historical Society of California, Texas Woman's University, and American Association of University Women granted me the time and money for this research. Fellowships and other support from the Institute for Research on Women at Rutgers, the Rutgers Center for Historical Analysis, and a Schlesinger Library summer seminar, Sequels to the 1960s, allowed me to be part of rich, challenging conversations and to receive feedback that deepened my thinking about U.S. feminist histories.

During my travels and graduate work I had the good fortune to encounter activists, scholars, and scholar-activists who shared their wisdom and memories with me: Joyce Berkman, Marisela Chavez-Garcia, Mary Gehman, Judy Gerson, Sherna Berger Gluck, Mary Hawkesworth, Jill Jack, Karla Miller, Sandy Pickup, Aaron Silander, and Sandra Smith. There are also a few folks in archives and libraries who made me feel especially welcome, including Kimberly Johnson, Kären Mason, Bethany Ross, Desiree Yael Vester, Janet Weaver, and Nanci Young. And Maxine Wolfe, your profound commitment to preserving lesbian lives is a model for the refusal to separate theory and practice and makes the power of the archive palpable.

As editors of the series this book joins, Claire Potter and Renee Romano have guided me so wisely and expertly—and with great patience—through revisions and re-revisions and re-re-revisions. Thank you for seeing value in this project. Thank you, as well, to the anonymous outside readers who pushed me to sharpen my ideas with their insightful and thoughtful responses to the manuscript. I also have great appreciation for Mick Gusinde-Duffy for believing in my vision of the manuscript. Beth Snead, John D. Joerschke, and Ellen Goldlust deserve much gratitude for their assistance with all the big and small mechanisms of book production.

Since my first forays into underground publications, I have encountered many brilliant thinkers and mentors. Before I could have imagined this book, Caryl Flinn, Miranda Joseph, and Sandy Soto sharpened my thinking about underground and activist publishing as they worked with me on my master's thesis about zines. Bravely facing the untamed wilderness of early chapter drafts, Harriet Davidson, Joanna Regulska, and Trysh Travis offered invaluable guidance for my dissertation. And I offer deep gratitude to Judy Tzu-Chun Wu, who took seriously the ideas of a novice scholar whom she'd barely met, reading and supporting my work like it mattered. And I am a better writer because of the way I learned to treat words with care and wonder while Jonathan Johnson advised me during my master of fine arts in poetry. But, foremost, I am indebted to Nancy Hewitt and Elizabeth Lapovsky Kennedy. Liz brought me into the feminist fold when I was a new and naive master's student at the University of Arizona and shared with me the labors of editing an anthology, a gift for which my gratitude continues to grow. Nancy agreed to serve as my dissertation committee chair when I had only nebulous ideas about feminist periodicals. Even the most superlative thanks only partially convey my gratitude for the way her feedback helped me craft the first version of this book. I so admire the way both of you have modeled accountable scholarship, and I hope to follow in your footsteps.

I am fortunate to have the inspiration of the teaching, writing, and research of wonderful colleagues: Özlem Altiok, Rosemary Candelario, Jessica Gullion, Raina Joines, Rick Joines, Sandra Mendiola Garcia, Megan Morrissey, Chad Pearson, Whitney Peoples, Jennifer Jensen Wallach, and Mike Wise. More recently, the Dallas Area Social Historians provided a lively venue where I could present my ideas and connect with a thoughtful intellectual community. The frequency of our writing group waxes and wanes, but I am continually thankful that I can reach out to Anahi, Ashley, Steph, and Stina for feedback on works in progress and to talk through the sometimes knotty politics of academia. It is wonderful that the National Women's Studies Association conference reconnected me with Anne and Jessica thirteen years after we took our first class together in the fall of 2003 so that I could continue to learn from them.

My home department has a palpable impact on my intellectual life, and I am especially grateful to have worked with AnaLouise Keating, Mark Kessler, Jillian Morales, Gail Orlando, Danielle Phillips, and Claire Sahlin: because of you all, I look forward to going to work.

This web of support crosses many state lines and spheres of my life. A list of names is, like an iceberg, only the tip and incommensurate with the beauty you've brought to my travels: Allison Miller, Amanda Austin, Andy Mazzaschi, Ben Arenger, Bhavin Patel, Brandon Babbitt, Brandon Young, Christy Tronnier, Courtney Jacobs, Doug Campbell, Elaine Hess, Emily White, Finn Kolsrud, Karl Gossot, Liz and Elliot Hammer, Remington Pohlmeyer, Sarah Vaughn, Tristan Bynum, Yashna Maya Padamsee, and Zug Thompson. The serenity and joy that I find in Denton's Saturday morning tai chi group keeps me grounded and reminds me to be present: thank you to Jude, Linda, Ling Hwey, and Pip. And Julie Winnette, John Plevock, and Susan Paz—your welcoming energy, which includes early morning rides to the airport, cat care, and wise advice, makes Denton feel like home.

Happily, some folks move through multiple parts of my life and enrich it endlessly—in their astute ways of seeing the world, generosity and kindness, delightful company, fierce intellect, and commitments to justice. How lucky I am to have celebrated joyful moments with you, and how you have sustained me through the difficult ones: Allison Miller, Christopher Johnson, Clark Pomerleau, Heike Schotten, Janinne Milazzo, Laurie Marhoefer, Minnie Chiu, Stephanie Clare, Stephen Vider, Steve Kidder, and Sue Tyczinski. Among these lovely people, Julie Enszer stands out as an inestimable friend, collaborator, and coconspirator whose ability to write justice into this world continually astounds me. I can't wait to get started on our next project.

Mom, Dad, and Simon—you're the best. Sharing a life with you has allowed me to see the world with openness and curiosity. Jenny, how lucky I am that you've become part of this family, and how joyful it's been to get to know Evie and Julian with you and Simon. Thank you for your radiant creativity, generosity, love of learning, corny jokes, and boundless love, which leave me (nearly) speechless and have made me a better human being.

# Liberation in Print

# Origins and Reproductions

In the spring of 1971, the Hadley, Massachusetts, *Valley Review* sent a reporter to the Valley Women's Center (VWC) for a piece on the local women's movement. The reporter described her arrival at the center in detail:

> A small, inconspicuous sign, fastened to the door, invites the visitor inwards and upwards. I went in, climbed the stairs, passing a second floor beauty shop, and found the first of three rooms that serve as the Valley Women's Center office. The walls are painted a pristine white, with the exception of a handsome purple one at the far end of the room, and are liberally covered with bulletin boards, posters, and women's liberation stickers of various sizes and persuasions. A gaily colored davenport sits in front of a low black table; here too lie stacks of pamphlets, newsletters and communications from other women's groups around the country.[1]

Indicating the VWC's palpable presence in the community, a few months later another article appeared, this one in the *Smith Alumnae Quarterly*.[2] Seven photographs accompany it; almost all of them include what I presume to be the "handsome purple wall" covered in posters. A photograph on the first page caught my eye as I was doing research in the Sophia Smith Collection in 2009.[3] In the foreground a woman with long blond hair stands by a magazine rack filled with various ephemera, while the posters in the background demand peace, gender equality, freedom for Angela Davis, and reproductive rights. One celebrates August 26, 1970, the fiftieth anniversary of the passage of the Nineteenth Amendment granting women's suffrage. Another retells the creation story depicted in Michelangelo's *The Creation of Adam* by replacing God and Adam with female figures and adding the caption, "And god created woman in her own image." Still another proclaims, "The women's liberation movement is gonna get your mama . . . and your sister, and your girlfriend."

A little left of center, a poster shows a figure raising her left arm, fist clenched. The photograph's blurry background makes the details difficult to discern, but the figure it depicts and the accompanying text would have been familiar to feminists across the country at the time because it portrays Sojourner Truth, whose likeness appeared widely in 1970s feminist print culture. With a jolt of surprise, I realized that I had seen this image while reading issues of *Ain't I a Woman?*, a feminist newspaper from Iowa City. It was the front cover of the first issue of that paper, published in June 1970, portraying Truth with her familiar spectacles, white Quaker-style cap, and white collar. Unlike the usual representations, the dominant feature in the image is Truth's raised left arm, which frames text from the iconic "Ain't I a Woman?" speech she gave at the 1851 Akron, Ohio, Women's Rights Convention. Just as the newspaper's editors had found this image striking enough for the cover of their first issue, someone at the Valley Women's Center had been moved to affix the cover to the wall as a symbol of the center's feminist politics.

The richness of that moment in the archive has continued to reverberate for me, becoming an important point of origin for my project. The newspaper links two small, rural cities and very visibly signifies the way periodicals propagated connections, creating a web of political and social relationships that held together the women's liberation movement.[4] Small feminist collectives such as those in Iowa City and Northampton emerged throughout the country, seemingly spontaneously and independent of other local feminist groups and national organizations. Many developed through consciousness-raising groups and study groups, often meeting in members' homes or in borrowed community spaces in the late 1960s and early 1970s, before women's centers became prevalent. As Robin Morgan wrote in *Sisterhood Is Powerful*, "This is not a movement one 'joins.' There are no rigid structures or membership cards."[5] Consequently, networks formed idiosyncratically, and information traveled unpredictably, so periodicals were especially important mechanisms for creating and sustaining communication among feminists throughout the United States.

Thirty years after the women's liberation movement's formative moments, I first encountered one of those periodicals. In the spring of 2002, I was working on a master's thesis about zines and started to wonder what feminist underground print media had preceded those raucous, brash publications. I followed a path through the library catalog to microfilm reels of four different periodicals: *Ain't I a Woman?*, *off our backs*, *Rat*, and *It Ain't Me, Babe*. The bulky microfilm machine imposed thin horizontal lines on the pages and added a darker hue to everything, causing words and images to lose some of their detail. I printed out a few issues of each periodical and, as a financially challenged graduate student, tried to maximize the amount of information and minimize cost by condensing each periodical page to a letter-sized format, further distorting its content.

Five years later, I looked again at these printouts while preparing an application for a seminar sponsored by the Institute for Research on Women at Rutgers University. As I struggled to parse the text and decipher these copies of copies, I realized that I was likely missing part of the story these periodicals told. The Lesbian Herstory Archives in Brooklyn, New York, holds a number of feminist periodicals in its collection, so I planned a visit. One of the volunteers there led me to the second floor of the brownstone building in Park Slope, climbing stairs that creaked as only thick slabs of old wood do. I ran my hand over the smooth railing, imagining the women who had done so before me. Upstairs I found shelves full of periodicals, including the four I'd looked at in Tucson.

After clearing off a table in a room ringed by file cabinets, I opened the first box and was astonished. The microfilmed pages and their printouts had not prepared me for this encounter. Their size, the fragile newsprint, the dust tickling my nose, the photographs whose subjects suddenly became clear, the fact that I could no longer take in a single page with one glance, the way turning the pages brought the scent of musty paper—the experience was a sensory revelation. I cannot offer empirical certainties about the cognitive or semiotic effect of the differences between viewing the periodicals on the microfilm reader, as printouts on 8½" × 11" paper, and in newsprint, but the feeling of this difference has lingered, emphasizing the affective components of our textual encounters.

As touchstones I return to these experiences in the archive, reminded that for the women writing, editing, and reading them, periodicals served a number of different purposes: circulating information, building and reinforcing networks, creating an imagined community of feminists, articulating theories, and telling women's stories. The publications constituted sites where readers formed relationships with the women's liberation movement. For historians and researchers, these publications enliven and animate feminism in that moment: angry, explosive analyses of injustice; joyful celebrations of sisterhood; women's intimate reflections on their lives; editorials and announcements that detail the gritty struggles and labors of feminist organizing on the ground. Encountering the movement through periodicals, I, like so many women in the 1970s, hungered for more. Though their desires surely differed from mine, readers articulated their joy at feeling connected to feminism. Lee Walker began a letter to *Sister*, a Los Angeles newspaper, by proclaiming, "The religion issue of Sister is a holy marvel. It is sacred to me. Enclosed is my subscription check for a whole year."[6] Echoing the importance of these publications, Jo Sullivan wrote to the Cambridge, Massachusetts, group Female Liberation, "Dear Sisters, I DO want to continue getting the Newsletter. The contact and exchange is necessary for our action and sanity. I am a full-time graduate student so I don't have much money, but I really want to see it keep going."[7] And Nancy Savage told editors of New Orleans–based *Distaff*, "I was absolutely delighted by Susan Burns' article regarding the use of the word 'hon.' For many years I have waged what I thought was a one-woman campaign against this demeaning term."[8] Thousands of other women were moved to write similar letters, indicating that periodicals mattered not only because they provided information but also because they gave women a feeling of connection to others in a larger struggle.

From the hundreds of feminist periodicals published in the 1970s, I selected five to form the basis of this study: *Ain't I a Woman?* (Iowa City, 1970–74), *Distaff* (New Orleans, 1972–74, 1974–75, 1979–82), *Female Liberation Newsletter* (Cambridge, Massachusetts, 1970–74), *L.A. Women's Liberation Newsletter* (1970–72; later *Women's Center Newsletter* [fall 1972] and *Sister* [1973–79]), and the *Valley Women's Center Newsletter* (Northampton, Massachusetts, 1971–77). As the titles suggest, some are newsletters (mimeographed on letter- or legal-size bond paper), while some are newspapers (published through offset printing on newsprint). None of the periodicals had a single area of focus; rather, all are "multiissue" publications, reporting on feminism more broadly.[9] All also contain a mixture of textual genres: editorials; announcements; information about resources and services; advertisements; journalistic articles written by local women, copied from alternative news services such as the Liberation News Service and KNOW, Inc., or reprinted from both feminist and other print media; opinion pieces; calls to action; creative writing; photographs; drawings; letters from readers; comics; and informative pieces such as instructions for how to fix a record player.[10] Periodicals, therefore, provided women with information about different kinds of events and actions—study groups, public protests, letter writing, volunteer opportunities, film screenings, and classes, among many others. Each issue contained pieces from a variety of contributors, providing diversity in authorship, styles of writing, and viewpoints.[11] The periodicals thus featured a striking polyvocality and multitextuality that manifested feminism kaleidoscopically and presented more "objective" and descriptive pieces alongside more "subjective" and personal ones.

As serials, these five periodicals offer hundreds of different primary sources—myriad moments in which the women's liberation movement comes into focus as an assemblage of people, actions, texts, relationships, values, emotions, discourses, and materials. On the one hand, the breadth of this textual archive illuminates variation in feminism: different communities experienced sexism, racism, classism, homophobia, and other injustices uniquely because of their distinct geographic, historical, economic, social, demographic, and political characteristics. On the other hand, patterns emerged from my research. Certain words, phrases, and rhetorical tropes repeated. Certain political issues received coverage. Certain publishing practices predominated. Such patterns indicate that which held more powerful symbolism for feminists and point to one mechanism through which ideas became ideals in the women's liberation movement. Repetition was one of the primary devices through which the term *feminism* solidified as a collective identity for women's liberation activists, and periodicals are particularly useful for identifying and analyzing this process. They capture the dominant narratives that stabilized feminism and honor the dynamic qualities of identity formation as well as the heterogeneity of feminism in the 1970s.

In *The Fantasy of Feminist History*, Joan Wallach Scott argues that while historians have productively destabilized the homogeneity of identity categories, their studies have focused primarily on identity as a product rather than on the process of its formation. This work has "left aside questions about how identity was established, how women with vastly different agendas identified with one another across time and social positions." She continues, "What were the mechanisms of such collective and retrospective identification? How do these mechanisms operate?"[12] For Scott, fantasy—as structured through a psychoanalytic lens—proves useful for examining how subjects have come to see themselves as similar to and different from others across time and place. I take up Scott's probing questions from the perspective of feminist print culture—more specifically, feminist periodicals.

Feminism constitutes an accumulation of repeated discursive tropes that are performative, semiotic, and affective. Judith Butler's theory of performativity suggests that repetition causes characteristics to appear as if they are a natural and inevitable part of an identity category, creating the illusion that no other way of being, thinking, or doing exists. For example, the apparent ubiquity of sisterhood in all sorts of feminist media and cultural products made this concept inextricable from the women's liberation movement, as I discuss in chapter 4. Sara Ahmed describes another effect of repetition when she writes, "If a word is used in a certain way, again and again, then that 'use' *becomes* intrinsic."[13] For her, semiotic stickiness explains how concepts gain certain meanings at the expense of and in tension with others. Through repetition, some connotations tend to adhere, whereas others weaken or disappear.[14] Ahmed also demonstrates that emotion intertwines with meaning: "Signs increase in affective value as an effect of the movement between signs: the more signs circulate, the more affective they become."[15] Similarly, Victoria Hesford argues that repetition of rhetorical devices has produced an "'affective economy' in which particular objects . . . and figures circulated in the press coverage and worked to shape certain emotional responses to the movement."[16] In other words, repetition enables both semiotic and affective stickiness: when a sign circulates in a similar form and there is consistency in its connotations, both meaning and feeling accumulate and are affirmed.

However, a signifier is never repeated verbatim, which, for Butler, offers a method for resisting the hegemony of norms. This ontological instability—"the possibility of a failure to repeat"—makes transformation possible because individuals have the opportunity to "do" gender differently, to resignify "man" or "woman."[17] The possibility of repetition with a difference reveals gender's incoherence and disrupts the apparent naturalness of its existence, questioning not only the givenness of the traits associated with femininity or masculinity but also the givenness of the category itself. Repetition therefore allows us to investigate both the robustness and the plasticity of the narratives that frame our identities. While repetition reifies certain values as central or peripheral to feminism, individual instantiations of an idea and representations of a feminist issue did not always mirror the dominant discourses, demonstrating that norms are not only potentially hegemonic but also heterogeneous.

Following Margaret R. Somers, I avoid "categorical rigidities by emphasizing the embeddedness of identity in overlapping networks of relations that shift over time and space."[18] At the same time, I recognize that for an identity to be meaningful, it needs to maintain some coherence through space and time. Periodicals allow us to see the patterns—the overarching discourses—that became central to feminism by identifying which tropes stuck with feminism as the decade passed. However, periodicals also served as a disruptive force: a concept may be repeated, but variation in meaning can mark its iterations. This dialectic between consistency and difference tells an important story about how activists at different sites imagined and embodied feminism as a movement, allowing us to better understand one mechanism through which collective identity forms. Attention to repetition as a method therefore reveals consistency and variation in conceptions of feminism and suggests that some of these norms may have gained such power in the movement precisely because they were semiotically spacious: they could encompass and even encourage different interpretations that suited the needs of local communities and individuals without losing the core of their significance.

### Women's Liberation and Activist Print Cultures

The year 1968 represented a watershed for political activism. Throughout the world—in France, Mexico, Germany, the United States—students mobilized to protest the educational system, imperialism, capitalism, and social inequalities. This year also serves as one point of origin for the U.S. women's liberation movement because of public and publicly staged events. Widespread coverage of the 1968 Miss America Pageant protest in Atlantic City, New Jersey, has caused this event to be consistently evoked as catalyzing the movement.[19] But 1968 also brought the Jeannette Rankin Brigade's march in Washington, D.C., to protest U.S. imperialism in Vietnam and the first national Women's

Liberation Conferences in Illinois and Maryland. And activists would have found the first issues of feminist periodicals arriving in their mailboxes or through their local feminist groups: *Voice of the Women's Liberation Movement* appeared in Chicago that spring, then *No More Fun and Games* from Cambridge, and *Lilith* from Seattle.[20] The ripple effect of large-scale demonstrations and the early publications caused hundreds of women to seek out feminism, and the movement gained momentum, leading up to 1970, the year that both Bonnie J. Dow and Victoria Hesford identify as a "turning point."[21]

Through continued large protests and mass demonstrations, provocative zap actions, guerrilla performances, and other spectacular occupations of public space, feminism gained unprecedented visibility in 1970. Great numbers of women participated in events, such as the August 26 Women's Strike for Equality, which commemorated the fiftieth anniversary of the passage of the Nineteenth Amendment. In ninety cities across forty-two states, women organized marches and protests, public art projects, teach-ins, vigils, and re-creations of the suffragists' picket lines; an estimated ten to fifteen thousand women participated in New York City alone.[22] Also making feminism visible on a national scale, the National Organization for Women (NOW), the Women's Equity Action League, the National Association for the Repeal of Abortion Laws, and other groups had been established. They drew thousands of women to feminism but did not translate into a movement governed by the structure and ideology emanating from a single national organization. Although NOW provided a vital contingent of women who targeted legal, political, and cultural institutions and who shaped feminist activism throughout the country, neither the multitude of small groups that formed the bulk of the women's liberation movement nor the local NOW chapters themselves— which numbered more than 350 by 1973—consistently mirrored the group's structure or political message.[23]

A closer look at feminist activism on a local scale reveals that much of the women's liberation movement in the 1970s was decentralized, idiosyncratic, and informal, with many small groups emerging, shifting, and disbanding unpredictably.[24] These large-scale occupations of public space and national organizations therefore did not represent what the majority of feminists were doing and how they were doing it. Rather, as Jo Freeman described at the time, "The thousands of sister chapters around the country are virtually independent of one another, linked only by numerous publications, personal correspondence, and cross-country travelers. They form and dissolve at such a rate that no one can keep track of them. With time and growth the informal communication networks have partially stratified along functional lines, so that a within a single city participants of, say, a feminist health clinic, will know less of different groups in their own area than other health clinics in different cities."[25] Freeman's words offer us a glimpse of the dynamics that influenced the structure, politics, relationships, and practices of the incipient women's liberation movement. Freeman emphasizes the importance of communication networks. Without the overarching presence of a national organization, publications did the important work of connecting individuals and groups, sharing information, and creating an informal structure for the "thousands of sister chapters" that made up much of the women's liberation movement. A 1971 editorial from *Women: A Journal of Liberation* explained, "An important part of the women's liberation movement has been the many publications that have emerged from the struggle. They have been key in providing an exchanges of ideas and bringing new women into the movement."[26] Therefore, the role of periodicals in creating and sustaining an imagined community for feminism should not be underestimated: they allowed readers to see themselves as part of a much larger entity and to make connections with women on a local scale.[27]

A handful of these publications began appearing in 1968; by 1969, according to Martha Allen, 25 had been created. Despite this somewhat slow start, a distinct feminist print culture mushroomed over the next half decade, with more than 85 new feminist periodicals appearing in 1970 and the number of such publications topping 550 three years later.[28] Barbara Godard has estimated that around 300 feminist periodicals have been published in Canada since the 1960s, and at least some of them circulated in the United States, just as U.S. feminist media spread northward.[29] Produced by hundreds of small groups, newspapers and newsletters became a common type of feminist text in the early 1970s. In fact, Eileen Cadman, Gail Chester, and Agnes Pivot describe local newsletters and newspapers published in England during the 1970s as "the most typical women's liberation publications," an observation that holds true for the United States as well.[30] As offset printing replaced linotype printing in the 1960s and 1970s and as mimeograph machines became more affordable, even those who lacked money or technical expertise could publish periodicals.

Mimeograph machines in particular contributed to the growth of feminist print culture, although they have long since been eclipsed by more modern technologies. Female Liberation, for example, announced in its February 21, 1972, newsletter that its mimeograph machine had run one million pieces of paper. "No small part of this million," they explained, "comes from the Newsletter. In fact, the Newsletter accounts for about 5,000 sheets a week."[31] According to Charlotte Bunch, the "first large purchase" made by the women's liberation group in Washington, D.C., was a mimeograph machine, demonstrating the technology's centrality to the group's activism.[32] By mimeographing their own publications, women's liberation groups achieved a high level of control over their publications' contents, avoiding the time, labor, cost, and ideological compromises potentially involved in putting out a book or a for-profit periodical.[33] The proliferation of feminist periodicals in the 1970s illustrates the ease with which such publications could be produced.[34]

Other kinds of ephemera, books, posters, academic journals, and creative writing also spread feminism across the nation, and a feminist infrastructure emerged in concert with and in support of such endeavors.[35] A growing literature highlights many of these projects, which encompassed groups and businesses working at all points in a text's life cycle—feminist printers (the Iowa City Women's Press, Naiad Press [Tallahassee, Florida], Lollipop Power Press [Chapel Hill, North Carolina]); feminist bookstores (explored in Kristen Hogan's work); and distribution and information dissemination services (Pittsburgh's KNOW, Inc., Carol Seajay's *Feminist Bookstore News*, Women in Distribution [in the Washington, D.C., area]). Beginning in 1976, Women in Print Conferences reinforced this feminist print culture by bringing together activists in all these areas.[36]

The periodicals I examine were written and edited primarily by white women, as evidenced by the photographs that appeared in periodicals or were preserved in organizational records. As a result, my analysis continues to center the perspective of white women and potentially bolsters the narrative that such women bore most of the responsibility for activism countering gender oppression. Even when pieces by women of color were included, white-identified women likely chose to publish those works (though editors and contributors often were not named). Nevertheless, these five periodicals, as well as the dozens of others I read in the archives, complicate whiteness, illustrating the heterogeneity of white women's lives. They also did not shy away from grappling with the intersectional, interlocking forces that shaped women's oppression and frequently pushed readers to confront the realities of racism. Though the periodicals' antiracist, anti-imperialist work is noteworthy, writing about the Vietnam War, Angela Davis, or the sterilization of American Indian women without their consent did not necessarily mean that these white women worked to build coalitions across difference or actively resisted their race privilege.

Moreover, the publications explicitly associated with the women's liberation movement developed in conversation with and alongside a strong print culture connected with radical communities of color. According to Kimberly Springer, the National Black Feminist Organization, the National Alliance of Black Feminists, Black Women Organized for Action, and the Third World Women's Alliance put out serial publications during the 1970s.[37] In particular, the Third World Women's Alliance published at least eighteen issues of its newspaper, *Triple Jeopardy*, between 1971 and 1975 as well as small educational booklets with such titles as *Black Women's History* (1978), *Asian Women's History* (n.d.), and *Combat Liberalism* (1976) that offered more in-depth and nuanced explorations than they could present in the pages of *Triple Jeopardy*.[38]

Another group that Springer studied, the Combahee River Collective, did not publish periodicals, but some of its members, among them Barbara Smith and Cheryl Clarke, profoundly affected activist print cultures with their writing, and the group's "A Black Feminist Statement" (1978) has been reprinted and anthologized extensively. In addition, Toni Cade Bambara's 1970 edited collection, *The Black Woman*, provided much-needed analyses of sexism, racism, and classism. Though the collection is not an ephemeral publication, many of the contributions are reprints of items that originally appeared in periodicals.

Other women of color took up the tools of production to publish periodicals. Southern California was a hub for Chicana political and textual activity. The Chicana Service Action Center published a regular newsletter from 1973 to 1977, while the Comisión Femenil de Los Angeles did so from 1973 to 1989. Las Hijas de Cuauhtémoc, a group at California State University, Long Beach, put out a few issues of a periodical in the early 1970s before some members started a more formal publication, *Encuentro Femenil*. In addition, a San Francisco–based group, Concilio Mujeres, published *La Razon Mestiza*.[39] I encountered fewer gender-focused periodicals from Asian American groups, though the Asian Women's Center in Los Angeles published a newsletter in the early 1970s, and a group of Berkeley students began publishing *Asian Woman's Journal* in 1971.[40] And despite a less visible print culture in certain groups of women of color, publications from U.S. Third World communities — the Black Panthers, the Brown Berets, Chicano nationalist groups, the Red Guard, and student groups on college campuses — show clear evidence of women contributing as activists and writers. Elizabeth Sutherland Martínez, for example, edited a radical Chicano newspaper, *El Grito del Norte*, between 1968 and 1973.[41]

## Methodology

As serial, multiissue publications, periodicals illuminate patterns in the representation of feminism, and I use these patterns to trace a map of the movement. To create such a map, I conduct close readings of periodicals by considering how they are part of a broader intertextual dialogue that forms across space and time. As Jonathan Gray points out, we read a text "not only in the sense of moving temporally and spatially *through* a text, but also in the sense of reading *via* other texts. . . . Other texts are always there with us as we work through a text."[42] The intertextuality characterizing these periodicals resulted in part from the range of different women who contributed, causing what Kathryn Thoms Flannery calls "a cacophony of ideas [that] may at times seem self-canceling or contradictory"; as a consequence, these publications "perform a riot of variations rather than a consistency of positioning."[43] Not only does a single issue contain a potential "riot of variations," a single page can do so as well. In these publications, a piece about a local film festival could appear next to an announcement about an upcoming election and in the same issue as a page full of poetry, a graphic of a woman with her fist raised in a Black Power salute, and an editorial requesting help putting out the newsletter. Therefore, my analysis considers text and imagery along with the other items on each page and the rest of the issue in which the article appears. Yet discourses outside a particular article or image shape its meaning: a single issue is in conversation with previous issues and anticipates future ones, and other feminist media and mainstream media also come into play.

Maylei Blackwell's approach to U.S. Chicana feminist activism has inspired my method. She argues for telling histories through the "gaps, interstices, silences, and crevices of the uneven narratives of domination," a process that results in "possibilities . . . for fracturing dominant narratives and creating spaces for new historical subjects to emerge." Her method entails not just making a record of the voices that have been subjugated but also attending to the way stories are told, listening for "the gestures, tones, and sighs—the literal performance of memory, how narrators rock themselves when they talk of difficult memories, how we stop the tape when tears flow."[44] The oral histories Blackwell conducted allowed her to gather knowledge based on verbal flourishes, nonverbal cues, and halting speech, all of which can be difficult if not impossible to translate to paper. I have thus adapted Blackwell's process for a different kind of archive.[45] Written texts are also performative, conveying some of what Blackwell attributes to her conversations with Chicana activists, and so I read feminist periodicals in a way that makes space for the embodied knowledge Blackwell sees in interviews to become visible.[46] For example, an editor's plea for volunteers to put together the newsletter is a gesture that adds context to the misnumbered pages or typographical errors in an issue. Could an ellipsis be like a sigh? Do the hand-sketched additions to a masthead indicate a moment of excitement in the production process? Scholars most often cite articles from feminist newsletters because of the topics they explore, so these traces of the production process—of those laboring bodies—effectively become silenced. We are likely to read around, over, and through them and not to read them *as* content. While I do not attribute a fixed meaning to these marks, I analyze them as an integral part of periodicals, practicing what Blackwell artfully describes as listening for "the non-dominant groove in the song."[47] And in an attempt to honor these moments in discourse, I have transcribed quotations from these publications without correcting (mis)spellings or typographical errors such as missing words.[48]

This analysis ultimately draws from a range of fields, including nineteenth- and twentieth-century history, social movement theories of collective identity and framing, geography, cultural studies, and visual studies as well as feminist theories about power, economy, and identity. These literatures are tied together by the history of the book, an interdisciplinary area of study that explores the cultural, discursive, and material facets of print communication and provides a framework that accounts for the content of text, its physical properties, and the processes through which it was published. Outlining his approach to a "study of written culture," book historian Roger Chartier begins with the refusal "to separate the analysis of symbolic meanings from that of the material forms by which they are transmitted."[49]

One of the most influential models for analyzing the life cycle of a printed text is Robert Darnton's communications circuit, which has helped me envision the relationships among the different stages in producing feminist periodicals and has provided a vocabulary for my analysis of their life cycles. This circuit encompasses the various phases of textual production and consumption by naming the figures who participate in it: authors, publishers, printers, shippers, booksellers, and readers. Darnton also recognizes that a text exists within a broader publishing context comprising "intellectual influences and publicity," "economic and social conjuncture," and "political and legal sanctions."[50] Of course, models almost inevitably impose order onto messiness, oversimplify how components interact, and highlight some aspects at the expense of others. Book historians and print culture scholars have critiqued Darnton's communications circuit and offered alternative paradigms that also have shaped my analyses. Thomas Adams and Nicolas Barker shift the focus from roles to functions in their circuit (for example, using *publication* rather than *publisher*), which creates space for different people to work on one process and for one person to work on multiple processes.[51] In my analysis of feminist periodicals, history of the book scholarship is more ghostly than palpable, but it nonetheless provides a foundation for my methodology. In particular, my focus on editorial and authorial practices in chapter 3 has been influenced by the way book historians situate the discursive and cultural significance of printed texts within the modes of their production. And I presume that how a print text came into being affects how a reader interacts with it, a presumption that is reflected in my attention to periodicals as material objects and as products of material processes.

According to Alberto Melucci, collective identity is an effect of the cognition, relationships, and emotions through which actors develop a shared discourse to frame their political values, objectives, allies, and opponents.[52] Also emphasizing the multifaceted process of identifying with a larger group, Francesca Polletta and James Jasper define collective identity as "an individual's cognitive, emotional, and moral connection with a broader community, category, practice, or institution. It is a perception of a shared status or relation, which may be imagined rather than experienced directly, and it is distinct from personal identities, although it may form part of a personal identity."[53] Dorothy Holland, Gretchen Fox, and Vinci Daro describe collective identity as a "realm of interpretation and action generated by participants of a movement through their shared activities and commitments that imagines the terrain of struggle, the powers of opponents, and the possibilities of a changed world."[54] These conceptualizations reinforce collective identity as a relationship that develops between an individual and a larger community. On the one hand, such relationships are discursive: discourses act as frames that shape the range of meanings available for a particular identity and allow activists to establish distinctions between *us* and *them*.[55] While a collective identity exists as an ongoing discursive process, it requires a material existence. This materiality manifests in the form of action: Holland, Fox, and Daro cite "shared activities" as a component of identity formation, and Melucci shows that social movement actors have incorporated organizational practices and structures into their sense of self.[56] Moreover, the ideas, ideals, values, and politics of a social movement must be objectified, even if, as is often the case now, those manifestations occur through virtual media.

Recent trends in social movement theories also emphasize collective identity as an effect of the feelings that accompany participation and nonparticipation. Extending into affective realms, identity is more than merely a name or category, the cognitive recognition of a commonality, or the effect of a logical assessment of the costs and benefits of joining with a certain group.[57] As Polletta and Jasper ask, "Why not simply admit the emotional satisfactions of collective identity?"[58] We create ties with others because of the way we feel around them, the emotions a name—like feminism—evokes, the joy of working toward particular goals, and the anger and disgust accompanying what we perceive as injustice. The "click" women cited as a moment of transformation reflects a cognitive as well as affective shift—a moment when the world gained new significance.[59] This letter to the *L.A. Women's Liberation Newsletter* indicates how these periodicals brought both information and joy: "Dear Sisters, . . . The newsletter is definitely wonderful—informative, and interesting and it always cheers me up a lot to know that somewhere other people are working too."[60]

After chapter 1 situates the five periodicals within the media landscape of the early 1970s and within their particular locational contexts, chapter 2 explores the places of and spaces for feminism. To identify with a social movement or a collective identity, people first must come into contact with the movement, and periodicals enabled people to find feminism in the late 1960s and early 1970s. They not only conveyed where feminism was happening in the local community but also offered glimpses of how women throughout the world were resisting gender-based injustices, enabling readers to see themselves as part of a larger imagined community of activists. This chapter makes one more analytical move, examining place and space through a temporal dimension. As serial publications, periodicals allow us to track spaces and places through time, which illuminates how feminist places were created, changed, and maintained as well as how they may have ended.

Whereas chapter 2 asks where, chapter 3 asks how. On a local level, women collaborated to publish newsletters, and these modes of periodical production illuminate how women understood feminism as a collective identity because periodical editors attempted not just to create a feminist product but also to create it in a feminist way. Decisions about content, form, and format; structure of the editorial group; where and how the group worked; and the publication schedule all manifest feminist ideals. A prominent feature of the feminist periodicals I study is the visibility of publishing process in the finished product—in editorials, brief notes and announcements, and features about the publication itself. Readers would have encountered these messages about what constitutes a feminist publishing practice, and the repetition of these messages cements them as part of a feminist political identity. In particular, this chapter investigates collectivity as a concept that informed feminist publishing through the way editors attempted to manifest their political ideals in their practices.

Chapter 4 analyzes the discourse of sisterhood. The term frequently becomes symbolic of a universal commonality among women as a consequence of either biological or social essentialism. However, a close look at the forms and instances of its repetition in feminist periodicals shows that this discourse both implied solidarity among women and presumed that it was not a fait accompli. I focus on the way *sister* was used in direct address to show that when periodicals hailed readers, they did not necessarily presume to be speaking to a homogeneous group of women who were always and already sisters. While my analysis reinforces the centrality of sisterhood to feminism as a collective identity, my close reading of direct address complicates the dominant denotation of sisterhood in feminist politics and shows that its meaning was not monolithic.

Chapter 5 explores affective aspects of identity formation by analyzing the representations of women of color as revolutionary freedom fighters. When placed within a larger context comprising mainstream media and New Left discourses, images and text depicting women of color indicate the ways that discourses are inflected by feeling. Those outside women's liberation treated feminism as trivial and diminutive, as concerned with petty issues, and as countering the efforts of "real" activist projects (such as the antiwar movement), so the fierce presence of women warriors—spanning the globe and extending back into history—served more than a denotative function and was not merely an uncritical deployment of universal sisterhood. Rather, these revolutionary bodies symbolized anger about injustice and a commitment to changing the world that spurred U.S. women to action. This chapter thus demonstrates that the visual and discursive tropes in the depictions of women of color countered not only sexism but also the implicit racism in dominant narratives characterizing the women's liberation movement. These tropes, through their repetition, reveal the interplay of ideology, politics, and affect in feminist collective identity formation.

The conclusion uses periodicals to rethink the historiography of late twentieth-century U.S. feminism and explores two broader implications of my methodology. Constructing history through print culture allows me to interrupt the conventional wave narrative used to historicize feminism and interrogate the epistemological relationship between our primary sources and the histories they tell. Periodicals offer important insights into feminism that might not be gleaned from more formally published texts, oral histories, or other ephemera. In addition, because print culture can illuminate similarities and differences in a social movement across time, and because social movements generally incorporate and use texts, my methodology has applications for the study of a social movement's development across space and time.

# CHAPTER 1

# Printing Feminism

In August 1971, the *L.A. Women's Liberation Newsletter* announced that women would be taking over the *Los Angeles Free Press* for an issue:

> The Free Press belongs to women! (For the Aug. 27 issue). The women on the staff of the Free Press will have total control of editorial policy. They will have women covering the news and will feature articles of special interest to women.
>
> They need artists, photographers, and writers. Here's your opportunity to get published and paid for it!
>
> Aug. 20 is the deadline. Contact Sue Marshall at YES 1970 if you have something to contribute.[1]

As promised, the August 28–September 3 edition of the *Free Press* featured contributions from women and was produced by women, though the following week the paper returned to business as usual. The preceding fall, the women who worked on Atlanta's *Great Speckled Bird* had made a similar move: as Becky Hamilton wrote in the paper's October 1970 issue, "The men were editors and business people (i.e., circulation, keeping the books, understanding the finances). That left typing for women. Women fought for control of layout, which was the one creative outlet allowed to women." As a result of these practices, women on the paper formed a caucus, and out of the group's first meetings "(not at all confined to *Bird* women) came an idea for a 'women's issue' of the *Bird*. We would prove ourselves to the men. We would write, type, layout—everything."[2] Earlier that year, perhaps the most visible example of such a feminist occupation of New Left media had occurred: in January 1970, a coalition of New York City women activists had seized the production apparatus for *Rat*, an alternative paper whose male-dominated editorial crew was just as likely to print images of nude or seminude female figures as to print articles about feminist activism. The first feminist issue of the paper, published in February 1970 under the title *LibeRATion*, indicted these sexist politics with Robin Morgan's "Goodbye to All That," which declared, "If men return to reinstate the porny photos, the sexist comic strips, the 'nude chickie' covers (along with their patronizing rhetoric about being in favor of Women's Liberation)—if that happens, then our alternatives are clear. *Rat* must be taken over permanently by women—or *Rat* must be destroyed."[3]

Although feminists were much more likely to start their own publications than take over existing ones, these actions hint at the broader media landscape of the late 1960s and early 1970s, when feminist periodicals began to emerge. Two main forces catalyzed the upsurge in feminist periodical publishing. First, mainstream periodicals were becoming more corporatized: the number of daily publications decreased, ownership of periodicals consolidated, and control of these publications remained primarily with white men. Martha Allen has described the media industry of the late 1960s as run by local monopolies, leaving most Americans "no choice in their local printed news, since 97 percent of all cities with daily newspapers had only one company printing the news."[4] Social movement groups across the nation thus took textual production into their own hands, and feminist publishing became part of a diverse media counterpublic that covered events and issues that mainstream, for-profit news outlets marginalized and distorted.[5] The *Valley Women's Center Newsletter* acknowledged these omissions when it printed a December 1972 letter from the Los Angeles Feminist Women's Health Center, which was engaged in legal battles regarding self-help health classes it offered: "We want to keep everyone informed of the deliberations and events inside and outside of the courtroom. As we all know, the straight media does not offer us any means with which to do this. So . . . we have decided to have our own 'feminist press' to cover this event. Everyday after court, we will return to the Health Center to transcribe the day's activities. WE WANT THE WORD TO BE SPREAD!"[6] Similarly, Brenda Davillier, a New Orleans woman who ran for the U.S. Senate in 1972, discussed her difficulties working with mainstream media in *Distaff*'s January 1973 issue: "The worst thing was that the media refused to take me seriously. When I called a news conference, few reporters came, and the coverage they gave me quoted statements out of context and didn't give me a fair chance for rebuttal. Channel 4, for example, showed me saying I was a mother and that I cooked for my family myself, because I couldn't afford a maid, but they didn't give one second of time to air my views on the important political issues that the campaign was about."[7] And one of the earliest issues of a Minneapolis publication, *Female Liberation*, explained that it would "print anything submitted by any woman": "We feel that since women are not allowed real access to the media, a female paper is important to give women this opportunity. It is a space where women can express themselves and not be ignored."[8] Moreover, the New Left, despite its aggressive critiques of mainstream media and other centers of power, did not necessarily extend its politics to include a thoughtful representation of feminism.[9] *Voice of the Women's Liberation Movement*, often recognized as the first women's liberation periodical of the 1970s, bestowed its March 1968 Male Chauvinist of the Month Award on Warren Hinckle III, editor of the left-wing magazine *Ramparts*.[10]

As a response to the "dildo journalism" of the New Left, some feminists attempted to bring change to the "straight media" itself, staging protests such as a well-publicized March 1970 sit-in at the *Ladies' Home Journal* office and filing lawsuits against *Newsweek* for its discriminatory hiring practices.[11] Other women, like those at the *Los Angeles Free Press*, the *Great Speckled Bird*, and *Rat*, mutinied, demanding that New Left and underground media put into practice their rhetoric regarding social justice and participatory democracy. The five periodicals I examine, however, represent a break with both industries rather than a direct engagement with them and circulated primarily within existing feminist communities.

Nevertheless, these feminist periodicals both form part of the long history of alternative and underground media and pushed back against it. Dissidents turned to ephemera in their activism long before the 1960s, producing materials not only as a response to the dominant narratives in mainstream media but also as a way to, in the words of Black Panther Huey P. Newton, "produce new values, new identities [and] mold a new and essentially human culture."[12] The category of alternative and underground publications could thus be seen to include such disparate media as seventeenth-century pamphlets from the American Revolution, the little magazines that published avant-garde material in the late nineteenth and early twentieth centuries, and the zines of the late twentieth century. Robert J. Glessing identifies the *New England Courant*, published in the 1720s by James Franklin (with contributions from his younger brother, Benjamin), as the first underground paper in the United States because it used humor to challenge certain accepted ways of thinking.[13] More than a century later, abolitionist papers such as the *North Star* and *The Liberator* publicized the perspectives of those who lacked access to the dominant media outlets. Socialist, communist, and anarchist newspapers (for example, *The Firebrand*, *Appeal to Reason*, and the *Daily Worker*) flourished at the start of the twentieth century, the same era that saw the rise of a rich women's activist counterpublic through Margaret Sanger's *The Woman Rebel*, Emma Goldman's *Mother Earth*, Susan B. Anthony's *The Revolution*, *The Suffragist* (published by the Congressional Union for Woman Suffrage), and other publications.

Marking another vibrant period of alternative media production, New Left activists in the late 1960s responded to the consolidation and monopolization of mainstream media with newspapers that included *Avatar* (Boston), *Fifth Estate* (Detroit), *Berkeley Barb* (California), *Helix* (Seattle), *Austin Rag*

(Texas), *Kaleidoscope* (Milwaukee), among many more. The Chicano movement, Asian movement, and Black Power activists also relied heavily on their own media networks and produced a rich archive of newsletters and newspapers, among them *Black Panther*, *El Grito del Norte*, and *Gidra*.[14] In many ways, the mimeograph machine symbolized these countercultural and political activists' intense and energetic commitment to print media. Taped to the wall in the national office of Students for a Democratic Society (SDS), for example, was a drawing of a mimeo machine with the handwritten caption, "Our Founder."[15] And John McMillan explains, "various multihued pamphlets and flyers, densely printed newspapers, crude bulletins, circular letters, and delicate, smudgy carbons—this was the stuff from which SDS would change the world."[16] Thus, shifts in technology made do-it-yourself printing possible for those who could not or chose not to use mainstream media to convey their messages.

The combination of a fecund political climate and accessible printing technologies catalyzed the proliferation of feminist periodicals, with the Chicago-based *Voice of the Women's Liberation Movement* leading the way in March 1968. Though it lasted less than a year and only a few other periodicals emerged before 1970, hundreds soon followed, among them *Ain't I a Woman?* (first published in 1970), the *L.A. Women's Liberation Newsletter* (1970), the *Female Liberation Newsletter* (1970), the *Valley Women's Center Newsletter* (1971), and *Distaff* (1973).

On the one hand, these publications are common and ordinary, reflecting the characteristics evident in many multiissue feminist periodicals published at that time. According to Allen, such periodicals shared eight qualities: "(1) women speaking for themselves, not reporting for others, (2) preference for collective rather than hierarchical structures, (3) sharing instead of competitive, (4) analysis of mass media's role relative to women and women's media, (5) a nonattack approach toward different women's views, (6) 'open forum' emphasis [inviting any woman to contribute], (7) provision of information not reported in the mass media, and (8) an activist orientation."[17] The five periodicals I have chosen to study are thus broadly representative of feminist practices and politics at the time. On the other hand, each of these periodicals is unique. Despite their similarities to other feminist newsletters and newspapers, most women's liberation periodicals had a local orientation that shaped their content and how feminist ideals manifested in the papers.

## Choosing Periodicals: Geography and Genre

I chose periodicals to represent different regions of the country and cities that are not usually foregrounded in the narrative of U.S. feminism. Most feminist groups in the 1970s did not operate from feminist hubs, which tended to be large northeastern urban centers such as New York, Boston, and Washington, D.C.[18] Despite their undeniable importance, these sites have too often stood in for feminism, as in *The Feminist Memoir Project*, an anthology that sought "to capture memories from the early days of the contemporary United States women's movement." While this important collection presents a wide variety of views and highlights the heterogeneity of feminist politics in the 1960s and 1970s, it focuses on only a few geographic areas, devoting fifteen of its twenty-seven essays to New York City and five to the Boston/Cambridge area.[19] None of the volume's contributions discusses Los Angeles, where feminist activism frequently connected with issues of race and racism and where substantial amounts of feminist art and popular culture were produced and disseminated. Indeed, Los Angeles rarely appears at all in national histories of U.S. feminism.[20] One exception is Sara Evans's *Tidal Wave: How Women Changed America at Century's End*, which mentions not only Los Angeles but also Iowa City in a list of women's liberation journals.[21]

Activism in the well-documented hubs reverberated throughout the country and merits careful analysis, but decentering these hubs is useful in two ways: it recognizes not only that a vast network of vibrant—albeit diffuse and informal—feminist communities existed throughout the country but also that the activism in the hubs was not necessarily representative of the issues and politics in other locations. After traveling across the nation to promote *Sisterhood Is Powerful* in the early 1970s, Morgan came to realize that "the exhausting debates that consumed her in New York were fundamentally irrelevant to most of the groups springing up across the country."[22] Morgan's observation does not mean that New York City and New Orleans, for example, were completely disconnected. Therefore, studying the feminist movement in smaller cities and cities outside the Northeast not only fills in gaps in the historiography but also allows us to complicate dominant narratives, honor the decentralization of feminist practices, and analyze the relationship between a social movement's structure and the construction of its collective identity.

I also chose periodicals to reflect a variety of forms. Most feminist periodicals emerged from small, grassroots collectives and were not formally connected to national organizations, and most also were not identity-based or focused on a single issue.[23] Therefore, I excluded from my sample publications that explicitly adopted a particular editorial focus (for example, women's health or art) and those published by formal groups such as the National Organization for Women, the Women's Equity Action League, or any of their local chapters. Feminist journals were also in the minority. Such publications were usually longer than newsletters and newspapers and generally published at most three or four issues a year. Cell 16 in Cambridge, Massachusetts, for example, published six issues of *No More Fun and Games* (ranging between 80 and 190 pages) between 1968 and 1973, and *Heresies* generally appeared two or three times a year during its lifespan (1977–93). Journals likely included contributors from across the country with a similar breadth in distribution, reflecting the editors' goal of reaching a national rather than regional audience.[24] These journals tended to have higher circulation numbers as well: *No More Fun and Games* distributed more than ten thousand copies of its first issue in April 1970, while *off our backs* (published in Washington, D.C.) had a circulation of fifteen thousand in 1977.[25]

Representing an even smaller minority than journals were feminist magazines. *Ms.* is perhaps the most well-known because of its circulation (250,000 by 1972) and relationship with the mainstream, for-profit media industry. According to Amy Farrell, the first issue was made possible by twenty thousand dollars in seed money from a publisher and stockholder of the *Washington Post* and because the editor of *New York* magazine agreed to incorporate a preview issue of *Ms.* into an issue of his magazine and to split the profits with the *Ms.* editors.[26] Because most editorial groups lacked Gloria Steinem's cultural capital and access to the mainstream media industry, their print runs stayed in the hundreds to low thousands and remained regionally focused. Unlike *Ms.*, most feminist periodicals did not attempt to make a profit, and many feminists in fact developed a deep distrust of capitalism and chose a publishing practice that actively resisted the values of this economic system.[27]

For many reasons, then, most feminist newspapers and newsletters highlighted feminism in the locale where they were published and consequently had relatively small subscription lists. I chose to study periodicals that fit this profile: regionally focused, small-scale newsletters and newspapers.[28] The *L.A. Women's Liberation Newsletter* was distributed to around forty-two hundred people in September 1970; the *Valley Women's Center Newsletter* claimed three hundred people on its mailing list in April 1971 and more than seven hundred a year later; and by late 1970, editors of the *Female Liberation Newsletter* were mimeographing 500 copies of each issue.[29] *Distaff*, which described itself first as a "New Orleans monthly feminist forum" and later as a "dialogue for southern women," had a peak circulation of about three thousand.[30]

These forms and modes of publishing mattered because they reflected the way scale had more than a quantitative impact. The *Female Liberation Newsletter*, for example, was not merely a smaller, more regional version of Female Liberation's quarterly magazine, *The Second Wave*. A pamphlet put out by the organization's Speaker's Bureau explained, "Our quarterly magazine, THE SECOND WAVE, serves nationally as a forum for feminist writings and discussion," while the newsletter "serves as an information exchange for women throughout the Greater Boston area."[31] Scale of publication thus related to the kind of audience the periodicals' editors imagined. In addition, frequency of publication shaped content. Appearing monthly or weekly, newsletters and newspapers included information that might be outdated by the next issue;

in fact, delays in publication occasionally meant that announcements for events appeared after they had already occurred. Newsletters and newspapers also tended to feature a greater number of discrete pieces—especially if each announcement or other small item is considered an individual piece— and longer pieces were more likely to resemble journalistic writing. Journals generally contained longer essays as well as academic writing, meaning that each issue had more pages but fewer distinct contributions.

In addition to serving different purposes and audiences, the *Female Liberation Newsletter* and *The Second Wave* embodied different economies. The inaugural issue of *The Second Wave*, published in the spring of 1971, was forty-five pages and cost seventy-five cents, and by August of that year the editorial collective announced that each issue would have to sell seven thousand copies to turn a profit.[32] In contrast, the *Female Liberation Newsletter* was free for nearly two years, until the editors announced in April 1972 that this model could no longer be sustained: "THE FEMALE LIBERATION NEWSLETTER WILL BE GOING ON A SUBSCRIPTION BASIS IN ONE MONTH. WE'VE BEEN PUTTING OUT THE NEWSLETTER FOR ALMOST TWO YEARS, WITH ONLY DONATIONS TO SUSTAIN IT. FINANCIALLY THIS IS NO LONGER POSSIBLE."[33]

The Valley Women's Center presented a similar narrative. An editorial from October 1975, when the Valley Women's Union was firmly established, explained, "We are charging non-dues-paying people $3 for a year's subscription to the newsletter. Any non-members who do not reply to this mailing will be dropped from our mailing list."[34] The emphasis on subscriptions suggests that the group could no longer support the periodical without such funds. In contrast, *The Woman's Journal* cost twenty-five cents at the start. A booklet-like periodical that the VWC published from the spring of 1971 through the summer of 1972, its higher production value required greater financial input to sustain.

## Location Matters

As studies of U.S. feminism show, location matters.[35] The content of a periodical depended on the women who worked on it, their priorities, and the interests of their readers as well as their budget, printing options, and the labor women contributed. Local politics shaped what *would* be included in the pages of an issue; local resources shaped what *could* be included. Theories developed and transformed in conversation with a place's history, geography, demographics, communication networks, and economy, and these factors manifested in relation to the coalitions and factions that formed among and within activist groups. Some campaigns, such as those to pass the Equal Rights Amendment and to free Angela Davis from incarceration, galvanized women across the country, and many local publications offered readers a section or a page devoted to national or worldwide feminist news.[36] Yet women's energies tended to be influenced predominantly by more immediate and local needs and possibilities. The local/regional quality of these periodicals arose in part because publishing collectives and women's centers consistently struggled with financial stability and lacked the finances and labor to expand their distribution. According to Charlotte Bunch, feminist publishers faced various challenges, but "perhaps the greatest limitation is the small distribution and circulation of most such works."[37] The *Female Liberation Newsletter* told readers, "With the recent increase in postal rates it now costs *$64.00 a week* just for postage for the newsletter. It now cost *$250.00 a week* to operate the office. This includes money for the supplies, newsletter, and all our activities excluding *The Second Wave*."[38] *Distaff* explained in January 1974, "For a long time now, the paper has depended on 2 or 3 women to do all the organizing of staff, fundraising, distribution, errand running public relations, writing, and production. Besides holding down full-time jobs, being wives lovers, mothers, and whatever else our private lives demand."[39] The focus on coverage of local and regional events meant that these periodicals were unlikely to appeal to many readers in different cities, and editors generally lacked the funds, time, or energy to expand availability.

*Ain't I a Woman?* and the *Valley Women's Center Newsletter* illustrate another aspect of the impact of location. Though both were published in relatively rural areas, those areas had different qualities. Northampton is only 100 miles from Boston and 160 miles from New York City, and the Valley Women's Center (VWC) was connected to both cities: women traveled to and from Boston and Cambridge with relative ease, and New York City was an important destination and resource for women from the Pioneer Valley seeking abortions. Amherst Women's Liberation, the group that started the VWC and its newsletter, was connected with Boston from the start. Pat Sackrey, a VWC organizer, explained that "right away, we had contacts with Boston feminists. [A] woman from Boston, if I recall, helped start a support group out here and gave us technical assistance on that." This connection was reinforced through the circulation of texts and ephemera: "We read underground papers on feminism, primarily from the New England [Free] Press in Boston though all the papers weren't written there. They had a very radical political view, which fit in with a good many of our politics already, personal politics, working in the radical movements of the time."[40]

Iowa City, in contrast, was much more isolated from sites of activism, with the closest feminist metropolis, Chicago, 230 miles away. The editors of *Ain't I a Woman?* did not express a sense of political kinship or demonstrate the same kind of political exchanges with the women in Chicago that existed between the VWC and Boston. *Ain't I a Woman?* explicitly contrasted Chicago with Iowa City: "Women from smaller cities can easily fall into feeling that they are less obvious than sisters and groups from big cities. Usually the national media features groups and actions which are happening in places like New York, Washington, Chicago, etc."[41] *Ain't I a Woman*'s editors in fact felt a stronger bond with Minneapolis (300 miles away), as evidenced by the paper's inclusion of references to and essays by groups in that city.

## "Freedom of the Press Is Guaranteed Only to Those Who Own One": Five Feminist Periodicals

In keeping with *New Yorker* journalist A. J. Liebling's 1960 observation that "freedom of the press is guaranteed only to those who own one," women's liberation activists across the country began publishing newsletters as a means of both sharing information and expressing opinions without being subject to the censorship of mainstream media gatekeepers.[42] On June 26, 1970, the first issue of *Ain't I a Woman?* (figure 1) appeared in the already politicized University of Iowa community of Iowa City. Students were mobilizing around national issues such as the Vietnam War, U.S. militarization, South African apartheid, and the civil rights movement as well as local issues such as proposed tuition hikes, racial discrimination on campus, free speech and the university newspaper, the requirement that all males at the university take two years of ROTC classes, and the university's curriculum more generally.[43] In 1969, students conducted a three-day boycott of classes to protest tuition increases, and militancy intensified after the May 1970 Kent State shootings. Hundreds of University of Iowa students were arrested for participating in a demonstration that involved burning campus buildings and that ultimately curtailed the 1969–70 school year. University president Willard L. Boyd moved his office off campus, and many students opted not to finish out the semester, choosing to "make up the work later, accept a grade of pass or withdrawal, or take a grade based on course work completed through May 3. The option to leave was taken by 11,796 students, effectively closing down the university early."[44] The *Iowa Defender* (1959–69), a weekly alternative newspaper and counterpart to the university's more conservative *Daily Iowan*, reported on many of these activities.

This radical climate nurtured a number of specifically feminist activities. The Iowa City Women's Liberation Front served as an umbrella for a number of loosely organized and dynamic cells, including those focused on day care, gay women, health, revolutionary art, political study, and a speaker's bureau.[45] Iowa City was also home to the Emma Goldman Clinic for Women (a feminist health clinic that published *Emma's Periodical Rag*), the Iowa City Women's Press, Grace and Rubies (a women's restaurant project), Plainswoman Bookstore, a women's coffeehouse, a lesbian alliance (which published *Better*

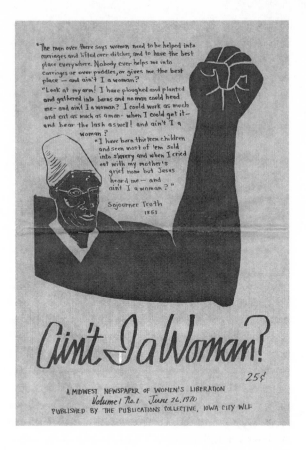

FIGURE 1. Front page of *Ain't I a Woman?*, June 26, 1970. Lesbian Herstory Archives, Brooklyn, New York.

*Homes and Dykes*), the Women's Resource and Action Center (which affiliated formally with the university in 1971), and lesbian and gay pride conferences and events.[46] And the university's Action Studies Program offered courses on African American studies, human rights, Vietnam, and women and gender. With the notable exceptions of the Emma Goldman Clinic and Women's Resource and Action Center, these events, collectives, organizations, and businesses were for the most part short-lived, and *Ain't I a Woman?* ceased publication in May 1974.

The first issue of *Ain't I a Woman?* lists the names of the editors—Vicki, Pat, Debbie, Lori, Linda, Dale, Penny, Carole, Julia, Anne, Carol, Pat, Sue, and Linda. However, most later issues identified them only as a group—the "Publications Collective of the Iowa City Women's Liberation Front," "the Angry Independent Amazon Women," or "a collective of 8 (plus one travelling sympathizer) functioning as a world-wide conspiracy of Radical Lesbians."[47] Most members of the editorial collective also lived together, a practice unique among the periodicals analyzed here, although not unique among feminist periodicals more broadly.[48] Shared housing meant that the editors' living space was also a workspace and that group members pooled resources to ensure the paper's continued existence. *Ain't I a Woman?* was also unusual in that it did not frequently ask readers for written contributions or for donations of money, time, and skills. Not until the paper's twenty-sixth issue, published in August 1972, did the collective reach out to readers for assistance: according to the editors, an office flood had resulted in the loss of "a lot of production materials, precious volumes of back issues, a large portion of our library and furniture. Also, the delay has resulted in a bottleneck in the mailing of orders and correspondence. We still have to re-locate and re-organize, so we ask you to bear with us, and to help us out if you can, it's been a hard-licks birthday."[49]

*Ain't I a Woman?* at times solicited contributions from women and feminist groups across the Midwest but was much less likely than the other publications examined here to print open calls for assistance in publishing or for written pieces.[50] The editors thus quite carefully guarded the boundaries of their group and identified their closeness as a strength.[51] Perhaps not surprisingly, therefore, the pages of *Ain't I a Woman?* focused heavily on politics, theories, and practices relating to collectivity: "In Iowa City we have tried to work out collectively this getting-the-work done problem. We certainly don't claim complete success, but the sacrifices in efficiency seem justifiable in terms of what we have gained in collective consciousness and responsibility. We have tried to rotate office work monthly to a group consisting of one person from each small collective. Often the work just hasn't gotten done, but we maintain that if the work to be done is decided on collectively (which it should be), it should be done collectively."[52] In addition to these self-reflective pieces, the newspaper frequently included lengthy explorations of other experiments with collective living and working and of the place of collectivity in revolutionary movements more generally.

Yet the editors also emphasized the importance of building larger-scale political networks. The first issue discussed the "special need to increase communication between sisters in the Mid-West. . . . Women in the mid-west, with the exception of the few large urban areas, find themselves working in their city's only women's liberation group." The editorial concluded, "We hope that AIN'T I A WOMAN will serve as a forum of communication between women in the mid-west about ideas, actions, and events. This issue is mostly by and about Iowa City Women's Liberation Front—we hope that won't happen again."[53] To this end, the editors invited women's liberation groups from New Mexico to Ohio to take responsibility for a page in the paper.[54]

*Ain't I a Woman?* initially was published twice a month.[55] In October 1970, the collective announced that the paper would appear every three weeks because the original schedule was too "grueling."[56] In early 1972 the publishing schedule became more erratic, and the last extant issue, dated May 1974, lacks

FIGURE 2. Front page of *Distaff*, October 1973. Mary Elizabeth Gehman Papers, Manuscripts Collection, Newcomb Archives and Vorhoff Library Special Collections, Newcomb College Institute, Tulane University, New Orleans.

volume and issue numbers. It also offered no explanation for the unpredictable publication schedule or any indication that it would be the final issue.

*Distaff*, a New Orleans newspaper, began publishing in early 1973 (figure 2), as *Ain't I a Woman?* neared its final issue. According to a 1980 editorial, *Distaff* originated with local candidate Barbara Scott's 1972 bid for the state House of Representatives: "To publicize her feminist platform [Scott] put out an 8 page tabloid called DISTAFF, a word meaning women's work. The campaign was not successful, but Scott became the impetus behind getting women together to seriously plan the publishing of a newspaper. She left town in 1972—now runs a restaurant in Biloxi—but her friends carried through with the idea, and in January 1973 the first issue of DISTAFF appeared."[57] This issue was labeled a preview, and February 1973 marked the official first issue. Though Scott inspired the paper, its backbone was Mary Gehman, a journalist who had experienced sexism in the mainstream media and sought to give women a voice and medium for communication. Unlike most feminist periodicals from this era, *Distaff* very much depended on the labor and initiative of a single person throughout its life span. As a result, it could exist only when she had the ability to publish it.

Also unusual was *Distaff*'s publication schedule. Between January 1973 and March 1974, issues appeared almost monthly. Then, after a short break, Gehman and Donna Swanson, former coworkers at the New Orleans welfare office, collaborated to publish ten issues between September 1974 and July 1975. The two women formed New South Feminist Press, hoping it would allow them to work full-time on the paper as "co-editors and co-everything."[58] This partnership is noteworthy not only because of the business model the pair developed but also because Gehman is white and Swanson is black. Although one example of interracial collaboration does not overturn the dominant narrative of U.S. feminism as an overwhelmingly white movement, it does provoke a closer look at the dynamics that often prevented but sometimes facilitated the building of cross-racial feminist coalitions. Swanson felt that "we're all in this together," and her commitment to *Distaff* evidenced this feeling of inclusion.[59] After a little under a year, however, Swanson and Gehman ended their coeditorship, and the paper remained dormant for four years. It reappeared in November 1979, triumphantly observing, "*Distaff* is like the proverbial cat: they say it has nine lives, but no one keeps a close count. The important thing is that it does come back, and always to a warm welcome."[60] The paper subsequently appeared monthly until January 1982, with Gehman maintaining her optimism about the paper's future and the importance of publicizing women's work and activism.[61]

As the 1970s progressed, *Distaff* came to resemble a conventional newspaper, and Gehman made various attempts to incorporate it. The February 1973 issue invited women to join the board of directors as *Distaff* became incorporated as a nonprofit organization.[62] And according to a 1980 editorial, "Our purpose is to print on a monthly basis news and events of interest to southern women, to serve as communication between women and women's groups, and to provide an outlet for the work of women writers, journalists, photographers and artists. The newspaper is operated as a business. We are not associated with any groups or organizations."[63] Few other feminist newspapers adopted such a corporate model, but Gehman imagined professionalism and collectivity as coexisting.[64] Indeed, an editorial in the first issue set up collectivity as a standard for the paper: "We want to invite all women to join us in this venture. DISTAFF is a feminist newspaper collective, open to any woman who wants to participate."[65]

*Distaff* accompanied a range of activism by and for women in New Orleans, including a NOW chapter, a television program occasionally hosted by *Distaff*, the nationally known Southern Female Rights Union, feminist art exhibits, a Women's Work Collective, a guerrilla theater group, the New Orleans Women's Caucus for Art, a Free University based at the main public library branch, and other local feminist and gay periodicals.[66] Both Tulane University and Loyola University established women's centers in 1975, with other such centers developing independent of the universities. In addition, beginning in the mid-1970s, New Orleans women participated very publicly in the local political machinery, working to ratify the Equal Rights Amendment, to dismantle sexist legal codes (particularly those related to reproductive rights and marriage), and to produce political parity by fighting for basic resources such as a women's bathroom in the state capitol building.[67] It was within this context that *Distaff* traveled its somewhat rocky road.

Feminists in Los Angeles, like those in New Orleans, produced a periodical that experienced significant shifts over its ten years of publication. From the summer of 1970 through the spring of 1972, the mimeographed *L.A. Women's Liberation Newsletter* appeared. From the summer of 1972 through the fall, the publication was named the *Women's Center Newsletter*. Finally, it finished life as *Sister*, its title from January 1973 to the summer of 1979 (figures 3 and 4).

From the outset, the *L.A. Women's Liberation Newsletter* defined its connection with a specific locality:

> The Women's Center is a non-partisan organization whose primary purpose is to serve all the women of Los Angeles. All women are invited to share in our activities and to avail themselves of our services, and to use the Women's Center as a springboard from which to explore the various women's liberation groups.
>
> The Women's Center Newsletter is published to inform the women of Los Angeles of Women's Center programs and activities of interest to women's liberation. Material from all women and women's liberation groups is welcomed. Viewpoints are those of the authors and do not necessarily represent an endorsement on behalf of the Women's Center.[68]

The Women's Center, initially located at 1027 Crenshaw Boulevard, was affiliated with the University of California, Los Angeles (UCLA). Although the campus was located more than eight miles from the center, a number of its founders were part of the university, and they secured funds from the Associated Students of UCLA.[69] The center's offerings included abortion and contraception resources, legal referrals, self-defense and automobile repair classes, emergency housing, and psychological and vocational counseling. The center also sold literature, published the newsletter, developed a speaker's bureau, and hosted nine different women's liberation groups, including the Socialist Women's Organizing Project, the Working Women's Group, the National Organization for Women, and a theater group. As the proportion of students participating in the center's activities decreased and the number of community members increased, the center began to depend more on literature sales, money received through the speaker's bureau, and donations. With this shift in the feminist community, the leaders struggled to accommodate and respond to the center's growth and to stay afloat financially. When the Crenshaw Boulevard center closed on December 31, 1972, feminist energy and

# L.A. WOMEN'S LIBERATION NEWSLETTER

VOLUME II   NUMBER II         WOMEN'S LIBERATION CENTER
SEPTEMBER 1971   MARILYN MONROE   1027 SO. CRENSHAW BLVD.

## NEWS

The Equal Employment Opportunity Commission has proceedings before the FCC to determine whether AT&T and the 24 Bell Co.s discriminate in employment against women, blacks and Spanish-surnamed Americans. The EEOC is preparing its case for fall presentation and wants information about 1)nature of the telephone company's recruitment program among women; 2)how women see placement and promotion opportunities at Bell; 3)women's experiences re: placement and promotion. If you have any info please write: Katherine Mazzaferri--Legal Intern, Task Force on AT&T, EEOC, Washington, D.C. 20506. It will help sisters.

- - - - - - - - - - - - - - - - - - - - - - - - - - - - - - - - - - - - - - - -

A bill (H.R. 1746) that goes far toward assuring women full and equal rights in employment is scheduled for action in the House of Representatives shortly after Congress returns in September. This bill introduced by Cong. Hawkins (Ca.) would strengthen the Equal Employment Opportunity Commission by giving it the

right to order an employer to "cease and desist" from sex discrimination. It would also broaden coverage of women workers to include those in small companies or unions, in local and state government and in educational institutions--not now under the jurisdiction of the EEOC. The Commission would then have the power it is lacking now. You (and your WL group) should 1)try to visit your House members when they come back home during summer recess--Aug.-Sept. 6; 2)If you can't visit them, write individual letters citing your personal experiences. Mail is running against the bill now; 3) Urge House members to vote for H.R. 1746 and against the substitute bill and against all amendments. 4) Urge them to be present when the bill is taken up.   Signed, Bella Abzug, Shirley Chisholm and Patsy Mink.- - - - - - - - - - - - - - - - - - - - - - - - - - - - - - - - - - - -

Sybil Brand Institute (SBI) for Women (that's a nice name for the women's jail) is hostessing a charity (????) ball on September 11th at the Coconut Grove. Any women interested in leaf-leting to point out that all women in jail are political prisoners of a sexist/racist system and the need for basic changes in the correctional (??) system should call the Center and a meeting will be called as soon as possible.

MARCHING, COMT. MARCH ON THE PRESIDIO! Sept. 4, Noon--San Francisco. According to the leaflet the Woman's Center received: "On Sept. 2, 1945, after centuries of struggle, the Vietnamese people declared their independence.... Inspired by the courage of the Vietnamese, we will march with the strength of sisterhood against Pentagon West (Presidio) to defeat the enemy's plan to build a biological war, and center there (to create diseases that affect only Asian people). Schedule of events: Thurs. Sept. 2--films, theatre and education projects in celebration of Vietnamese Independence Day--2012 Pine St., S.F. 7:30 pm. Fri, Sept. 3--leaf-leting, street theater--1380 Howard St. Party at 2012 Pine St., 7:30 pm. Sat, Sept. 4, Noon--March from Embarcadero Plaza to the Presidio. Sun, Sept. 5--Woman's Festival in Delores Park. **Carpools are leaving from L.A. Try the Women's Center to find a car or riders. In San Francisco call days: 861-6466 or come by 1380 Howard. night address for housing, etc. is 2012 Pine St.

- - - - - - - - - - - - - - - - - - - - - - - - - - - - - - - - - - - -

AFI AFI AFI AFI AFI AFI AFI AFI AFI AFI AFI AFI AFI AFI AFI AFI AFI AFI AFI AFI AFI AFI AFI AFI

The American Film Institute's Center for Advanced Film Studies was founded three years ago with funding from the Federal Gov't, Ford Foundation, National Endowment for the Arts, and the Motion Picture Association of America. During those three years it has constantly discriminated (ignored?) against women: 13 screen-writing grants, one to a woman; 24 men apprenticed to established directors, no women; of 60 grants, 3 went to women; of 40 fellows at the Institute 2 are women; of 20 trustees, 4 are women. In December, 1970, 60 women from 'Women for Equality in Media' (WFEM) met with AFI director George Stevens'Jr. to present 12 demands: that 53% of grants, scholarships, internships, and administrative positions be given to women, that a temporary review board be set up to review previously rejected woman applicants, and that a permanent board of women be set up 'to combat discrimination and stereotyping of women.' None of the demands were met during the following 8 months of negotiations. Aug. 5, 1971, about 35 women picketed AFI with such signs as 'Creativity has no sex' and 'No token women'. It was also announced to the press that WFEM and EIPJ (Entertainment Industry for Peace and Justice) are preparing a lawsuit against AFI on the basis of Sex Discrimination.

FIGURE 3. Front page of the *L.A. Women's Liberation Newsletter*, September 1971. Los Angeles Women's Liberation Movement Collection, Southern California Library, Los Angeles.

FIGURE 4. Front and back pages of *Sister*, January 1973. Woman's Collection, Texas Woman's University Libraries, Denton.

the newsletter shifted to the Westside Women's Center, located at 218 Venice Boulevard in Venice.

At first glance, the *L.A. Women's Liberation Newsletter*, the *Women's Center Newsletter*, and *Sister* appear to be three different periodicals, and in a sense they are. The *L.A. Women's Liberation Newsletter* was mimeographed on legal-size paper, and was stapled in the top left corner and folded in half for mailing. In the summer of 1972, when the publication became the *Women's Center Newsletter*, it shifted to a tabloid format, printed on newsprint folded in half to measure about fourteen by ten inches. Announcing this change, the editors proclaimed, "The newsletter staff, after months of searching, finally found a printer who would print our newsletter for what it cost to run off the newsletter ourselves. Bless the Mother-Goddess! What a relief it is not to have to struggle with the mimeograph machine which each month found a new way to break down and became quite unreadable."[70] When the publication became *Sister* six months later, it continued to resemble a newspaper. The inaugural issue, a January 1973 special feature on "Women and the War," marked its connection with the *Women's Center Newsletter* via a subtitle, "a monthly publication of the Los Angeles Women's Center." However, the second issue of *Sister* contained a small item on page 10 announcing that the newsletter was now being distributed from the Westside Women's Center in Venice, distinguishing it from the *L.A. Women's Liberation Newsletter* and the *Women's Center Newsletter*, both of which were based at the Crenshaw Boulevard center.[71]

As with Mary Gehman's curation of *Distaff*, editors Nancy Robinson and Joan Robins provided continuity for the Los Angeles periodicals.[72] Both women's names appear as editors of the *L.A. Women's Liberation Newsletter* and *Sister*, and Robins (but not Robinson) worked on the *Women's Center Newsletter*. The stability provided by the connection with a women's center and the editors' tenure as well as the fact that the *Women's Center Newsletter* and *Sister* continue the volume/issue sequence from the previous publication make clear that these three periodicals are part of one decade-long serial publication.

Los Angeles had a strong, diverse community of women activists during the 1960s and 1970s. Two aspects of this movement are especially significant for analyzing the *L.A. Women's Liberation Newsletter* and its offshoots: the feminist self-help health projects and the array of feminist periodicals. Carol Downer was an important figure in the community for her work establishing the Feminist Women's Health Center and promoting the self-help health movement, and she gained national renown after she and another clinic worker were arrested on September 21, 1972, for practicing medicine without a license.[73] The women's trials and Downer's eventual acquittal on December 5, 1972, received widespread coverage in the national media as well as through public relations efforts undertaken by supporters.[74] In addition, the Los Angeles area had a notable range of feminist periodicals during the 1970s, among them local NOW newsletters, *Everywoman, Woman Worker*, the *Free Angela Davis Newsletter*, the *Asian Women's Center Newsletter, Sisters United!*, the *Los Angeles Women's Liberation Union Newsletter*, the *Chicana Service Action Center Newsletter*, the *Lesbian News*, the *Lesbian Tide, Women West, Born a Woman*, and *Encuentro Femenil*.[75] Some focused on specific issues, such as labor, welfare, or sexuality; others had an identity-specific orientation, targeting Asian American, Chicana, or black women; still others, among them the *L.A. Women's Liberation Newsletter* and its successors, sought to promote feminism more generally. The range of activist projects and the feminist networks that crisscrossed Los Angeles certainly shaped the *L.A. Women's Liberation Newsletter* and the editors and writers who created it.

Similar to the Los Angeles periodical, the identity of the *Valley Women's Center Newsletter* (figure 5) was closely tied with a particular place, although the VWC remained at a single location for its life span (1971–77).[76] A local group, Amherst Women's Liberation (AWL), began the *Amherst Women's Liberation Newsletter* in June 1970, publishing it on an almost monthly basis. In April 1971 it became the *Valley Women's Center Newsletter* after the establishment of the VWC. The name changed to the *Valley Women's Union Newsletter* in 1975 and retained that title until publication ceased in early 1977.

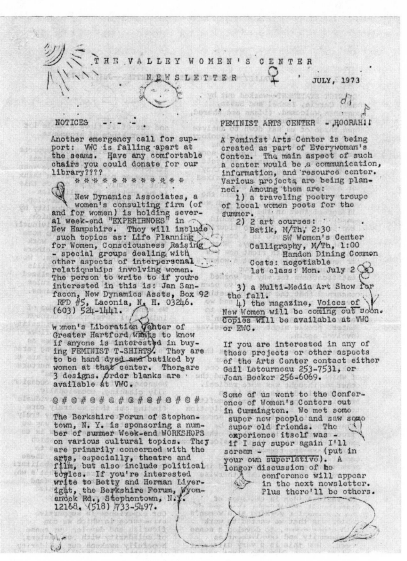

FIGURE 5. Front page of the *Valley Women's Center Newsletter*, July 1973. Valley Women's Center Records, Sophia Smith Collection, Smith College, Northampton, Massachusetts.

In 1969, the AWL started meeting at a member's house. The newsletter initially served as a forum in which the AWL's smaller action groups reported their activities and printed announcements for local events. After several months of publishing, the group announced in its October 16, 1970, issue, "VALLEY WOMEN'S CENTER—A REALITY. . . . AT LAST. . . . A PLACE OF OUR OWN!!!"[77] The April 8, 1971, issue was the first to bear the title *Valley Women's Center Newsletter*. Despite AWL's desire to serve all women in the region and despite the fact that the center was located in Northampton, about eight miles from Amherst, the group's presence continued to dominate. Through mid-1972, the newsletter featured information about general women's liberation meetings, describing them as AWL events. The center also retained the workgroup structure formed by the AWL, and in July 1972, as the staff worked to make the center more welcoming to readers, the newsletter clarified,

> Many women have said there is confusion over the nature of the monthly meeting. Although the name of the group which calls the meeting is Amherst Women's Liberation, the members of that group are from all over the Valley, from Holyoke to Greenfield and Wendell to Ashfield. This is the open "big" meeting which discusses policy and strategy for women's liberation in this area. The Valley Women's Center is a place for implementing these programs and for the community to interact with Women's Liberation. Any woman is welcome at the monthly meeting as well as at the Center.[78]

Because of its association with the VWC, the center rather than any particular person played the primary role in the newsletter's publication, especially after 1972. The editors published minutes from the center's general, staff, and business meetings and from the meetings of action groups that used the center. The newsletter also publicized these meetings as well as the VWC's resources—study groups, feminist literature, a lending library and archives, and welfare and abortion counseling. In addition to announcements and reports, readers encountered dialogues and debates about the role of the center in the local community, the organizational structure and political ideology, whether or how men should be involved, and whether or how to pay women on the staff. And the newsletter frequently printed announcements about the center's need for funds, equipment, and volunteers. A mid-1972 call to readers is typical: "HELP!!! We need contributions. as of Jan. 20, we have only $120. in the treasury. It costs approximately $240/mo. to run the center. So we/you definately need our/your support. Especially considering the big phone bill that is soon expected. we are also looking for an electric typewriter and another, really and truly functional this time, mimeograph machine. Help?"[79]

Starting in 1973, concerns about the center's structure and services became more prominent in the newsletter, appearing in meeting minutes and position papers. The January 1974 newsletter began, "This issue of the newsletter is a report on the January 13th meeting of the Valley Women's Union. Several months ago some of us who had noticed that the Center was no longer functioning as it had in the past began to meet regularly to evaluate and reorganize it."[80] Seeing the center as "apolitical" and viewing the Everywoman's Center at the University of Massachusetts, Amherst, as drawing women away from the VWC, the group was determined to "create an organization which would direct energy toward accomplishing real political change."[81] Six of the issue's eight pages outlined a structure for the new group, its working principles, and its socialist-feminist philosophy. Despite the proposed changes, members of the collective averred their commitment to continuing the newsletter by proposing a workgroup that "would be responsible for the production of a monthly VWU newsletter(paper?). We feel that the newsletter must be more than a collection of news items and should reflect our philosophy and principles, and be an organ of education and communication between Union and area groups, as well as providing commentary on national issues. Members of this work group would coordinate articles from the workgroups as well as research articles on their own, and from other publications."[82] When the newsletter became a project of the union in early 1974, it did not change in format, and not until October 1975 did the newsletter officially take on a new name: "This is the first issue of the latest version of the Valley Women's Union Newsletter."[83]

Despite the upheavals of 1973–74, the center remained a vibrant site of feminist activism in the Pioneer Valley.[84] Open for only four months when the first issue of the newsletter appeared, the center already hosted sixteen action groups, including those devoted to sexism and imperialism, the free store, archives, auto mechanics, orientation committee, family planning, and the newsletter.[85] The staff kept a daily log that recorded the wide variety of services for which women asked. Women came to the center for help with welfare-related, personal, vocational, and legal counseling and called for help locating housing, babysitters, dentists, and feminist literature. The center also provided space for a feminist film co-op that distributed films throughout the country as well as the Lesbian Gardens, which held meetings and other events at the center. Along with the specifically woman-centered spaces and resources, the mimeograph machine (despite its constant state of disrepair) was part of the center's heart, as suggested by the number of references to operating, maintaining, repairing, and replacing it in the daily logs and the newsletter. Used primarily for the *Valley Women's Center Newsletter* and other center groups, it also served as a resource for outside groups, including the United Farm Workers, the local food co-op, the Greenfield Women's Center, antiwar activists, and those working locally for George McGovern's presidential campaign.

The local community of activists also encompassed women's centers at the University of Massachusetts at Amherst, Smith College, and Mt. Holyoke College as well as the feminist student collective at Smith, which published its own newsletter. The region also had a strong network of antiwar and peace activists, and the range of people involved in reproductive rights activism indicates that this issue was a political priority.[86] Proximity to New York City and Boston shaped the Pioneer Valley's activist community as well: women

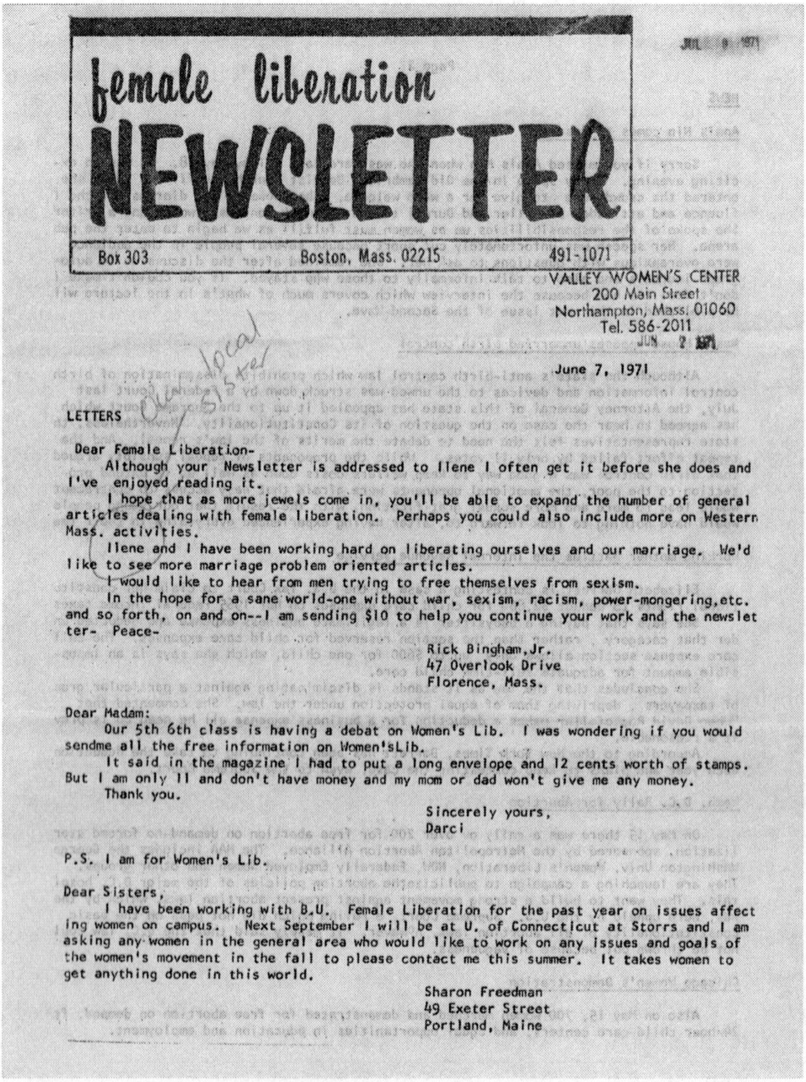

female liberation
NEWSLETTER
Box 303 Boston, Mass. 02215 491-1071

VALLEY WOMEN'S CENTER
200 Main Street
Northampton, Mass. 01060
Tel. 586-2011

June 7, 1971

LETTERS

Dear Female Liberation-
Although your Newsletter is addressed to Ilene I often get it before she does and I've enjoyed reading it.
I hope that as more jewels come in, you'll be able to expand the number of general articles dealing with female liberation. Perhaps you could also include more on Western Mass. activities.
Ilene and I have been working hard on liberating ourselves and our marriage. We'd like to see more marriage problem oriented articles.
I would like to hear from men trying to free themselves from sexism.
In the hope for a sane world-one without war, sexism, racism, power-mongering,etc. and so forth, on and on--I am sending $10 to help you continue your work and the newsletter- Peace-

Rick Bingham,Jr.
47 Overlook Drive
Florence, Mass.

Dear Madam:
Our 5th 6th class is having a debat on Women's Lib. I was wondering if you would sendme all the free information on Women'sLib.
It said in the magazine I had to put a long envelope and 12 cents worth of stamps. But I am only 11 and don't have money and my mom or dad won't give me any money.
Thank you.

Sincerely yours,
Darci

P.S. I am for Women's Lib.

Dear Sisters,
I have been working with B.U. Female Liberation for the past year on issues affecting women on campus. Next September I will be at U. of Connecticut at Storrs and I am asking any women in the general area who would like to work on any issues and goals of the women's movement in the fall to please contact me this summer. It takes women to get anything done in this world.

Sharon Freedman
49 Exeter Street
Portland, Maine

FIGURE 6. Front page of *Female Liberation Newsletter*, June 7, 1971. Sophia Smith Collection, Smith College, Northampton, Massachusetts.

from those cities—Robin Morgan, Florynce Kennedy, and Jill Johnston, for example—traveled to western Massachusetts, while women from the valley could access these urban hubs fairly easily.

Like the Los Angeles and Northampton periodicals, the *Female Liberation Newsletter* (figure 6) also existed as a project of a specific place, though the group operated from several different addresses in the early 1970s.[87] The first extant issue of the *Female Liberation Newsletter* is undated but likely was published in the spring of 1969; the next extant issue appeared in the fall of 1970, and according to Female Liberation, the newsletter was first published in 1970.[88] Between September 1970 and February 1972, it appeared weekly; thereafter, editors voted to publish every two weeks because of lack of funds and staffing.[89] The collective sustained this schedule until late 1973, when a financial crisis led the group to publish only one newsletter in December.[90] The next extant issue, published on March 4, 1974, was the publication's last: "This is the final Newsletter from Female Liberation. It is so late getting out because it took time for us to clear up the business of disbanding F.L., moving out of our office and the Second Wave moving to a new office in Harvard Square. We also spent a lot of time writing up the Press Release, which is the main body of this Newsletter, in which we have attempted to present an honest analysis of the major factors leading to our disbanding in the hope that other women and women's groups can use what we learned through our struggles to avoid or recognize similar situations."[91] The press release characterized the disbanding as an effect primarily of a debate "between those who wished to circumvent the power structure and those who wished to attack it directly."[92] Other points of contention, such as the relationship between the personal and the political, group leadership, and group structure, exacerbated the struggle. Such statements are rare: the final issues of most feminist periodicals generally did not indicate that another would not be forthcoming.

Like the *Valley Women's Center Newsletter*, the *Female Liberation Newsletter* remained a mimeographed publication throughout its four-year existence. These two groups also kept the size consistent—using 8½" × 11" bond paper—though Female Liberation used pink, blue, yellow, and orange as well as white paper. Most but not all issues consisted of a single color of paper, though multicolored issues appeared more frequently in 1972. Neither the newsletter nor the group's archived records elaborate the rationale behind the use of colored paper, though frequent requests for readers' financial help suggests that this decision was related at least in part to costs.

Female Liberation and thus the newsletter faced a crucial moment when a disagreement developed with another feminist group, Cell 16. The two entities initially collaborated and shared office space and finances, and in July 1969 they jointly issued a statement introducing and recruiting women to feminism.[93] By late 1970, however, a factional fight between these groups reverberated nationally. According to a statement Cell 16 sent to feminist groups throughout the country, women from the Young Socialist Alliance took over the office and then "joined" Female Liberation, co-opting the feminist energy and compromising feminist politics. Cell 16 also referred to political coalitions that Female Liberation made "with which [Cell 16] had no political agreement," thus "impeding [the movement's] efficiency and diluting its message."[94] The December 2 issue of the *Female Liberation Newsletter* responded to these accusations, agreeing with some and challenging others. In particular, members of Female Liberation emphasized their efforts to support coalition building and the importance of being "open to all women who want to work on feminist issues regardless of their other political affiliations." The authors continued, "Very few individuals have total 'political agreement'. However, we feel we have 'common goals' with most women and therefore seek to form coalitions for specific actions aimed at these 'common goals.'"[95] After the two groups parted, Cell 16 continued to publish *No More Fun and Games*, a monthly journal, while Female Liberation published the *Female Liberation Newsletter* and *The Second Wave* from its new office on Massachusetts Avenue.

The Cambridge/Boston area is often presented as a hub of U.S. feminism, so for those familiar with feminism in the 1970s, these cities need almost no introduction.[96] One of the earliest locations of women's liberation (along with New York and Chicago), this area was home to the Boston Women's Health Book Collective, which published *Our Bodies, Ourselves*, as well as to groups that have become archetypes of radical (Cell 16) and socialist (Bread and Roses) feminist collectives.[97] Much like Los Angeles, Boston/Cambridge had numerous feminist periodicals, among them the *Bread and Roses Newsletter*, *On Our Way* (from the Cambridge Women's Center), *The Second Wave, No More Fun and Games, Hysteria*, the *Boston Area Socialist Feminist Organization Newsletter*, the *Women's Liberation Newsletter* (which covered all of New England), and *Battle Acts* (published by the Women of Youth against War and Fascism). The New England Free Press, based first in Boston and later in Somerville, also supported women's liberation by publishing and distributing feminist pamphlets and position papers.

These vignettes point to the way location thus affected the production, content, circulation, and consumption of these serial publications. Such factors as the cost of rent for offices and women's centers, the availability and politics of area printers, proximity to other cities and feminist groups, and local political concerns affected and were reflected in the production of periodicals, thus shaping how feminism was presented on the page both materially and ideologically. At the same time, certain concerns crossed local communities, and a great deal of feminist content also circulated through towns, small cities, and other hubs, helping to forge a collective identity amid diversity.

Although most periodicals provided information about women throughout the nation and the world, they generally focused on a very local audience. Though each individual publication had only a small print run and limited reach, such publications proliferated as numerous groups created their own serials as a means to maintain connections with other feminists, learn about the women's liberation movement, and share information. Such a structure reinforced the polyvocality of the women's liberation movement and created space for a multitude of voices.[98] Through these voices and these periodicals, the women's liberation movement grew and spread through hundreds of cities across the United States.

CHAPTER 2

# Locating Feminism

In June 1972, Female Liberation published a letter from feminist writer and activist Marge Piercy:

> Dear Sisters,
>
> Laura Murra of the Women's History Research Center just sent me a copy of your newsletter. I was active in women's liberation in New York and I'm now living on the Cape [Cod] year round.
>
> Please send me the newsletter. That's my address above. Do you know of groups on the Cape?[1]

Tracing the route through which information circulated so that Piercy could find feminism in her local community, we begin in Cambridge, where the *Female Liberation Newsletter* was published. One of these issues crossed the country to the Women's History Research Center in Berkeley, California, which archived feminist periodicals from around the country. From there, the center's founder, Laura Murra, sent a newsletter to Piercy in Wellfleet, Massachusetts. And then Piercy's letter traveled another hundred miles to Female Liberation. Although Cambridge is only about sixty-five miles from Cape Cod, and although the *Female Liberation Newsletter* circulated primarily along the East Coast, Piercy learned of Female Liberation from someone across the country and after the newsletter had traveled more than six thousand miles.

Also reflecting the idiosyncratic pathways connecting women to feminism is an August 1970 letter in which Rena Szajman asked Female Liberation for information about a place where she could read and borrow women's liberation literature.[2] While such a query was common, Szajman's return address bears note. She wrote from Toronto—about nine hundred miles from Cambridge—to learn more about feminism in her home city. Toronto had a thriving community of feminists—as early as 1966, women affiliated with the University of Toronto had established a women's liberation group, and the socialist-leaning Toronto Women's Caucus had formed in 1970—but the city's feminist presence remained invisible to Szajman, and she had to write to a distant organization in her search for local resources.[3]

Though neither Szajman's nor Piercy's letter appeared in the *Female Liberation Newsletter*, similar missives did. In 1971, for example, the paper printed several such communications:

> Here in France my chief problem is isolation. There is no feminist movement here and even the radical students are very much into a chauvinist bag.[4]

> We're so far out in the country, comparatively, that sometimes we feel completely isolated from the movement, and your Newsletter helps us keep going.[5]

> In this small Virginia town, I have no contact with the movement— Depressing![6]

Receiving the *Female Liberation Newsletter* gave these women some connection to the women's liberation movement, but their words imply that they desired more. Although France and a "small Virginia town" were quite distant from the conventional hubs of feminism, the second letter came from Cape Ann, Massachusetts, only forty miles from Boston. Feminism's vibrant presence in the Boston/Cambridge area might have been expected to extend that far, yet the writer certainly felt that it did not, reflecting the uneven, idiosyncratic emplacement of feminism in the early 1970s. This sentiment was common enough that the Female Liberation office staff wrote an editorial addressing it: "Women who are in groups in different areas of N.E. please send in information on your group, description of aims and members, where you meet, how often and phone number to contact. Women call us all the time saying 'I am moving out to . . . , who can I contact about getting into a women's group?' Therefore, we are starting a file on suburban groups. Thanks for your help."[7] Recognizing a similar challenge in the circulation of information about and visibility of feminism, the Valley Women's Center (VWC) included an announcement in one of its earliest newsletters:

> Because it is important for all of us to know as much as possible about what is happening in the area in terms of action projects, and because it is sometimes hard for women new to Women's Liberation to know where they might use their energies and talents, the next page contains a descriptive listing of current action groups. As far as possible, this list is up to date, but please feel free to call in changes right away to the VWC. The VWC staff will try to keep current on changes, actions, problems, personnel in each group in order to facilitate communication between groups and between individuals.[8]

In the early 1970s the women's liberation movement gained unprecedented visibility in mainstream media, and the rapid increase in periodical publication signaled a similar growth in new feminist groups. Yet these letters show that such visibility did not guarantee that feminism could be found or accessed. Wrote *Distaff* editor Mary Gehman in a 1973 overview of women's liberation in New Orleans, "Look in the phone book under W: nothing but Woman's Clinic and Woman's World Beauty Salon. The yellow pages offer women's apparel as their sole listing. And calls to the YWCA or the City Hall Answer Desk yield little helpful information. The guided tours and tourist bureaus of the city do not list any women's organizations. People on the street might vaguely remember having heard of the National Organization for Women (NOW) but have no idea how to contact them."[9] Gehman correlated the movement's invisibility with the stereotype that the U.S. South was less progressive than the rest of the country when she wrote that others believed that "women's liberation simply hasn't infiltrated the southern swamps."[10] Considering the ways in which mainstream media represented feminism primarily in large cities and primarily in the Northeast, rarely giving commensurate attention to actions outside these hubs, Gehman's observation makes sense: if public events had become synonymous with feminism, then the absence of such events in a city would signify the absence of feminism.

Another activist described her firsthand experience with this phenomenon: "I remember being twenty-one and looking in the *phonebook* in Minneapolis, and I was looking through it trying to find the *women's movement....* I couldn't find it in the phonebook: What do I look under? Where do I go?"[11] Anne Enke calls out this paradoxical situation, asking, "How does one locate a movement that could reach a woman in her home and at the same time seem utterly inaccessible to her? A movement that was 'everywhere' and yet nowhere the same?"[12] And while it may seem unusual for a woman to query a group in another country about feminism, as Szajman did, Jo Freeman notes that women wrote to the White House to ask how to join a feminist group, which suggests the widespread need for the women's liberation movement as well as the challenges of locating it.[13] Offering another version of this sentiment, a Tucson woman wrote to the Valley Women's Center in December 1971 about her "abysmal luck trying to contact any of the people that were working in the women's center last summer" and about how she had been the only person to show up for a meeting at the women's center.[14] In other words, the *existence* of feminism in the 1970s could be taken for granted, but the *locations* of feminism could not. Women knew that *spaces* for feminism existed but could not find the *places* where it materialized.

As maps of the women's liberation movement, periodicals reflected, created, and materialized feminist activism in the 1970s, providing one site where people could connect with the movement. Each issue located feminism in both place and time and thus conveyed where, when, how, and why liberatory work was taking place. June Arnold's observation that "the first thing any revolutionary group does when taking over a government is to seize control of communications" suggests that the existence of feminism co-incided with the appearance of feminist media in that place, so periodicals mark not just the presence of the women's liberation movement but also its incipient moments, giving a city both a place and a time on this map of feminism.[15] Noting the geographic spread of feminism "from major cosmopolitan cities into suburban areas and smaller cities," Joan Cassell cites the publication of a newsletter as symbolizing the movement's arrival.[16]

This chapter's analysis of spatiality and temporality offers two primary interventions: first, by detailing the different ways periodicals gave feminism a place, we gain a better sense of feminism's richness and vibrancy, especially at the local level. Periodicals granulate feminism, opening it through the local, quotidian labors that sustained the movement and allowing us to see the multitude of micropractices that gave it meaning. As Benita Roth has put it, "Looking at grassroots journals and underground publications is essential for understanding how feminists viewed things on the ground."[17] Enke's analysis of feminism also provides an important rationale for the study of space and place in a social movement. Ideas and ideologies as well as identity must be not only conceivable but also materializable—that is, they need a place to exist. Enke artfully brings to life the bars, bookstores, softball fields, and coffeehouses that women occupied, arguing that feminist institutions are "a product of social movement dynamics that can be better understood through analyzing the contested ways in which women *took place*."[18] The ambiguity of *took place* points to the general significance of a social movement's emplacement and to the specific power dynamics involved in taking a place, with or without permission, and transforming how it is used. From the living room, where consciousness-raising and study groups met, to mass marches along city streets, women took places and made them into sites of feminism.[19]

Second, in alignment with Daphne Spain's claim that "feminist places were sites of identity formation and radical action," a consideration of place also illuminates how collective identity is an ontology and a process.[20] "To be is to be some*where*," Robyn Longhurst has stated, emphasizing that our sense of self is tied to our sense of place.[21] And, as James Martin elaborates, "spatiality is widely recognized as a key dimension in the formation of social identities: identities are understood to be generated in relation to specific places, territorial and social."[22] Places are more than sites of activism: they are sites where individuals build relationships and affective connections with a movement.[23] Furthermore, the types of places available to and selected by activists for their political work shape who identifies with those politics and who takes part.

My analysis of feminist collective identity formation treats place and space according to one of the dominant models in human geography: spaces are the discursive and relational structures through which specific places become meaningful. In other words, place is "where everyday life is *situated*" and where the ideas, ideologies, conceptions, and imaginaries that construe space become lived.[24] Sara Ahmed, for example, has described the heterosexualization of public spaces: norms create heterosexualized *space*, with the result that some bodies fit better than other bodies in particular *places*.[25] More crudely, place reifies space, at least momentarily. At the same time, however, place refuses stasis—refuses to be homogenous, stable, or fully knowable. Places are polysemous, with meanings that are socially produced, and different people experience the same place differently. Places also constantly form and re-form. Space, moreover, is not a blank canvas that exists prior to its instantiation as a specific place and on which we create places.[26] Rather, spaces and places interact dynamically and dialectically with each other and within social, ideological, and material contexts to become meaningful. In the case of feminism, ideas about what constitutes a feminist space (for example, that feminist spaces are nonhierarchical) affect the creation and experience of specific feminist places (for example, a women's center or a public demonstration), and experiences of these places shape conceptions of feminism, which, in turn, inform how feminist spaces are imagined.[27]

This chapter does not examine places themselves but instead analyzes the production of place and space through feminist periodicals. Periodicals gave feminism a place in a very pragmatic way, telling readers where to find feminism and reporting on places where feminist events have happened and will happen. Publications thus created space in which feminism's existence could be imagined across different locales. The diffuse, informal structure of the women's liberation movement, combined with the broader social and economic structures that isolated women, put great weight on print culture's role in building a feminist collective identity.

Benedict Anderson's attention to space and community offers a useful framework for understanding the significance of feminist periodicals, since he argues that the circulation of publications enabled readers to identify themselves with a group of compatriots that extended beyond their specific locales. First, these publications made readers aware of the multitude of people who shared their particular language. Second, the rate of language change slowed as reproduction of texts was no longer subject to the idiosyncrasies of individual scribes.[28] Third, certain languages, which Anderson calls "languages-of-power," dominated because they became the most common print-languages.[29] As a result, people started imagining themselves as part of a national community, a much larger group than anyone could ever experience concretely. In this sense, an imagined community is a *space*, a discursive construct that gives meaning both to specific places and also to a reader's sense of self.

Feminism, too, resulted from such a discursive process, and the spaces and places necessary for this community could exist in periodicals. But a feminist imagined community encompasses more than just a vast, potentially trans-national expanse. When a woman writes about her conversation with her doctor or about the dynamics of a living collective, she affirms that feminism exists in the intimate, private spaces to which outsiders are not privy. Thus, some of the movement's complexity is lost if this community is located only at scales larger than the local.

To be somewhere, a person, thing, idea, or action must also be somewhere in time. Therefore, when women wrote to periodicals about being unable to find feminism and about the invisibility of the local women's liberation movement, we can read between the lines of their requests to understand that they also did not know *when* the movement was happening. Periodicals gave feminism an existence by showing readers where and when feminism was, is, and will be.[30] In calendars of events and announcements, periodicals gave feminism a place in the future; periodicals also reported on events that had already occurred, thus giving feminism a past. And through each issue, periodicals repeatedly situated feminism spatially and temporally, making se-riality a key facet of the process through which these publications supported the formation of a feminist collective identity.[31]

### Periodicals Created Places

"Please don't eat at Joe's Café," urged the cover of the February 1974 *Valley Women's Center Newsletter*. The cover also announced "Behind the Great Wall of China," a photography exhibit at Smith College; a women's show on WMUA, a student and community radio station hosted by the University of Massa-chusetts at Amherst, every Tuesday evening between eight and nine o'clock; and the Spark Bookstore and a health care project testing for lead poison-ing in Florence. Finally, the newsletter encouraged readers to boycott the nearby Ramada Inn and to join the picket line at Joe's Café on Market Street in Northampton. Stimulating women's political participation and providing information about different events, these kinds of statements commonly ap-peared in feminist periodicals. The cover's layout, however, gives these an-nouncements an uncommon form. The page bears the label "VWU Topog-raphy" and includes some geographical landmarks to indicate that it is a map (figure 7). A hand-drawn Connecticut River bisects the page vertically, Route 9 connects Northampton to Amherst, and Interstate 90 (the Massa-chusetts Turnpike) runs horizontally across the bottom of the page. More important, though, and taking up more visual space, are political landmarks. The map foregrounds the women's liberation movement of the Connecticut River Valley, using roads, highways, cities, and rivers primarily to give a spatial context for feminist sites and events. And the cities mentioned—Florence, Northampton, Amherst, and Chicopee—appear to gain prominence not

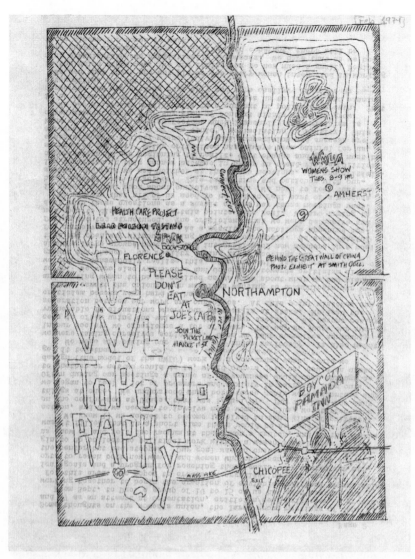

FIGURE 7. Front page of the *Valley Women's Center Newsletter*, February 1974. Valley Women's Center Records, Sophia Smith Collection, Smith College, Northampton, Massachusetts.

because of their size or population but because of their relevance to the VWC and to feminism in the region. For example, Chicopee had about five times the population of Florence, but Florence takes up more space on the map because of the density of feminist sites and activism there.

*Sister* also printed a feminist map qua map. It, too, features a conventional cartographic representation through the presence of highways but they seem to function only as markers that enable readers to locate points of (feminist) interest. The Woman's Resource Center sits just southwest of the Ventura Freeway and Santa Monica Freeway, the Chicana Service Action Center lies east of the Hollywood Freeway, and just southeast of the Pasadena Freeway is the Woman's Building. Although such maps were rare, each issue of a feminist periodical is in many ways a map of the women's liberation movement. Noting specific places where feminism has happened and will happen, periodicals gave feminism a place, diagramming it with announcements, advertisements, articles, essays, and photographs.[32]

Consistent with the scope and scale of the Northampton and Los Angeles maps, the periodicals examined here most often highlight feminism locally and regionally, and I offer just a few examples to show what a reader might encounter in them. In November 1972, the *Valley Women's Center Newsletter* announced the opening of the Everywoman's Center at the University of Massachusetts in Amherst, about fifteen miles away.[33] The *L.A. Women's Liberation Newsletter* let "all women" know that they were welcome to attend the Sherwood Forest Women's Collective's Tuesday evening meetings at the Sherwood Forest Bookshop, located "at 210 W. 3rd St., Santa Ana."[34] *Distaff* emplaced feminism with a "Guide to Women's Organizations in New Orleans" that listed contact information for a range of groups, including the Council of Black Women, the ERA Coalition, the Rape Crisis Clinic, and the National Organization for Women.[35] And *Ain't I a Woman?*'s special February 1973 double issue on child care reported on local activists who took over buildings at the University of Iowa to turn them into child care centers.[36] Periodicals also frequently included calendars (for example, *Distaff*'s list of events, "Don't Ms.") and commonly embedded information about events throughout an issue.

By including seemingly nonfeminist locations in the pages of a periodical, editors expanded the movement's scope spatially and ideologically. For example, while some groups in *Distaff*'s guide might not have explicitly identified as feminist, their presence in the newspaper allowed readers to imagine them as sites of the women's liberation movement. The September 1972 issue of the *Valley Women's Center Newsletter* announced a "multi-media show about women in the arts, which is shown Wednesdays at noon at the Danbury [Connecticut] Public Library through the end of October."[37] By occupying this place, the objects in the art show—and likely the people who went to see it—transformed the public library, even if only temporarily, into a site of feminism. In addition, the newsletter allowed those who could not experience the show firsthand to imagine it within the fold of feminism and, by extension, possibly to imagine public libraries more generally as places where feminism could exist. Even advertisements could politicize locations and give them feminist connotations. The September 1974 issue of *Sister* included ads for both explicitly feminist businesses (The Feminist Wicca and Sisterhood bookstore) and others (the Apple Room batik store and a mountain retreat), enabling the latter to become places where the idea of feminism might be realized.[38] The metamorphosis of nonfeminist places into feminist ones demonstrates that the creation of feminist places did more than give women an answer to the question of where the women's liberation movement was. Taking place and taking up space was a political act, rewriting both the purview of specific places and also how these places related to the existing topographies of power.[39] Readers may broaden their understanding of feminism by seeing the YWCA and the Ecology Center (both included in *Distaff*'s guide) as places where feminism could—and perhaps should—exist. Further, by going to or using these resources, readers may literally realize them as feminist locations.

Imagining feminism through a more regional scale, *Ain't I a Woman?*'s editors worked to make their publication be a newspaper of the Midwest, announcing in September 1970, "The voice of the Midwest needs to be heard in the Women's Liberation Movement. *Ain't I A Woman?* will print without editing any laid-out page from a Midwest (New Mexico thru Ohio) Women's Liberation group. We would like to encourage other women to start working collectively to avoid elitism and destructive power relationships that pit us against each other. We will send details on deadlines, page size, column length, etc. if you would like."[40] Various groups responded to this call, and the paper offered updates and information from Minot, North Dakota; Wooster, Ohio; Milwaukee, Wisconsin; Bloomington and Grinnell, Iowa; Kansas City, Missouri; and Cleveland, Ohio. As with other periodicals, *Ain't I a Woman?* more frequently highlighted nearby groups, but their connections to feminists as far as eight hundred miles away reflected their sense of the women's liberation movement in the region. This geographical range contrasts with the September 1971 issue of the *Female Liberation Newsletter*, which contained letters that offer some sense of the newsletter's circulation and thus the regional feminist community: women wrote from Brookline (about 4 miles from Cambridge), Newton (8 miles), North Weymouth (15 miles), Hardwick (66 miles), and Provincetown (118 miles). Such locations are representative: letters featured in other issues consistently came from eastern Massachusetts and particularly the Boston/Cambridge area. One reader even wrote to ask for more information on the rest of the state.[41]

Though their focus is mainly local and regional, periodicals locate feminism at different scales, from the intimate, personal, and individual to the international. Coverage of the Vietnam War and other Third World revolutions, for example, as well as letters from readers throughout the world reveal the movement's breadth. A few issues of *Sister* include "International News Briefs." The April 1975 edition reported on issues and activism in Italy, France, Israel, Germany, Kenya, England, and Eritrea, and the April–May 1976 issue took "International Feminism" as its theme. The Valley Women's Center staff sent a congratulatory 1971 telegram recognizing Norwegian women's election to city councils in Oslo, Trondheim, and Asker and announced those victories in the newsletter.[42] And women freedom fighters from Indochina and elsewhere received coverage in many feminist periodicals, which symbolically included these fighters within the scope of feminism.[43]

In addition to expanding feminism to encompass activism and politics at regional and international scales, periodicals made it visible at scales even more minute than the local—that is, the personal and the quotidian. These publications printed women's writing about their daily experiences, moments of transformation, instances of sexism, love and heartbreak, health concerns, and family dynamics. *Ain't I a Woman?* in particular frequently featured personal essays and poetry. The October 1971 issue presented "What I Did Last Summer," parts 1 and 2, in which a woman grappled with her shifting awareness of her sexuality, intertwining it with class, race, and ideologies of "rugged individualism" through mundane moments such as dinner conversation.[44] Combining description and reflection, she revealed her internal, psychic work to understand her interactions with friends, whom she began to see in a new light. And the form of the two pieces asks the reader to come even closer. The two pages contain cursive text on what appears to be lined notepaper, resembling a personal diary or journal.

Leading readers through another intimate moment, *Ain't I a Woman?* included information about the politics of reproductive health in its November 1971 issue. While the topic was common in feminist periodicals, the presentation in this issue is striking. A two-page piece about menstrual extraction (described as a form of birth control) included specific instructions for the procedure and two photographs of a woman performing the extraction. Her legs are spread and her vagina is visible as she uses a speculum, clamp, cannula (small tube), and syringe to extract her menstrual blood.[45]

In August 1973, *Distaff* printed a poem that adds another dimension to the intimate realm of feminism. Olive Schreiner's "I Saw a Woman Sleeping" presents a moment of self-determination through a dreamscape when a sleeping woman chooses freedom over love.[46] The page's layout textures this intimacy, as the poem appears beside Mei Kwang Lu's line drawing of a nude female figure. A side view depicts the woman with legs crossed, one arm cradling the other. The poem's left margin appears to trace the edge of her body, following the contours of the figure and creating an intertextual conversation between the poem and the drawing: the body physically shapes the structure of the poem and visually alludes to the intimacy that the poem explores. The significance of creative pieces such as Schreiner's often resides not in the depiction of facts or places but in the space for feminism they create by inviting readers into what would otherwise be private, perhaps unspoken, moments. Such content certainly aligns with the way feminism redefined the boundaries of the political as reflected in the sentiment "the personal is political." As much of the periodicals' content indicates, the home, the body, the psyche not only *are* sites of feminism but *must be*.

Periodicals are more than just containers of content: they are material objects, and their physical existence becomes meaningful as a feminist location. In December 1971, Audrey Brown explained to Female Liberation that the newsletter was her "only continuous and informative contact with the female liberation movement."[47] The following month, another *Female Liberation Newsletter* reader could "only say that getting the newsletter is of great importance to me; knowing that other women are actively involved in political activity is of great importance to me; knowing the office is there is of great importance to me."[48] In February 1973, yet another reader commented, "The Newsletter gives me the feeling of being 'in touch' with many things I can't actually participate in."[49] In these letters, the newsletter and the women's liberation movement coincide: the newsletter *is* the movement. As the Valley Women's Center became the Valley Women's Union in 1975–76, the women in the communications and outreach workgroup explained that they hoped "to make the Union more visible in the community by means of press releases and educational newsletters, to be able to take a stand on political issues, and to provide orientation for both old and new members."[50] Print texts thus became evidence of the workgroup's presence in Northampton, highlighting the important connection between the circulation of the organization's publications and its visibility.

*Ain't I a Woman?*'s editors offered another perspective on how a periodical becomes a proxy for a group. A February 1972 editorial expressed disappointment that feminists and activists in other parts of the country had not recognized the Iowans' work as activists and publishers, a phenomenon that reinforced certain cities as central to feminism: "Most people in the East wouldn't think that the Midwest (if they ever do think about the Midwest) has heard of Women's Liberation and therefore probably don't know about *Ain't I A Woman?* [and if] they have heard of AIAW then they probably don't listen to what we are saying. In other words we are invisible." The editorial concludes, "None of the writing we have done on lesbianism has been reprinted."[51] The women involved in *Ain't I a Woman?* saw their periodical's content as materially giving their activism a presence, so the newspaper's absence from the larger women's liberation movement equated to the group's absence from the movement. Serials constituted just one of many different cultural products that enlivened and materialized the women's liberation movement, so the publications' role must not be overestimated; at the same time, however, that role also must not be underestimated. The large number of periodicals and the volume of letters to the editor they generated demonstrate the importance of the physical existence of feminist publications, particularly for readers who could not find or physically join their sisters in feminist places.

Before moving on to a discussion of space, place, and collective identity, I offer one more mechanism through which periodicals gave feminism a place. Editorial collectives spatialized feminism through their labor. Women gathered in offices, homes, women's centers, and other places to compile contributions, type stencils for the mimeograph machine, edit, lay out content, and print and address newsletters. For the many women whose voices and tacit imprints shaped the final product, the production process made a place for feminism. Serials offered numerous opportunities to create these feminist places, and evidence of these feminist practices appeared explicitly in a finished product. An issue of a newsletter or newspaper, therefore, often drew a path of feminism, showing readers the previous moments and sites at which feminism appeared.

As Rob Cover has explained, "All depictions of identity and the forging of communities based on marginal identities require some sort of *source* for the performance and mutual recognition of groups and group belonging."[52] Specifically, he sees periodicals as a vector that links an individual's identity with a larger group's "symbols, rituals, institutionalised behaviours and norms."[53] Cover's reference to norms indicates that periodicals did not merely reflect an objectively existing reality. The particular places periodicals discussed and the content of these discussions did ideological work by tacitly or explicitly texturing the relationship between a location and feminism: Is it a place designed to nurture feminism, like a women's bookstore or coffeehouse? Is it a place of protest? Is it a public place? Private? What kind of feminist politic occurs there? Who occupies it?

In addition to recognizing the mechanisms through which periodicals produced and made a place for feminism and feminists, it is also important to pay attention to the moments during which places became unwelcoming, uncomfortable, dissonant, and exclusive. One moment of discord that reverberated far outside its point of origin occurred in the fall of 1970, between the feminist groups Cell 16 and Female Liberation.[54] Although the conflict was more complex than an argument about the use of the office, that specific place became an important site and subject of their discord. Cell 16 disagreed with Female Liberation's decision to use the office to establish "coalitions with groups with which [Cell 16] had no political agreement, only common goals — as when [Female Liberation] worked with anti-feminists on abortion law repeal."[55] And part of the way Cell 16 made this split official was to list its new mailing address on Lexington Avenue in Cambridge at the top of the first page along with an announcement: "We are no longer producing and distributing the Journal [of Women's Liberation] at the Boylston Street address [in Boston] because that office has been taken over and is being occupied by female members" of the Young Socialist Alliance.[56] Therefore, as the ideological, political, and organizational differences sharpened, they played out through the space of the office and were about the use of the office.

Cell 16 chose to distance itself from Female Liberation and the office space, but spatial dynamics also excluded those who wanted to feel a sense of belonging. A letter from Diana Diamond and Omie (?) E. West outlines an experience they had at the Valley Women's Center. On August 23 they brought a group of students from Springfield, Chicopee, and Holyoke high schools for a tour of the center and a lecture on birth control. The group was "hustled . . . upstairs with admonitions not to touch anything and to be quiet because of the beauty parlor next door" and then was "largely ignored; the women at the center did not make any effort to introduce themselves or to welcome our students or to explain what the center was about. In addition, although our students were obviously low-income, the women at the center gave no consideration to this fact and would not give any discount on the literature the students wanted to purchase." By the time Lee Porter, the woman facilitating the birth control lecture, arrived, "the students were already feeling hostile and out of place."[57] Center staffers' actions may not have reflected a specific political ideology but nonetheless gave visitors a message about whether they belonged. According to Ahmed, "To be comfortable is to be so at ease with one's environment that it is hard to distinguish where one's body ends and the world begins. One fits, and by fitting, the surfaces of bodies disappear from view."[58] For her, this comfort—this fit—relates directly to the ways in which one embodies norms. Norms—even if not explicitly stated—are manifest through space and shape how a place is made for certain bodies. Being out of place thus indicates that the norms of a place are unwelcoming. Based on Diamond and West's description of the day, the Valley Women's Center staffers apparently had treated the visitors as outsiders, conveying the message that they were also outside the scope of feminism.

The *Valley Women's Center Newsletter* remained silent about this issue although Porter raised the incident with the women's center staff, asking, "What are we doing as an organization of sisterhood when a group of 30 high school girls from Springfield (all but 6 of them were black), invited for group counselling and to visit the women's center, are greeted coldly and made to feel unwelcome? Is this the way we expect to reach our black and third world sisters?" Across the top of the page, Porter wrote, "PLEASE INCLUDE THIS IN THE NEXT VWC NEWSLETTER." A member of the VWC staff, Michelle Aldrich, stapled a handwritten note to Porter's statement: "It seems to me that if we print this we should add the statement by Cleo + Elana in the log, Aug 26."[59] In this log, the two staffers had written that "a warm welcome was extended" to the visiting girls and that "we gave the kids no reason to feel that we were 'white middle class' etc, unless they automatically assume that about *all* white women (which is understandable, but ridiculous to try to work with in ½ hour)."[60] These disparate accounts highlight the fact that different people experience places in different ways, and these differences are both implicitly and explicitly reflected in varying conceptions of feminism. In addition, by failing to present any of these perspectives in the newsletter, the center created another kind of place-based exclusion. If the newsletter served as a site of feminism—realizing feminism in its content and material existence—then its silence about this event further confined and silenced the visitors. The voices of the girls and their chaperones are literally written out of feminism, and the conflict itself is effectively erased from the public record of the women's liberation movement. The fact that many of the girls were people of color offers more evidence that white feminists struggled to practice their critical understandings of power and privilege in a way that reflected the intersectional qualities of identity. The incident also offers a useful reminder that although periodicals constitute rich chronicles of feminism's daily life in a community, they are curated and therefore give readers a selective image of the women's liberation movement.

### Ephemeral Feminism

Imagine this: it is midday and perhaps you are taking a break from the city's busyness to enjoy a little bit of shade. Perhaps you are sharing lunch with a friend, walking a dog, or reading a book. Regardless of your specific action, at this moment your attention shifts; you tilt your head and listen more intently as sounds slowly build, carried by the wind. You suddenly see an approaching mass of women. Those at the front carry a life-size statue of Sojourner Truth. Others carry signs with brazen slogans and bold imagery, chanting and singing. Someone comes up and hands you a sheet of paper labeled "Certificate of Sisterhood/Certificado de Hermanidad." In both English and Spanish, the page offers statistics about women and men in the workforce and the lack of available day care options for women across the nation. It also contains a list of seven demands, among them "free community controlled and staffed 24-hour child care centers funded by taxation of corporate profits" and "free self-defense classes for women starting at the junior high level."[61] Such a scene may have unfolded on March 8, 1971, when women from all over Los Angeles joined in a celebration of International Women's Day. The morning began with a gathering of representatives from the Women's Liberation Labor Committee, the Los Angeles Committee to Free Angela Davis, the Asian Women's Collective, Lesbian Feminists, and other groups as well as individual activists at East 11th Street and Santee Street, in the Garment District just southwest of the heart of downtown. The activists walked along 11th Street, turned right onto South Broadway, walked six blocks, and turned left on West 6th before ending the march at Pershing Square, which they renamed Sojourner Truth Square, transforming it from a memorial to a U.S. Army general into a site of feminist liberation.[62]

The *L.A. Women's Liberation Newsletter* described some of what happened once the group reached the square and the previously tranquil civic place had become a loud, raucous place of feminism: "Renee Harding read the speech Sojourner Truth gave before the Women's Rights Convention at Akron, Ohio in 1851, popularly known as 'And Ain't I a Woman?' [as] the statue of her was chained to the center flag-pole in the middle of Pershing Square. The women, with arms linked, joyously sang a feminist song, each one of them overpowered by the growing sense of sisterhood and strength the successful demonstration had given to each of them."[63]

Responses to such actions demonstrate that they were a powerful way to galvanize women. Building on the activist repertoires of the New Left and revolutionary groups such as the Black Panthers and Weathermen, feminists relied on marches, demonstrations, and zap actions to challenge power structures by reconfiguring public places: the 1968 Miss America Pageant protest in Atlantic City, New Jersey; the 1969 WITCH protests at bridal fairs in New York City and San Francisco; the 1970 sit-in at the *Ladies' Home Journal* office in New York City; the hundreds of marches during which feminist activists filled the streets.[64] Such events made the women's liberation movement visible, since they were more likely to garner mainstream media attention, especially if they presented some controversy.[65] As Bonnie Dow has remarked, despite the ways that media oversimplify and sensationalize activism, "movements need media to make news, and media need movements so that they can make news out of them."[66] Events that delivered these highly public "moral shocks" are useful in provoking affective responses that enabled outsiders to begin identifying with a movement's politics, reinforced the solidarity of those already involved, and pushed those in positions of authority to take the group seriously.[67] Regardless of the specific impact on individuals— through reports by media sources or through word-of-mouth feminism— actions like the International Women's Day march made feminism a force to be reckoned with for both movement insiders and outsiders.

These energetic, energizing feminist disruptions certainly gave feminism a place, but they were also ephemeral and spatially bounded. They temporarily overwhelmed and transformed public locations, creating space for feminism, but as soon as the events ended, evidence of feminism could be erased. Social movements, however, need resources to make themselves sustainable; they require labor that gives them a presence *through* time, not just as a spectacle *at* a specific time, or they limit their ability to transform oppressive systems. For the women's liberation movement in the 1970s, periodicals were integral to establishing this enduring presence, weaving a temporal and spatial fabric for feminism that allowed activists to experience a vibrant present moment, a sense of the movement's past, and a vision for its future.

Michel de Certeau's theorization of tactical and strategic actions offers a useful frame for understanding the significance and limitations of feminism's more guerrilla actions and helps elaborate the vital role periodicals played in creating and reproducing the women's liberation movement. This taxonomy categorizes and characterizes different social movement activities, allowing us to see their utility and their disadvantages. As with many models, the tactic-strategy distinction may be a little too neat, a little too simple, to reflect the ways in which people actually interacted with and experienced their activism and the places of a social movement. Accordingly, I also use periodicals as a medium to interrogate and complicate Certeau's model.[68]

Because of the continually uncertain, often guerrilla-style (ephemeral) occupation of a place, tactical action characterizes much of the work that feminists did and the sites from which women chose and were forced to work. Certeau explains that a tactic "belongs to the other. [It] insinuates itself into the other's place, fragmentarily, without taking it over in its entirety. . . . It has at its disposal no base where it can capitalize on its advantages, prepare its expansions, and secure independence with respect to its circumstances."[69] Tactics disrupt and interrupt: they "insert themselves into the accepted framework, the imposed order [so that the] surface of this order is everywhere punched and torn open by ellipses, drifts, and leaks of meaning: it is a sieve order."[70] Unpredictable and surprising, creating fissures and exposing the cracks so that a different set of rules can organize a place, tactics destabilize dominant epistemologies and reorganize (albeit briefly) the conventional uses of a particular place and the way people can relate to each other there.[71] Tactical actions would lack the same impact if they were regular occurrences, if they took place somewhere already designated as feminist, or if they did not occur in public. The Los Angeles International Women's Day event, for example, allowed for a carnivalesque eruption of feminism, a "temporary liberation from the prevailing truth and from the established order."[72] Therefore, strength can be found in these kinds of practices. They energize and mobilize and prevent institutionalized networks from falling into stasis.[73] Akin to performance art, tactical activism gains part of its power from its ephemerality and the unique interruption it creates.[74] But this transformation cannot last. The city—the assemblage of institutions that "properly" occupied the space— would not allow a permanent transformation, and the group organizing the event would not have the resources to maintain it. Reflecting this return to norms, the *L.A. Women's Liberation Newsletter* article noted that "Sojourner Truth no longer graces Pershing Square (the L.A. Park Development removed her within one hour after the demonstration had ended)."[75]

Aptly expressing this repertoire of tactical feminism, a St. Paul, Minnesota, activist who helped found a shelter for survivors of domestic violence described the group's practices: "We made do."[76] Inadequate funding, material resources, and staff/volunteer labor persistently dogged activists. The many announcements in feminist periodicals requesting reader assistance—for the group publishing the paper as well as for other groups—offer insight into the precarious place the movement occupied. In October 1970, the editors of the *L.A. Women's Liberation Newsletter* wrote, "At present money to support the Center comes in haltingly and sporadically."[77] Soon thereafter, they offered an update: "The recent Rummage Sale was a success thanks to those who cooperated so enthusiastically. But, we need many more such events if our Women's Center is to survive. Until very recently the Women's Center received monetary support from UCLA. That source of funds is no longer available. UCLA is now giving some support to our Legal Aid program. But, that's all!"[78] By December, the situation had become desperate: "HELP! HELP! HELP! We find ourselves in a self-perpetuating circle—not enough women down at the Center to do the necessary work so that future plans can be made and information given out and interest for the movement generated."[79] UCLA's withdrawal of support caused both spatial and temporal uncertainty and concomitantly uncertainty about the local movement's future.[80]

A tactical approach to activism, while a useful part of a movement's repertoire, is precarious, and a closer look at the distinction between tactics and strategies reveals the spatial and temporal dimensions of this instability. Because a tactical action is "determined by the absence of a proper locus," it manifests itself by taking a place and temporarily redesigning it transgressively.[81] As Certeau elaborates, a tactic "has at its disposal no base where it can capitalize on its advantages, prepare its expansions, and secure independence with respect to its circumstances."[82] Here he characterizes tactical actions as lacking stability in relation to place; in fact, he describes the place of the tactician as "nowhere."[83] Spatial instability implies a lack of stability in relation to time: without predictability in placement, a group likely lacks predictability in its future and cannot "prepare its expansions." In contrast to the contingency and ephemerality of tactical actions, strategic actions have a future, and, just as important, that future is predictable in part because strategies operate from a proper place.[84] Scientific writing, which falls into the disciplinary realm of strategies, illustrates the way Certeau's schema imbricates space and time: it "ceaselessly reduces time, that fugitive element, to the normality of an observable and readable system. In this way, surprises are averted. Proper maintenance of place eliminates these criminal tricks."[85]

Reinforcing the way space and time distinguish tactics and strategies, Certeau situates strategies as the province of those with power, whereas those resisting power must make do tactically. While this taxonomy is useful for understanding feminist practices, it nonetheless sets up a binary relationship between tactics and strategies: tactics are temporary, while strategies plan for the long term; tactics disrupt the dominant order, while strategies reinforce it; tactics connote uncertainty, while strategies reproduce knowability.[86] Within this frame, tactics necessarily correspond with resistance and strategies with hegemony, so according to this logic, maintaining a subversive stance requires social movement actors to be tacticians rather than strategists. However, if a social movement aims to endure, thinking strategically is important. As spatial interruptions, spectacular feminist events offered moments of introduction to and identification with feminism, supporting the protest cycle of a social movement, but they are less useful for doing the work of maintenance—that is, sustaining a social movement through time.[87] Recognizing the need for both tactical and strategic practices—the explosive dramatic moments and the daily, mundane, repeated labors—the article about International Women's Day in Los Angeles chronicles the excitement of the march and demonstration and ends with the call to readers: "If you too are interested in joining with your sisters in the struggle, contact the Women's Center for information."[88]

### Durable Feminism

A sustainable social movement needs predictability. It needs a future on which movement insiders can depend, which relies on access to a proper place. Periodicals produced a sense of this persistence for the women's liberation movement, not only because of the way their content enabled feminism to exist in time and space but also because of their serial format. Through coverage of events and issues as well as pieces about women in history, periodicals produced a feminist past. Announcements about upcoming events allowed readers to imagine and anticipate a future. And although this near future usually expired before the next issue was published, when the next issue arrived it produced another near future. Despite at times erratic publishing schedules, these periodicals regularly reminded readers that feminism had a place in the world and that this place could persist.

Letters to the editor particularly reflected readers' expectations regarding the arrival of a new issue and with it the present and future of the women's liberation movement. Women wrote to periodicals because they believed that their letters might be published or that their feedback might shape future issues. The *Female Liberation Newsletter* frequently opened with letters from readers, and one particularly noteworthy exchange began in the July 26, 1971, issue with a letter from a woman named Mary from Brookline, Massachusetts, who described her experience with voluntary sterilization at a local hospital. The exchange continued over an unusual temporal span—nine issues published over two months—and featured an uncommonly large number of participants, very clearly showing that readers interacted with periodicals in a way that imagined and created a future for feminism.

Mary's original letter began, "Dear Sisters, I am about to get myself sterilized, and would like to share my findings with you." Before she could receive the surgery, Mary had to have her husband's signature, and she wondered whether the requirement that men seeking vasectomies had to have the "wife's permission" were enforced comparably. Mary was "considering leaving the [husband's signature] line blank, or writing his name myself, or making up a crazy name just out of spite. But that might delay things, and perhaps I should spend the time and energy on more important issues, or at least more clear-cut issues. Comments, anyone? Yours in Sisterhood, Mary."[89] The next issue, published on August 2, included a response:

> Dear Sisters,
>
> In reply to Mary of Brookline about sterilization: my state senator, John F. Aylmer, is currently working on the first draft of a bill that would make it illegal for a doctor to refuse sterilization to any person desiring it unless there were medical contraindications. . . . Here's hoping this brings some good results. . . . I'll keep you posted on what develops.
>
> In sisterhood,
> Mary McDermott[90]

A week later, the *Female Liberation Newsletter* published two more letters on the subject. In the first, Sandy Kent wrote: "Dear Sisters: This is mainly to Mary who is about to be sterilized. I was sterilized in June and it was a positive experience except for the 'husband's permission' hassle. . . . Mary, I hope you are not going the old major surgery route. I had a laparoscopy. It's so much quicker, cheaper and less traumatic for your system." Kent also provided her phone number and encouraged Mary to call if she had any questions. The second letter came from Karen Lindsey: "Dear Sisters, This is in response to the letter from Mary on page 1 of your newsletter. I don't know anything of the situation in Mass, having just gotten here from New York. But now that I'm settling in Boston (Cambridge), I'd like to check it out." After describing New York feminist activism related to women's health issues, Lindsey provided her phone number and address and encouraged "Mary, or any other woman," to get in touch. She continued, "I've never done any kind of organizing, but if there were a few of us, maybe we could begin to do something," and she offered to help with Female Liberation's journal, *The Second Wave*.[91]

The exchange continued with another letter published on August 16 that began, "Dear Mary, I saw your letter in the *Female Liberation Newsletter* of July 26, and because I, like you, am interested in having myself sterilized, I thought I might try to answer some of your questions and ask some of you."[92] On September 20, the author of the first letter, Mary from Brookline, provided an update: the operation went well, and she persuaded some of the nurses to write postcards in support of the Equal Rights Amendment. She concluded, "I only feel guilty that I didn't forge my husband's signature. Let us all work on the legal aspect. And anyone who wants to call me to find out more about the operation, please call. . . . I have heard that there is even a simpler operation, an afternoon job, that will be available in Mass. sometime after Nov. As soon as I know for sure, I'll let you know."[93]

Female Liberation staff also participated in the dialogue, publishing a brief announcement on September 6 that voluntary sterilization was legal in every state except Utah and thus that the "difficult or demeaning requirements" imposed on women resulted from hospital policy rather than state or federal law.[94] Four months later, the newsletter published another letter from Mary McDermott with an update on her political work related to sterilization laws.[95] And in June 1972, ten months after Mary's initial letter appeared, the *Female Liberation Newsletter* printed an announcement for a book, *Foolproof Birth Control*, that includes essays about voluntary sterilization.[96] Lindsey, too, wrote again, with her August 1972 letter describing her positive sterilization experience: she had found a doctor through an earlier issue of the *Female Liberation Newsletter* and would be happy to talk with interested women about the procedure.[97]

This lengthy exchange reveals how readers relied on the newsletter, their assumptions about it, and how it created durability for women's liberation. Not only did the women who wrote expect that subsequent issues would exist to publish the letters, but these letters envisioned a future beyond that time horizon, as in Mary from Brookline's promise, "As soon as I know for sure, I'll let you know," and McDermott's pledge to "keep you posted on what develops." These sentiments reflect the presumption not only that an upcoming newsletter would print them but that Female Liberation would continue to exist, receive letters, and distribute information in the future. That the organization would do so via the newsletter is implied.

Despite readers' faith in the future of a periodical, which manifests their sense that the women's liberation movement occupied a proper place, editors continually struggled to procure the resources to maintain a publishing schedule, implying that these feminist groups still operated tactically, gathering what they could for the present moment. Seriality thus did not always live up to its promise. An editorial on the back page of the January 1982 *Distaff* eagerly anticipated the newspaper's upcoming issues: "*DISTAFF: 1982* will carry regular columns on women in the ARTS, in BUSINESS, in POLITICS, and in SPORTS. The DISTAFF DIGEST will recap the month's major local, state, national and international issues affecting women. OPINIONS, both yours and ours, will take greater prominence. The PEOPLE, RESOURCES, and SERVICES important to YOU will be close to you through DISTAFF's pages. The NEWS in the next decade is ours for the making. The NEW DISTAFF is ready to tell the story."[98] But no further issues ever appeared.[99] Discourse clearly was not sufficient to provide a future for a periodical. In another example of temporal instability, periodicals at various times instituted what were intended to be recurring columns, but these intentions were not always fulfilled. In January 1971, the *L.A. Women's Liberation Newsletter* printed on page 4 "What's Happening in Your Group?," which it described as "an on-going column attempting to somewhat bridge the communication gap and spread ideas between groups." The newsletter published updates from local feminist collectives, but such notes appeared unpredictably, not as a part of a named column. Therefore, not only is seriality not guaranteed, but promises made in one issue may not be fulfilled in subsequent issues.

The Valley Women's Center also demonstrates that longevity is no assurance of a continued presence or future. January 1977 marked a moment of crisis in Northampton. The newsletter's front page exclaimed, "EMERGENCY GENERAL MEETING, SUNDAY, JANUARY 16TH AT 12:30 PM AT THE VWU. All women are urged to attend. We are being evicted!!!!!"[100] The minutes of the meeting of the center's steering committee, which also appeared on the page, explain that the landlord had concerns, including "rent late," "use of building at night," and "posters all over." There is no indication of whether the eviction might be politically motivated and no attempt to rebut the landlord's claims, but the minutes do mention "a feeling that the center is gone." Though ambiguous, this sentiment indicates a shift in the way people were viewing and occupying the space of the center and further cements the fact that place matters to a group's activism. By this time, the newsletter had appeared regularly for almost seven years, and the Valley Women's Center had seemed a stable part of the local feminist community. Yet the eviction proved fatal for the center and the newsletter, with no other issues published.[101]

Seriality, therefore, reflects both durability and precariousness, encouraging us to complicate the tactic/strategy binary formulated by Certeau and adopted by other scholars.[102] Periodicals embody and enable a repertoire consisting of both tactical and strategic operations and open up paths for a broader consideration of how social movements can draw from both in their activist projects. Thus, a sustainable social movement needs predictability— *and unpredictability*. The women's liberation movement needed a proper place so that women could find it, but it also needed to be emplaced unexpectedly, surprisingly. It needed a firm foundation as well as space for flexibility and spontaneity. Joan Cassell explains that "decentralization maximizes experimentation, which may give a better chance of hitting on new solutions to problems. But it minimizes the possibility of long-term coordinated work toward (or against) specific goals."[103]

Seriality also allows us to better understand the nuances of tactics and strategies, and such an analysis provides a lens for understanding activist repertoires in social movements. Reading a periodical over multiple issues illuminates how repetition reinforces and complicates feminist politics and identity. When something—an idea, issue, person, or whatever—appeared frequently in a periodical, it became part of what made feminism meaningful as a collective identity. The series of letters about sterilization, for example, reinforced the idea that the doctor's office and the family were sites of feminist intervention. The *Female Liberation Newsletter* enabled the writers' perspectives to coalesce into a more unified voice stating that part of women's reproductive health care involved the right to voluntary, efficient, safe sterilization procedures. This repetition also affirmed the centrality of reproductive justice to women's liberation and highlighted sterilization as a meaningful part of this struggle.

At the same time, seriality creates a mode of repetition that refuses closure. Because the current issue of a periodical always anticipates a future issue, its depiction of feminism is necessarily unfinished and incomplete. Each subsequent issue brings a new panoply of voices and perspectives that add to the formulation of feminism, both reinforcing and adding nuance to certain aspects of it as a collective identity. Even though the sterilization letters express some consensus, they do not reduce sterilization to a singular narrative. Lindsey's 1972 letter contrasts with Mary of Brookline's letters in that the latter discussed the challenges she faced, while the former presented a more positive experience. Moreover, two weeks after Lindsey's letter appeared, the newsletter announced that the SPEAKOUTRAGE Project was seeking local participants to share their encounters with the medical establishment in areas including denial of voluntary sterilization or sterilization without consent.[104] This announcement extends self-determination to encompass not just the ability to access the procedure but also the ability to refuse it.

Another example of the way multiple issues of a periodical can disrupt the solidification and simplification of a feminist praxis occurred in Los Angeles as women grappled with ideas about leadership. On the one hand, the reappearance of this topic in the *L.A. Women's Liberation Newsletter* reinforced its significance to theorizing and practicing feminism. On the other hand, although the editors identified a nonhierarchical group structure as a preferred way of organizing, they published pieces that offer different views on this topic. In October 1970, Coralee Webb, Marie Colaneri, and Heidi Chrissos expressed their opposition to "the prevailing myth that that no singular woman has the intellectual fortitude to lead, to direct, to shape the cause or movement" and suggested that the women's liberation movement needed to be open to forms of organizing other than the purely nonhierarchical collective: "How can there be a collective leadership without leaders?"[105] Two months later, Mary An stridently declared, "We cannot and must not imitate the inadequate political structures of the male system which places all the power in the hands of the few"; "leaders are dangerous to our Movement."[106] After changing its name to *Sister*, the newspaper published a list of local resources for readers, indicating that feminism encompassed groups with different leadership practices. According to the editorial note accompanying the list, "The politics of these groups range from radical feminist or socialist to moderately liberal, and their structure ranges from collective to traditionally hierarchical. All define themselves as feminist."[107] The periodical's seriality consequently allows us to see leadership as a concept and practice that continually unfolded and that women debated without necessarily resolving. And while collective and nonhierarchical structures may be more visible as an ideal at both the local and national levels, feminist structures were not envisioned or practiced in identical ways. Periodicals show that this variation occurred both in different places and across time in the same place.

Serving as a kind of mobile bulletin board for the local women's liberation movement, feminist periodicals created a spatial collage of feminism and a space for its future. As such, periodicals—and printed materials more generally—were integral to women's liberation. Women's centers almost always had libraries that collected books and other women's liberation ephemera and usually sold these kinds of materials as well. The *L.A. Women's Liberation Newsletter* reminded readers that "for the latest information on feminism in all its aspects come down to the bookstand at the Center. We have pamphlets, magazines, newspapers, bumper stickers, pins and posters. Keep reading and be informed about the movement."[108] According to the first issue of the *Valley Women's Center Newsletter*, the center's archives "are files of pamphlets and clippings—from newspapers & magazines—dealing with problems relevant to our movement. There are three file drawers in the VWC: a publisher-author file; and two subject files. The material is kept available for research. New material is constantly sought; old material is constantly filed."[109] And the Female Liberation staff noted that "more and more books and pamphlets are coming into the bookstore now. In addition to the new listings in last week's Newsletter we have *Feminism: The Essential Historical Writings* edited by Miriam Schneir which excerpts some of the most exciting writings and speeches made by feminists of the last century."[110]

But texts more generally have provided alternative maps of places for a wide range of marginalized populations. Martin Meeker has written about the ways that space became coded through lesbian and gay publications in the 1960s and 1970s. According to Meeker, Ann Aldrich's nonfiction books about being a lesbian in New York City, *We Walk Alone* (1955) and *We, Too, Must Love* (1958), gave lesbians not just a place but a place in the public sphere. Hungry for information about where to find lesbians and lesbian-friendly places, women came to New York City "with images and expectations in their minds that had been shaped in part by the words of people like Aldrich."[111] These books offered evidence for the existence of identities because they located such identities in particular places and facilitated a gay imagined community—that is, a reader could imagine other gay women in these places. Fiction, too, mapped identity onto place, as Michèle Aina Barale shows in her close reading of the cover of a lesbian pulp novel, *Beebo Brinker*. Barale describes the novel in material terms as a guide to the city and in figurative terms as illuminating a cartography of desire.[112] Texts thus constitute various forms of spatiotemporal maps: they identify and name places to visit and avoid, they set up boundaries and produce relationships, they draw the past and connect it to the present, they create space in which the future can be imagined and possibly materialized, and they populate a world of people with whom the reader might identify. In a metaphysical sense, texts are part of the ordering of space (turning space into place) by serving as guides that implicitly and explicitly make intelligible bodies, objects, ideas, fantasies, and feelings.

These maps that periodicals created and constituted did not merely describe space, and their spatial inscriptions are not neutral assignments of meaning.[113] To make a map enacts and reproduces ideologies and epistemologies; as we name places, we create them, and there is power in choosing what to name, what to make visible. Naming also gives meaning both to the place and to the space it occupies.[114] Calling a building a women's center or proclaiming that a street has become Sojourner Truth Way confirms these sites as part of the realm of feminism. This is not to say that places do not exist independently of maps; rather, the process of naming and demarcating makes a claim to a territory. The Connecticut Valley map on the cover of the *Valley Women's Center Newsletter* creates places in relation to feminism—whether as in need of feminist intervention (Joe's Café) or as identifiably feminist (a radio station on Tuesday nights). Each issue of a periodical is a static representation of feminism at a particular moment in place and time but nonetheless also allows us to see feminism as dynamic, as a shifting assemblage of spaces and events, people and ideas, power and resistance.

# CHAPTER 3

# Doing Feminism

A short piece in the *Valley Women's Center Newsletter* alerted readers to a 1972 gubernatorial campaign: "CISSY FARENTOLD has put the fear of god in the hearts of Texas politicians. She is now in the special run-off primary for the democratic nomination for Governor of the state. Winning the democratic nomination is tantamount to winning the election."[1] Despite its focus on local and regional events and issues, the newsletter regularly informed readers about women in politics and highlighted news across the country and occasionally internationally, so readers would not have found such a piece anomalous. But the campaign's political importance was not the sole reason for the item's inclusion. The next sentence explained, "This election is getting local coverage because Cissy is Annebowen's older sister's godmother, annebowen did this newsletter's typing." This seeming afterthought does not add to readers' knowledge about the election's political issues or the candidates. A historian might be interested in the kinship connection; a sociologist might use this example to analyze the way informal networks can function in social movements. For me, although the location of the final phrase—"annebowen did this newsletter's typing"—almost gave readers permission to overlook it, it captivated me. Initially drawn to its information about the publishing process, I found myself pulled into the political, grammatical, and textual stories it told. A close, intertextual reading of this sentence illuminates broader patterns in feminist publishing. These patterns, in turn, contributed to the dominant frameworks that characterized feminism as a social movement identity.

Bowen's statement offers a kind of transparency about the way this issue was produced by foregrounding a facet of production—typing—that does not usually become visible to readers. Readers of any early 1970s mimeographed document would likely know on some level that a person had typed the words even if those readers did not know the details of the mimeographing process. Despite their integral role, typists rarely receive credit in the finished product.

In this case, however, the requisite labor becomes visible because the person doing it named herself. Feminist periodicals in various formats commonly made the labors and processes of production visible, a practice that both reflects and constitutes feminism as a collective identity. Inspired by comments such as Bowen's, I consider the cumulative significance of the way these periodicals use repetition to suggest ways of being and doing feminism.

Juxtaposing a state election and periodical production brings different scales of political action into the feminist fold and suggests that both hold equal feminist significance. Farenthold's campaign occurred at a macro scale, primarily at the state level, but also became visible outside Texas. Periodical production occurred at a local scale. Although periodicals covered the globe, the actual production—typing, laying out text and graphics, printing, preparing for distribution—happened in one place, usually a women's center or office. And the personal scale surfaces as well. The connection between Anne Bowen and Cissy Farenthold exposes something that professional journalists would avoid to maintain the appearance of objectivity in their reporting. Bowen, however, made no attempt to distance herself from the event—on the contrary, she actively expresses her sympathies by articulating her kinship with the candidate.

At the risk of putting even more symbolic weight on Bowen's run-on sentence, I return to grammar, specifically syntax. In most publications, the editorial process would alter a run-on sentence and regularize the spelling and capitalization of Anne Bowen's name, but such was not the case in the *Valley Women's Center Newsletter*. Though the linear syntax of English necessitates that we read one idea before the other, putting two independent clauses together in this way creates a horizontal relationship between the Texas election and periodical production: both the state election and the local newsletter's production process are newsworthy items, and, at least syntactically, one clause is not subordinate or auxiliary to the other. Moreover, the comma splice reflects an absence of the sort of editorial oversight exercised in mainstream print publications. Nothing in the organizational records of the Valley Women's Center (VWC) indicates that anyone systematically or consistently copyedited the newsletter. Rather, the women who produced this publication prioritized getting information to readers and often chose not to devote time, labor, or resources to retyping stencils or reconfiguring pages.

These periodicals are filled with inconsistencies and errors—typos and misnumbered pages; changes in font, formatting, and layout for no apparent reason; and varying ways of presenting information (for example, features that recur unpredictably, differences in citation formats, and location and presence of mastheads)—but this feminist print culture was based in part on an understanding that readers would not correlate syntactical or typographic errors with accuracy of content. Though readers wrote in to critique these publications and correct misattributions, such errata were not among the things they brought up. Somewhat counterintuitively, in fact, these signifiers of amateurism could have a positive effect by conveying to readers that even those who were not professionals or experts could participate in the publishing process. Just as the discourse of sisterhood encouraged women to see themselves as connected to others in the women's liberation movement, amateurism in publishing invited readers to see themselves as potential writers, editors, and distributors of feminism.[2]

So although a comma splice is not inherently feminist, in this case it opens a space in which to analyze feminist politics through some of the micropractices that produced it. Form and content, therefore, did not just inform, were not just effects of a particular publishing technology, and were not just errors. They also conveyed meaning about feminist editorial practices and about feminism more generally. They reflect a certain publishing method strongly and explicitly informed by a particular value system and through their repetition tell a story about what feminism was. Since such practices—rather than the large public events that tended to be visible in mainstream media— constituted the foundation of feminist organizing, these micropractices also constituted an important foundation of a feminist identity. Analyzing the civil rights movement, T. V. Reed has drawn attention to the "countless hours, months, and years of work by local activists"—most often women. A focus on media stars and male leaders thus obscures "the majority of the movement."[3] Similarly, a focus on the feminist spectacles and national events can obscure the "backbone of the struggle," and small regional periodicals are invaluable for the way they chronicle these daily labors.[4] And if these periodicals describe themselves as forums for feminism, then the way they include information about their production allows us to read periodical production as a proper part of feminism. The women's liberation movement consisted of myriad actions including marches through the streets, letters written to politicians, and showings of feminist films—as well as of the labor needed to publish the serial ephemeral publications that covered these splashier events.

This chapter examines the way feminist periodicals depict the processes of their production, showing that representations of the people who contributed to and worked on these periodicals as well as their labor reflect and constitute a crucial component of feminist collective identity formation. This analysis relies on the premise that "identity is produced through doing" and more specifically on the idea that these actions "must be sustained in order for the identity to continue to have meaning."[5] When Female Liberation asked readers to volunteer to collate the newsletter, when *Ain't I a Woman?* asked midwestern women's groups to contribute pages, and when *Distaff*'s masthead explained the publication's submission policy, they were articulating their visions of feminism through their modes of periodical production. Some feminist presses also attempted to hire only women and to use women-owned businesses for tasks that could not be done in-house.[6] Charlotte Bunch, who was deeply embedded in 1970s feminist activism and publishing, argues that feminist reading, writing, and publishing are a necessary part of resisting the forces of patriarchy because they expand women's literacy, giving them the intellectual and material tools to imagine and create alternative ways of being: "We need to look at the specific role and importance of feminist publishing and writing. If the written word is important, then where, why, and how we do it matters also."[7] Feminists took this sentiment to heart, recognizing that their ideals and values were imbricated in their material practices. It mattered not just to produce something—a protest, a book, a film, a women's center—but to produce it in a way that manifested their feminist politics. The members of *Ain't I a Woman*'s editorial collective showed their commitment to a feminist process only three months after publishing the first issue, when they grappled with their participation in the same politics they had renounced: "We should be concerned about appearing as a group against the system, not a group that looks like part of it. We cannot afford to not question such actions as incorporating, applying for mailing permits that require a subscription list be supplied to the government, or hiring full-time staff people."[8] Something as simple as using bulk mailing to distribute an issue could implicate groups in the (sexist) status quo. And if an identity also relies on creating boundaries between Us and Them, then the ways in which feminist periodicals differentiated themselves from mainstream publishing become part of a practice of identity formation.

These words and actions conveyed to readers not just "this is feminism" but "this is how you do feminism." Trysh Travis elaborates the politics of the women in print movement as based on the presumptions that "feminist theory—accurate ideas about what women are and where they are situated within the structures of power and culture—develops in concert with and as a result of women's development of practical skills" and that "the simultaneous development of women's heads and hands was necessary to prevent a divisive split between radical theory and practice."[9] This feedback loop between theory and practice translated into concerted efforts to embody feminism in editorial and publishing labors. As a result, doing feminism informed what it meant to be a feminist, and those who were feminists shaped the definition of acting in a feminist way.[10]

I situate these manifestations of the publishing process within the context of the issues in which those manifestations appear as well as in relation to the periodical as a whole. Read in isolation, the comma splice in the *Valley Women's Center Newsletter* could have a range of different connotations. In conventional media it would simply imply sloppy editing. But the newsletter's identification as feminist, the announcements about local and national events, and VWC meeting minutes give readers insight into the center's non-hierarchical organization and allow the run-on sentence to be understood as an effect of this praxis. Similarly, the presence of a more formal masthead in *Sister* suggests that the publication is or aims to be professional, but inconsistencies that signify amateurism appear across different issues: the masthead is printed on different pages in different issues and sometimes is omitted entirely. I also dialectically read text and paratext with and against each other. As theorized by Gerard Genette, the paratext comprises textual marks that fall outside the "text proper" and instructs the audience about how to "read properly according to the author's designs" by fitting the text into a genre of writing and by indicating how the text could or should be consumed.[11] Paratextual components can include page numbers, authorial attributions, typeface, layout, and titles. For periodicals, such components can also include advertisements, graphics and clip art, and traces of the mailing process. These paratextual marks are part of what let a woman know she was reading a periodical. Mimeographed on 8½″ × 11″ paper, stapled in the top left corner, and folded in half for mailing, essays such as Anne Koedt's "The Myth of the Vaginal Orgasm" and Pat Mainardi's "The Politics of Housework" circulated as pamphlets or position papers that had the same form as a newsletter.[12] But onetime publications were distinguished from serial publications by the absence of graphics, advertisements, and masthead information—paratextual marks.

My analysis of feminist publishing takes into account these different markers of the publication process across the full communications circuit and considers their messages about feminism. I first outline how the periodicals made visible their paths to publication, showing how the modes of periodical production are sites of identity formation in the way editors and writers actively distanced themselves from mainstream media. I then discuss the construction of a feminist identity through collective modes of working and the representations of authorship that actively aligned with feminist values and politics.

### "We Are Not Newsweek"

*Distaff* editor Connie Dorval-Bernal wrote a farewell essay about the work of production in November 1980: "All copy in and now it comes down to the wire. This is layout weekend, time for counting pennies, biting nails, and placating a suddenly active ulcer. Measuring copy down to the tiniest fraction of an inch, spending hours over the dummy and trying to ease everything in. And oh those harrying decisions of what must be cut when it gets down to the final squeeze. Then you spend long hours bent over the layout table, sometimes hot as summer, sometimes cold as winter, waxing, stripping in, straightening, squeezing, finding the right graphic, making last minute corrections and additions, racing back and forth from the typesetter for headlines and then suddenly, miraculously, you're ready to print." She described the sense of anticipation while waiting for the issue to be printed and the joy of seeing it "all tied up in great bundles, still smelling faintly of ink and looking proud and beautiful." This moment, though, quickly evaporates: "But wait, you're not finished yet. There is the addressing, labeling, sorting of zip codes, bundling, labeling again, and trundling the whole lot off to the post office, in the wan hope that the Postal Service sees fit to deliver them promptly. Then you make the rounds of the DISTAFF distribution points, and THEN you kick off your shoes, bib your wine, and start thinking about next issue."[13]

The issue of *Distaff* that included Dorval-Bernal's farewell devoted two more of its sixteen pages to celebrate a year of continuous monthly publishing after the newspaper's four-year hiatus.[14] The anniversary spread included nine photographs of women working on the paper with captions that described the action—"Drumming up ads," "Writing stories," and "The final step, pasteup"—and named the person portrayed. Columns of text by Mary Gehman framed the photographs and chronicled the paper's history, emphasizing the collective structure and the volunteer labor the periodical required. Because these two pieces appeared in the same issue, readers could place them in an intertextual conversation. Dorval-Bernal depicted publishing with evocative detail and specificity, confronting readers with the bodily motions and labors that each issue demanded—measuring, waxing, stripping in, straightening, squeezing, racing—and foregrounding the hours and energy women expended to write, edit, and compile the issue and then to ensure that it reached readers. And a few pages later, photographs of the tasks Dorval-Bernal described gave readers a visual context for and complement to her words.

The extent to which *Distaff* opened up the production process within this issue is unusual, but feminist periodicals published in the 1970s consistently let readers into all stages of the communications circuit that Robert Darnton has outlined: writing, publishing/printing, selling and distributing, and reading.[15] An issue might contain editorial statements (often printed near the front of the issue and meant to guide readers through current, previous, and/or upcoming issues), essays by editors (longer, more reflective pieces that might appear anyplace in an issue), shorter editorial notes (primarily informative pieces, often appearing toward the beginning or end of an issue), calls for assistance in the production process, masthead information, subscription slips, errors and other marks of amateurism, and feedback from readers. All of the periodicals I examine contain examples from most if not all of these categories, though in varying forms and degrees.

The format of a newspaper encouraged longer and more self-reflective explorations of the publishing process, many of which focused on obstacles to publishing. For example, a *Sister* editorial elaborated its editors' decision to take a short hiatus: "Suspending publication gave us time to talk about the problems, the low energy and our commitment (or lack of it)." The subsequent addition of new members reenergized the publication, and the editors returned to reflect on and restructure their work: "We discussed the mechanics, the shitwork, the need for clearly defined departments with a communication system between them, more business-like management of ads, subscriptions, distributions, correspondence, etc."[16] The demands of the newspaper similarly required the editors of *Ain't I a Woman?* to change the publication schedule:

> We have decided to start publishing the paper every three weeks instead of every 2nd and 4th Friday. It is the quickest collective decision we have ever come to. We all found a two-week publishing schedule grueling. It wore us out physically and left us functioning with limited spirit, creatively, not to mention our mental awareness. We are hoping that we can use the extra time to put out a better paper, to talk and to learn from each other with less pressure, and to be engaged in other Women's Liberation work beside publishing so that our relationship to the women's movement is not limited to only writing about it.[17]

And a *Distaff* editorial explained why, after a year of publishing, the paper had been shortened from twenty to twelve pages: "The reasons are at once simple and complex. There isn't enough money to pay the typesetter, our professional layout woman quit the staff because she ended up doing almost everything on the paper and felt exploited. We simply don't have volunteers with enough time and expertise to put more than a minimal 12 pages together."[18]

These editorials generally appear toward the front of issues, whereas other signifiers of the production process tend to be placed on the last few pages. For example, page 10 of the February 1973 issue of *Sister* invited readers to "hawk the newspaper! Keep 15¢ on each copy you sell. See Donna Cassyd and/or pick up a bunch at the Westside Center," with a brief piece offering tips for selling the paper.[19] Readers were also likely to find subscription information, and sometimes a slip to cut out and send with their money, near the end of an issue.

The newsletters in my sample were more likely to give briefer descriptions of the mechanics of publishing, both through freestanding notes and announcements and through embedment in editorials with other information. Near the bottom of page 3 of a summer 1970 issue, the *L.A. Women's Liberation Newsletter* expressed its "thanks to Betty and Loretta at the Commit office for their patience and assistance they have given us with the mimeoing of our newsletter."[20] *Female Liberation* put out a call to readers in the fall of 1970: "Help mail out the Newsletter at the office. Free coffee etc."[21] Highlighting the labor of publishing as well as the group's constant need, a calendar told readers that on February 9, 1972, "F.L. Office. All day. Newsletter is typed and run off on mimeo. Anyone who wishes to come in to help type, run it off, proofread, answer phones, etc. would receive all our love and admiration."[22] And in June 1972, the *Valley Women's Center Newsletter* reminded readers, "All Labor for the publication of this newsletter was donated."[23]

Finally, the modes and processes of production become visible through the masthead. In mainstream print media, the masthead lists staff who contributed to the issue and may also include who published and distributed the periodical and the location of the editorial office. Such information appeared in the periodicals in my archive, albeit with great variation. With varying degrees of consistency, often depending on the publishing collective's structure and whether the periodical was a newsletter, newspaper, or journal, feminist periodicals provided this information. Although the reality of the publication process might have been messier than the masthead indicated, the representation of editors and staff nonetheless gave readers a message about how the publication had come into being by making visible the structures of production. Among the publications I studied, *Distaff* and *Sister* most regularly included mastheads and did so in a form that most resembled a conventional periodical. *Sister*'s July 1973 issue listed people in specific positions, among them "editorial," "production," "distribution," "poetry advisor," and "July's theme editor."[24] *Distaff*'s last issue presented Gehman as editor and other people as production staff, contributors, and correspondents and as working in management/advertising and distribution.[25] When read intertextually, these instances signal that a reader is not holding a conventional periodical.

Such categories did not indicate an exclusively feminist production process. Mainstream media staff also solicit, edit, and lay out text. However, the presence of comments about the process in the finished product is a feminist characteristic. Professional publishing erases traces of those bodies "bent over the layout table," whereas these feminist periodicals highlighted the labors of publishing to bring them to readers' view. Naming oneself as the typist and thanking people for help with mimeographing calls attention to the fact that a periodical is not just a being but also a doing and in turn asks readers to consider that feminism is created through both its products and its processes. The first book the Iowa City Women's Press published, a mimeographed collection, *All the Women Are Welcome to Read Their Poetry* (1972), included a preface in which the press staff addressed the politics of publishing: "Many women will run mimeo machines sometime in their lives for their bosses, or even for political lovers, hardly any women will be allowed near a more sophisticated press. We want to break that cycle by acquiring our own press, but first we wanted to break it by respecting people's labor within the limitation of the only machine allowed to us."[26] In addition to being a perhaps incongruous introduction to a poetry anthology, this preface explicitly revalues the women and the work of publishing. Thus feminist praxis involves not just making labor visible but also giving it new meaning, an approach that is also reflected in the large body of feminist analyses of work more broadly.

The masthead, while connoting a more professional and formal approach to publishing, also marks these periodicals as distinct from mainstream publications. Characteristics of the masthead's presentation—particularly in the Los Angeles periodicals—indicated nonprofessional status. The October 1971 *L.A. Women's Liberation Newsletter* represented the members of the editorial collective with five hand-drawn faces placed above the women's names (Dixie, Shari, Joan, Liz, and Nancy) in cursive and the note, "We're the Newsletter regulars. D., S and I did the editing. We ran out of energy to give you the news—so help us next time to edit and we'll include your picture here . . . like the rest of us" (figure 8).[27] The following January, the editors made themselves visible in a small space between a short announcement about a judge giving women and men different kinds of community service sentences (men work in the forest camps while women are assigned to scrub floors in a local hospital) and a letter about the treatment of women in topless bars. The handwritten text, "The happy, happy newsletter staff," is surrounded by what appear to be small self-portraits (each about half an inch in diameter) by nine different women. Readers do not learn the women's names but nonetheless are reminded that there are laborers who produced the issue. When the *L.A. Women's Liberation Newsletter* transitioned to become *Sister* in January 1973, the newspaper's layout appeared more professional, but the periodical retained these marks of amateurism. Starting in May 1975, the paper fairly consistently placed the "Staff Box" on the back page with an accompanying graphic; the staff names were more likely to be typed as well. Yet despite this relative professionalization, the staff credits still occasionally appeared in different places, and the second issue of *Sister* had staff names ("Carol, Gertrude, Z, Donna C, Joan, Jo, Donna Lopez, Janet") handwritten at the bottom right corner of page 5 under the typeset label "The Sister Staff."[28] The women listed as editors for *Sister*'s July 1973 issue are similarly formatted: "Nancy, Ozone, Donna L., dixie, Z, Maria."[29] The ways in which women are named not only marks these editors as amateurs but also points to a feminist sensibility. The inconsistencies in the usage of initials, first names, and last names suggest that each person decided how she wished to be represented.

The other three periodicals I examined were even more informal about naming those who worked to produce issues. *Ain't I a Woman?* rarely included bylines. The first issue, published in July 1970, listed each editor's name handwritten in different script, but this practice quickly disappeared. The fifth issue, dated September 11, was the first to refer to the editors only as a group: "*Ain't I a Woman?* is published by the Publications Collective of the Iowa City

Maud Russell, editor of THE FAR EAST REPORTER, will speak about "WOMEN IN CHINA and HOW THEY LIBERATED THEMSELVES", at the Women's Center, Sunday night, October 17, at 8:00 P.M. Question and answer period to follow. There will be pictures, books, cards and various other items from China, on display and for sale. Ms. Russell has lived in China for many years, and is well informed about the position of women in both Old and New China.
\*\*\*\*\*\*\*\*\*\*\*\*\*\*\*\*\*\*\*\*\*\*\*\*\*\*\*\*\*\*\*\*\*\*\*\*\*\*\*\*\*\*\*\*\*\*\*\*\*\*\*\*\*\*\*\*\*\*\*\*\*\*\*\*\*\*\*\*\*\*\*\*\*\*\*\*\*\*

Feminist song and poetry magazine would like literary contributions. "Thunder in the Sun", 4224 University Way, Seattle, Wash. 98105.
\*\*\*\*\*\*\*\*\*\*\*\*\*\*\*\*\*\*\*\*\*\*\*\*\*\*\*\*\*\*\*\*\*\*\*\*\*\*\*\*\*\*\*\*\*\*\*\*\*\*\*\*\*\*\*\*\*\*\*\*\*\*\*\*\*\*\*\*\*\*\*\*\*\*\*\*\*\*

Hope Blocker (399-6939) and several other women are doing a show every second Tuesday at 3:30pm. They information, particulary on "women and labor".
\*\*\*\*\*\*\*\*\*\*\*\*\*\*\*\*\*\*\*\*\*\*\*\*\*\*\*\*\*\*\*\*\*\*\*\*\*\*\*\*\*\*\*\*\*\*\*\*\*\*\*\*\*\*\*\*\*\*\*\*\*\*\*\*\*\*\*\*\*\*\*\*\*\*\*\*\*\*

The Southern Calif Regional Anti-War Conference will be Oct 2. There will be a woman's workshop out of which will come the woman's contigient. Contact the LA Out-Now Coalition 461-3337.

JINGLE THE CAN FOR THE WOMEN'S CENTER!!!!!!!!! TIME TO MAKE THE STREET SCENE!!!!!!!!!!!!!
We are going to shake the cans for donations at busy downtown locations to raise money for the Center and to raise conciousness about the Women's Center and the women's movement. Volunteers to help are desperately needed. Volunteers meet at 10:30 on payday - Friday, October 8. For more info call Z at 876-0875.

\*\*\*\*\*\*\*\*\*\*\*\*\*\*\*\*\*\*\*\*\*\*\*\*\*\*\*\*\*\*\*\*\*\*\*\*\*\*\*\*\*\*\*RAPE & COUNTERRAPE\*\*\*\*\*\*\*\*\*\*\*\*\*\*\*\*\*\*

The FBI says that a woman is raped every 13 minutes. They also say that the real number of rapes (many are never reported) is probably 10 times that. That adds up to over 310,000 rapes a year. \*\*\* There will be an Anti-rape Squad meeting at 4450 Lockwood, Apt. 101 (right off of Vermont across from LACC) on October 1st, at 7:30

ROOMMATES WANTED-I am looking for 3 or 4 other free women, in their 30s, who are involved in the women's movement to start a small living collective. Bea Free 821-5177.
\*\*\*\*\*\*\*\*\*\*\*\*\*\*\*\*\*\*\*\*\*\*\*\*\*\*\*\*\*\*\*\*\*\*\*\*\*\*\*\*\*\*\*\*\*\*\*\*\*\*\*\*\*\*\*\*\*\*\*\*\*\*\*\*\*\*\*\*\*\*\*\*\*\*\*\*\*\*

REPORT ON THE SUBCOMMITTEE ON EDUCATION-There were hearings held in the House in summer of 1970. A 2 volume report with terrific material-statisics-facts, etc etc.--free-just write your Congressman. In so doing you will alert him to the fact that women are interested in themselves and their condition and he will pay more attention to our demands. For the Calif. Report on Women write-your senator &/or congressman-also free. Edith Green.
\*\*\*\*\*\*\*\*\*\*\*\*\*\*\*\*\*\*\*\*\*\*\*\*\*\*\*\*\*\*\*\*\*\*\*\*\*\*\*\*\*\*\*\*\*\*\*\*\*\*\*\*\*\*\*\*\*\*\*\*\*\*\*\*\*\*\*\*\*\*\*\*\*\*\*\*\*\*

### I Like to Think of Harriet Tubman

I like to think of Harriet Tubman.
Harriet Tubman who carried a revolver,
who had a scar on her head from a rock
thrown by a slave-master (because she
talked back), and who
had a ransom on her head
of thousands of dollars and who
was never caught, and who
had no use for the law
when the law was wrong,
who defied the law. I like
to think of her.

**Susie Griffin**

FIGURE 8. *L.A. Women's Liberation Newsletter*, October 2, 1971, 4. Woman's Collection, Texas Woman's University Libraries, Denton.

Womens Liberation Front. We are a group of 10 women."[30] As the group's values took hold more strongly, these notices came to include editorial notes such as, "We are a collective of eight women functioning as a world wide conspiracy of Radical Lesbians."[31] The *Female Liberation Newsletter* rarely named the people who worked on issues and much more frequently referred simply to "newsletter staff." And the *Valley Women's Center Newsletter* never formally listed the women who worked on the publication, also using "newsletter staff " or occasionally "work group," so readers learned about these women and their roles only when someone named herself, as Anne Bowen did.

Editors occasionally became present as individuals when mistakes or production hiccups could affect readers' experiences. A VWC staff member wrote an introduction (which itself contained several errors) to a series of position papers about the role and function of the center in the January 1975 issue: "Ann Ferguson's paper is printed on pages 3, 4,+5, ~~and 6~~ which are on the backs of pages 1, 2, and 3. Daphne's is on page 6, Elana's on pages 7 & 8, Seburn's is on page 9 & 10. Unfortunately this is another VWU newsletter put together to test your ingenuity and eyesight."[32] Though this example is somewhat extreme, feminist periodicals frequently contained small paratextual disruptions. The August 1971 issue of the *Female Liberation Newsletter* offered a disclaimer: "A note from your sister, the typist: please overlook such errors as sudden changes in type smudges and general disorder. There was a problem with the typewriter and with correction fluid. Hope the messages come through clearly anyway."[33] And in June 1980, after a decade of publishing, *Distaff* editors offered "profuse apologies to all you faithful readers who must fight your way through this unevenly typed issue. Isn't there anyone out there with some good equipment? We hope to resolve this problem by next issue, but we wanted to deliver your June DISTAFF on time."[34] One of *Ain't I a Woman?*'s editors injected some humor into her production struggles: the top third of the paper's subscription form contains evidence of her attempts to write a word: the first line has *subscriph* crossed out with a large *X*; below it *subscrib*— is also crossed out; the third attempt was successful enough, with *subscribe*—. To the right the editor wrote, "No shit—I really can't use one of these pens."[35] As if to emphasize the mismatch between the user and her tools, the subscription form features "AIN'T I A WOMAN?" handwritten messily in capital letters with the question mark squashed in because the writer ran out of space. Whether the production staff consciously decided not to amend mistakes, simply did not catch them, or chose to embrace them, these marks add to our understanding of the relationship between feminist publishing and feminism.

The informality and inconsistency in the content and layout of these feminist periodicals accumulated in a way that clearly albeit indirectly reinforced their status as social movement publications. However, mistakes in the product and struggles in the process of course are not qualities only of feminism; for this reason, it is valuable to read intertextually, since these periodicals offered more explicit messages about feminism as an identity and set of practices in relation to publishing. In addition to the discussions about and characterizations of feminist activism that constituted much of these periodicals' content, editors distanced themselves from the mainstream publishing industry and from larger economic, legal, and political institutions more generally. They did so by including messages about what feminism is, what feminists do, and who feminists are as well as what feminism is not.

*Sister*'s December 1976–January 1977 issue featured an editorial that announced, "We Are Not Newsweek." According to the piece, the distinction resulted from the mechanics of publishing rather than from specific content: "We want you to know we are different so that you can forgive us our occasional errors and celebrate with us the miracle of putting out once more a pretty good, getting-better-and-better, issue of *Sister*."[36] The editors suggest that *Newsweek*'s ability to publish predictably and without (or with few) typos was another sign of its mainstream status. From its first issue, *Ain't I a Woman?* expressed practical reasons for its distance from "pig media": "We want no hierarchy of editor, assistants, staff, etc. All the people working on the paper should be involved in the decisions and policy.... We want new structures that do not allow people to fall into leader/follower. We don't want to work in any situation in which we are oppressed or in any situation in which we do oppress."[37] The mention of "new structures" signals the editors' rejection of the patriarchal and capitalist investments that support conventional publishing structures, a position elaborated in the newsletter's second issue:

> Ain't I A Woman and many other publications by sisters around the country began as we felt a need for alternative media. We have to communicate without the constraints of the pig press where we've always had our page for recipes, fashions and advice on how to please a man. Working conditions in the pig media demand that any woman who works there must accept a male definition of what women are and should be. Women who work as reporters work for the Man. Usually the man with the most contempt for women sits as their editor. Little wonder that the women survive by seeing themselves as exceptions.[38]

Echoing the idea that the mainstream media were unwelcoming to women, Joslyn McGuire wrote in a January 1974 *Distaff* editorial that the newspaper offered "an open opportunity for women to learn journalistic skills in a nonsexist environment. It is an alternative to the local media for women who want responsible jobs in journalism." She continued, "Because we are a communal effort we do not feel that we can define ourselves as the DAILY WORKER or the TIMES PICAYUNE."[39] Such statements identify conventional media as sustaining and reproducing patriarchal values whether they were tacit, insinuated, or explicitly acknowledged. Embedded in the feminist rejection of the publishing industry are presumptions about the relationship between politics and practice. The statement introducing a radical feminist collection of writings, *Notes from the Second Year*, refers to an editorial policy of publishing pieces "uncut and only minimally edited." The editors attribute this decision to a politics of antiprofessionalism and situate it as part of the movement's "new daring, a willingness—eagerness—to tear down old structures and assumptions."[40] These feminist publications suggest that it is not enough merely to write about feminism: writing also needs to follow a feminist path to publication.[41]

A final way in which these periodicals constructed a feminist identity apart from and against mainstream publishing relates to the obstructions and disruptions editors faced at all stages in the communications circuit. In an August 1973 editorial, *Sister* explained, "As most of our readers know by now the July issue of Sister was almost suppressed by the male printing establishment. First off, our regular printer, Norco, in Orange County deemed the pictures of Self-examination and Carol Clement's cartoon obscene and refused to print the issue. After many phone calls and many hassles we finally found a printer in Riverside County, a two hour drive away and more expensive."[42] Relying on an outside printer left the editors at the mercy of one person's sexism or squeamishness about photographs of a woman inserting a speculum into her vagina.[43]

Editors not only had to navigate the challenges of printing and publishing but also had to figure out the distribution process. Six months after finding a new printer, another *Sister* editorial described how the *Los Angeles Times*, the *Los Angeles Herald-Examiner*, and the *Santa Monica Outlet* attempted to persuade the city to pass an antiobscenity ordinance. Though these mainstream newspapers were not directly targeting *Sister* or feminism, *Sister*'s content meant that the ordinance would prevent newsstands from selling the publication.[44] For *Distaff*, the expenses and labor associated with distribution proved arduous, costly, and time consuming. Donna Swanson proclaimed in December 1974 that distribution was "the most difficult part of this business." Because *Distaff* had a circulation of only a few thousand, the paper would have lost money had it used a commercial distributor, so Swanson and Gehman personally approached newsstands about selling the paper. The women encountered a range of reactions, including apathy, resistance, and hostility. The manager of one establishment on Bourbon Street "particularly enjoyed calling us 'sweetie' and lamenting over the fact that two 'cute little things like us were involved in 'Dyke stuff.'" Another newsstand told a would-be purchaser that *Distaff* had sold out but later returned all but one copy of the issue to Swanson and Gehman. According to Swanson, "In a futile attempt to control my temper, I very politely asked him why he had told customers that he did not have any papers left. His reply was: 'I don't have time to be bothered with women's stuff.'"[45]

Even when editors could bypass the newsstands and distributors, the post office and other delivery systems could present moments of friction. Administrators at a minimum-security prison in Alderson, West Virginia, refused to allow inmate Deborah Turney to receive the newspaper because "Sister has been found to be detrimental to the security, good order, and discipline of this institution because of its advocation or support of homosexuality."[46] As with the Los Angeles antiobscenity ordinance, Turney's experience undoubtedly did not result solely from sexism or antifeminism, but the effect was the same: the communications circuit remained incomplete.

Some subscribers also expressed concerns about the U.S. Postal Service, leading editors to question whether the problems resulted from deliberate attempts to suppress feminist publications. In response to reader feedback, the *Female Liberation Newsletter* noted in October 1971, "We have received a number of complaints from people who have not received newsletters or who received the 9/20 issue with the 9/27 issue—i.e., a week late. We have talked to the post office about this and we have to find out which areas are having trouble."[47] In early 1975, *Distaff* asked its readers to weigh in on when they received the newspaper, since "the U.S. postal system is not always the most efficient."[48] Subscribers to the *Female Liberation Newsletter* and to the *L.A. Women's Liberation Newsletter* mentioned their suspicions about deliveries: "Dear Sisters," Sandra Kent wrote to the Cambridge paper, "first, thanks for the Newsletter. I look forward to its being in the mailbox the first of the week. (unfortunately, however, sometimes the mail*men* don't get it to me until the end of the week)."[49] And Susan Thees wrote to the Los Angeles women, "Dear Sisters, Enclosed is $2 to remain on your mailing list. I was having trouble receiving the Newsletter for a while and soon found out the Post Office was at fault. I called the Post Office and put at tracer on it & 2 days later it arrived. (Funny, I got all my junk mail on time.) How many other sisters have had this problem?"[50]

Beyond the editors' decisions to publish letters about postal service, the fact that readers were inquiring about it fits into a feminist politics and praxis. Subscribers refused to accept status quo practices and discrimination, and publicizing such incidents reflected an awareness of the personal as political: a private, often domestic, moment—getting one's mail—had broader political implications. These letters also exemplify a limitation of Darnton's communications circuit that Simone Murray has pointed out. Darnton's model "has little regard for what founders in the system, for what remains unwritten, for that which is rejected for publication, or for books refused retail space or denied distribution outlets." Murray thus proposes that a feminist communications circuit could usefully look for "hiatuses, disruptions, and silences" in the process of publication as well as for the ways that a publishing institution also can constitute an "instrument for *non*-communication."[51]

## Collectivity as a Value

If identity exists through doing, then collective practices were central to the formation of feminism. Regardless of a feminist group's specific form, content, ideology, or objective, the praxis of collectivity structured much of the women's liberation movement, and so prevalent were discourses of collectivity that Francesca Polletta argues that they became "an essential component of what being a feminist was."[52] Judith Ezekiel's study of the women's liberation movement in Dayton, Ohio, describes the activists' commitment to this form of organizing: they set up monthly meetings to facilitate participation from a wide range of women, rotated the role of chair, and strove for consensus in decision making.[53] In the words of one Dayton woman, "If we sacrifice this process we have sacrificed the principle upon which our movement was built and which is an integral part of the society we are building."[54] The ties between practice and politics are evident in the repetition of certain terms in the names of 1970s feminist groups: the Boston Women's Health Book Collective, the Minot Women's Collective, the Asian Women's Collective, the Sherwood Forest Women's Collective, the Philadelphia Women's Health Collective, the Radical Therapy Collective, the *OURS* Collective, the Power of Women Collective, and the Women's Press Collective. These groups were among the many feminist organizations that published periodicals. And even though the publishers of the *Female Liberation Newsletter* referred to themselves as a committee, the June 1972 *Valley Women's Center Newsletter* described them as the "Female Liberation Collective."[55] Collectivity thus formed a foundation for the women's liberation movement, as if a collective were a unit of measurement for a small group of feminists (though the National Organization for Women and other larger groups were not characterized as collectives).

The extent of collectivity as a value and practice throughout the women's liberation movement makes it no surprise that this form predominated in feminist publishing.[56] Eileen Cadman, Gail Chester, and Agnes Pivot open their book about women in publishing by explaining, "The notion of collective working appears throughout the book as it is a crucial practice of the Women's Liberation Movement." They continue, "It is only by dismantling hierarchical relationships and sharing skills that we will achieve change."[57] Margaret Blanchard, moreover, claims that writing collectively was how "feminism became real, how the theory got lived out, how a new way of looking at and relating to the world got expressed."[58] And this principle was so deeply embedded in feminism as a praxis and thus as an identity that even one of the most professionally published U.S. feminist periodicals, *Ms.* magazine, exhibited collectivist principles.[59] Such sentiments fit easily into the framework of feminist organizing that Murray attributes to the feminist presses she describes as radical. For her, these presses have both adopted a specific structure—"collectivist organisation, non-hierarchical operating practices, job rotation, skills sharing"—and actively rejected mainstream political and economic systems.[60] She frames feminist publishing as a binary system in which "collective" and "corporate" gain meaning oppositionally. Regardless of the ways that the two poles were manifested in practice, this dichotomy reflects a specific value system in which feminist publishing equated to collectivity while mainstream publishing equated to corporatization. Women's presses and publishers, many of which attempted to turn a profit, thus struggled not only to survive but also to situate their work within a feminist movement that in many ways "harboured a deep-seated suspicion that profit-making is inimical to political credibility and that to make money from popularizing a political cause is, inevitably, to dilute the purity of that cause."[61]

Resisting hierarchies and enacting a radical sense of equality, periodical editors manifested an ethic of collectivity by inviting women to participate at all stages in the production process. The publications' repetition of *anyone*, *any woman*, and *all women* reinforced the horizontal structures that feminist activists saw as necessary to reach their objectives and *as* one of their objectives. The January 1973 *Distaff* declared, "This preview issue is the collective effort of a large group of women. The staff box represents only one tenth of those who have participated and contributed. We welcome all women who want to work."[62] The next issue affirmed, "We want to invite all women to join us in this venture. DISTAFF is a feminist newspaper collective, open to any woman who wants to participate."[63] Similarly, the third issue of the *L.A. Women's Liberation Newsletter* invited "anyone who wants to become involved in the Women's Center and is also interested in the newsletter . . . to join our newsletter staff. We meet at the center on Thursdays and Fridays. Please telephone and ask for a member of the newsletter staff."[64] And the VWC staff offered, "Anyone with news, announcements, requests, etc. which they want distributed in the Newsletter send them as you want them printed up to the women's Center or come to the Center."[65] The five periodicals studied here incorporated practices of collectivity into the publication process: they welcomed readers to submit content and to help with production, they blurred lines between different roles in the production process, and they resisted the hierarchies, divisions of labor, and monetary priorities that characterized mainstream publishing. At the same time, ideals and collective practices differed among groups and could shift over time within a group. Moreover, the groups had distinct organizational structures, as evidenced by their representations of themselves and their practices of production.

*Ain't I a Woman?*'s publications cell expressed the most active, explicit, and self-reflective investment in collectivity. The group avowed a commitment to razing hierarchy and bureaucracy, and as time passed they manifested this practice through a tighter and more closed group. A shift early in the paper's life span offers one example of how members curated their collectivity. The initial issues invited any midwestern feminist collective to submit a page of material to the newspaper, but the offer disappeared after the fifth issue. This apparent trend is reinforced by the absence of open calls for reader assistance in writing and editing the paper. Acknowledging this shift, the group wrote in May 1972,

> The strength of a tight collective should be recognizable from this fact that we have stayed together and productive for two and a half years. Half of the present collective was in the original cell that started AIAW. To keep our political direction progressive but stable we limit the collective to women of very similar political orientations, so that we are in agreement on all basic issues we feel are important. We therefore work in a less publically controlled way than groups who have a loose turnover of members.[66]

Therefore, although the women in the publications cell put extraordinary effort into practicing their theories and politics of collectivity, they undertook fewer collaborations with outsiders than did other editorial groups, at least according to what readers would have encountered in *Ain't I a Woman?*[67]

At the other end of the spectrum, the *Valley Women's Center Newsletter* and the *Female Liberation Newsletter* most indirectly expressed collectivity and most vocally requested reader contributions. The self-described committee that published the *Female Liberation Newsletter* operated out of an office rather than a women's center (although it offered resources and programming similar to those at the Valley Women's Center and Los Angeles Women's Center). Members also tended to use *committee* to refer to smaller, task-oriented groups (the orientation committee, magazine committee, fundraising committee). In keeping with the group's vision and practice of collectivity, it incorporated as a nonprofit business in the fall of 1971.[68] Doing so meant adopting an externally imposed structure that resembled conventional corporate hierarchies (a president, four vice presidents, a secretary, a treasurer, an assistant treasurer, and a board of directors), thus formalizing Female Liberation's enactment of collectivity.[69] Yet the newsletter's frequent calls for readers' assistance indicate a certain informality in the sense that writing or editing the publication required no expertise or even experience.

Periodicals also discussed collective practices not directly related to their groups or to their publications. According to the *Valley Women's Center Newsletter*, the objectives of Mother Jones Press, a Northampton business, included teaching "women (starting with ourselves) printing skills which they usually don't have an opportunity to learn. And we wanted to do this by working in a collective, non-hierarchical way. With each of us learning all the various processes involved in printing."[70] Collectivity was thus the axis along which the press aligned with feminist practices (avoiding hierarchy, training women) and distinguished itself from conventional businesses. More specifically, the press affiliated with the VWC as a workgroup, explaining that "When the Valley Women's Union was formed, we felt that our goals fit well into the workgroup criteria of service, education and action, and we welcomed the opportunity to belong to a larger women's organization which would provide organizational links to other women in the area."[71] Moreover, the fact that several pieces by and about Mother Jones Press appeared in the *Valley Women's Center Newsletter* implies that the press's politics overlapped with the center's.

The piece on Mother Jones Press begins on the same page of the newsletter as an update from the VWC's education workgroup, explaining its plans for a "political school for women" that would "get away from the oppressive roles and structures usually implied by the terms—school, teacher, student, classrooms, etc."[72] The group asked "any woman with ideas or skills she wants to share this summer in a women's sch school" contact the center.[73] The issue also contains a report from the graphics workgroup that refers to its "collective creativity."[74] And the Spark Anti Profit Bookstore Collective is described as having "anarchis and feminist" politics and an interest in "developing a community of local-based collectives."[75] While none of these pieces explicitly situates the newsletter's publication practice as collective, taken together, they indicate the centrality of this concept-praxis to the local feminist community.

The women who created *Distaff* and *Sister* instituted more formal organizational structures. In the second issue of *Distaff*, Gehman announced her intention to structure the publication as a business, though a year passed before her efforts reached fruition.[76] Although *Distaff* categorized the different roles that went into its production, it consistently welcomed all women interested in participating, and the same editorial that announced the intention to incorporate also featured an open invitation to readers: "Any women interested in serving on the board of directors for the paper should send name, address and phone number to DISTAFF ... by March first. We also need help now in typing, subscriptions, fund raising and distribution. And of course we are always glad for suggestions, articles, graphics and literature—or just some encouragement; so let us hear from you."[77] And an October 1973 request for help with "reporting, advertising, distribution, proofreading, [and] layout" also noted, "No experience necessary."[78]

Collectivity, however, could fall short of feminist ideals. One of the first issues of the *L.A. Women's Liberation Newsletter* closed with a notification of the submission deadline and the weary note, "Thanks. Your Tired Newsletter

Staff."[79] Even a tight and cohesive group like the *Ain't I a Woman?* publications cell struggled with distribution of labor: the editors wrote in April 1971 that "the shit work has not been very collective, mostly falling on one member or two at times, and this has been difficult for us to deal with, causing some resentment. We talk a lot among ourselves about subjects we deal with in the paper and about other things important to us. For some of us—most of us—AIAW collective is our priority, our project, support, and consciousness-raising group."[80] The phrase *for some of us—most of us*—implies that some members lacked that commitment and were not practicing feminism to the same degree. And Female Liberation's four-year existence ended in part because of dissonance connected to its theories about working together. According to the press release published in the final issue of the *Female Liberation Newsletter,* "We must admit that for the last two years, most of our energy has been absorbed by conflicts within the group. One of the main conflicts that has split us apart has been over different approaches to dealing with power. Some of us have sought to eliminate power, other to achieve it. . . . This basic conflict underlay differences in both the content of our politics and the style, or process, of our work."[81] Studies of 1970s feminism often frame these gaps between ideas and practices as the result of ideological shortcomings of individuals and groups, as the critiques of sisterhood I discuss in chapter 4 exemplify. Yet such gaps also result from material factors. The announcements and editorials that draw attention to the publishing process show that feminism as a concept needs a form in addition to resources to create and sustain these forms.

Periodicals offered an extraordinary transparency regarding processes of production but did not reveal all the obstacles they faced—what Murray describes as that which "founders in the system."[82] A 1972 exchange in the VWC's organizational records illustrates the problems that could arise from what Jo Freeman has termed the tyranny of structurelessness.[83]

> Pages 1 and 2 of the newsletter are done and runoff (copies on the table). Part of pg 3 typed on top of mail cubbyholes. what a pleasure the new machine is! cleo
>
> CLEO we run page 2 on the back of page 1. No harm done—we can create a bunch of stuff for the back of page 1 if necessary.
> Page 1A?
> appendix to page 1?
>
> CLEO Page 1a is a good idea. I will leave a note for Trish to see if she can edit material for thurs. night. MLA[84]

Despite the apparent consensus to create a page 1a, the back of page 1 became page 3. Regardless of the reason for this issue's pagination, it was not an effect of editorial oversight or carelessness. Rather, it symbolizes the group's sense of collectivity, which allowed any woman to work on any task at the center, and offers a way to trace the impact of material factors on specific feminist labor practices and, by extension, on a feminist praxis more generally.

In 1973, the center's log reflects additional confusion, this time surrounding the bulk mailing process:

> This note is about the mailing labels. Some misguided soul began retyping them from the old labels instead of from the zip code box like you are supposed to do. as a resi;t some new people are added in later. There is a longer note about this on top of the zip code box. roz
>
> sorry, it was me — we need a procedure card
>
> The Newsletter was mailed . . . today. It is one page and didn't go out to everyone because some of the labels were missing. c'est la vie. roz[85]

In response to this incident, Michele L. Aldrich added to the log a few days later, "ADDRESS LABELS: Since confusion is rampant on how to do same, I have created a procedures file card on the subject. Please read and edit for clarity and completeness."[86]

Such notes in the daily logs were available to anyone at the center and were necessary to convey information since different people worked on the newsletter. This aspect of structurelessness can be invitational, encouraging women to undertake new tasks such as typing stencils, running the mimeograph machine, and preparing the newsletter for mailing. At the same time, however, the absence of structure inevitably led to mistakes. Though some (the misordering of pages, for example) were minor and likely had little impact on readers, others were more significant: the bulk mailing miscommunication meant that the newsletter did not reach all intended recipients. The inclusion of some women (inexperienced volunteers in the office) resulted in the exclusion of others (those who did not receive the issue and were thus prevented from accessing information about the movement and possibly from learning about and then attending future events).

Jo Freeman's "tyranny of structurelessness," a phrase she coined for a 1972 article published in *The Second Wave*, provides a frame for the challenges that accompanied collectivist methods of political activism. Freeman developed the concept by bringing together her formal academic training (she held a doctorate in political science) and her activism in the movement.[87] According to Freeman, this leaderless form had become prevalent among women's liberation activists in response to an "over-structured society" and "the continual elitism of the Left."[88] Nonetheless, she argues, structurelessness stunted the development of feminism as a political movement by hindering the formation of widespread, accessible communication networks; facilitating the formation of unofficial elites within a group; and deterring the move from talk to action.[89] Polletta has also recognized that a group shaped by informal ties can be exclusive and unwelcoming to new members, can resist the imposition of formal decision-making procedures, and can be more difficult to sustain when people leave.[90]

### Authorship

The August 1974 issue of *Sister* featured an editorial note with a somewhat professional tone:

> Upcoming themes are:
> > September: Heroines/Role Models (deadline: Aug. 15)
> > October: Women in Politics (deadline: Sept. 12)
> > November: Social Control/Women in Prison (deadline: Oct. 10)
> > December: Mothers and Daughters (deadline: Nov. 14)
> > January: Rich Women-Poor Women (deadline: Dec. 12)
>
> We hope you will send us articles, thoughts, etc., relating to these themes. Please do. Some of the best articles have been unsolicited. Please include a stamped, self-addressed envelope if you want your article returned and be prepared for a long wait. We will edit for length and clarity only. Any major editing will be done only after consulting with the writer—so enclose phone numbers where you can be reached.[91]

Unlike the calls that encouraged "all women" or "any woman" to contribute, this notice suggested topics for would-be authors and contained specific information about the editorial process, suggesting that it had been standardized. The page with this note also has a list of *Sister* staff members, information about how to sell the publication, and advertising and classified rates. Other items in the issue reinforce the paper's professionalization. An announcement for a "News Writing Workshop" explains the editors' desire to develop "a team of professionally trained correspondents, investigative reporters and news analysts" to cover feminism locally and nationally.[92] Local journalists would instruct attendees in such areas as "interviewing techniques, investigative reporting, news analysis, and reviewing art and literature," and in return, "each participant in this workshop will be expected to write at least two stories for *Sister* following the workshop or to make some financial contribution to be worked out in advance." Despite this formality, *Sister* had not shed its practice of collectivity. The workshop invited all readers, regardless of their affiliation or expertise, into the women's liberation movement: "Anyone interested in joining the *Sister* staff or those interested in developing their own writing skills are urged to attend." This call reinforced the horizontal, dialogic relationship between editors and readers and specifically encouraged women to see themselves as writers.

In various ways, feminist periodicals repeatedly urged, "Sisters, send us your writing!" Editors sought letters, photographs, announcements, and creative writing; pieces inspired by personal, daily experiences and articles about large public events; praise and criticism; ideas and feedback. Informal newsletters produced entirely in-house, newspapers with designated editors and sent to a press for publication, and all sorts of periodicals in between consistently encouraged readers to become engaged not only as subscribers, typists, and hawkers but as contributors.[93] Readers consequently became sources of knowledge, experts in their own right—not just "consumers of the word" but "creators of the word."[94] Not to be underestimated, "ordinary women breaking into print," according to Kathryn Thoms Flannery, was a radical activity, in part because it enacted feminist values by blurring the reader/writer and amateur/expert binaries.[95]

Even though periodicals quite definitively tell readers "*we* see you as a writer," women did not necessarily respond to this form of interpellation. *Ain't I a Woman?* indicated one aspect of this struggle in a short piece that began, "I can't write" and went on to express other misgivings about becoming an author: "If I try to write something, no one will like it, but they'll be afraid to say so, so they'll print it anyway, and it will ruin the paper."[96] Whether the writer related her true feelings or intended the piece to be ironic, its presence in the paper's first issue reflected the idea's social power. Some women may have believed that what they wrote did not fit into the categories of (publishable) "writing." Some women may have wanted to write but lacked the time because they not only served as the primary caregivers in the home but also worked outside it.[97] Audre Lorde highlights the material factors that enable and constrain authorship when she reminds us, "A room of one's own may be a necessity for writing prose, but so are reams of paper, a typewriter, and plenty of time."[98] And women who finally did put their ideas down on paper could encounter obstacles in mainstream media. When Anita McClellen started working in trade publishing in the late 1960s, one editor refused to publish Emily Dickinson's poetry "because he already published a New England poetess."[99] Trinh T. Minh-ha notes yet another potential deterrent to claiming the label *writer*—that is, getting published may mean participating in and reproducing a racist, classist, sexist industry.[100]

Feminist periodicals thus helped to maintain and sustain the women's liberation movement not only by making feminism visible on a large scale but also by including individual women. This inclusion mattered because publishing women's words mattered, but editorial practices also recognized the power dynamics involved in publishing. Decisions about whom to publish, how to present contributors' voices, and how to give credit to writers reveal one mechanism of feminist praxis—that is, one way in which feminists signaled their feminism.

Letters sections in feminist periodicals reflected both editors' commitments to presenting a range of different women's voices and readers' willingness to take the position of writer, even if informally. All the periodicals I examined published letters, though in varying quantities. The *Female Liberation Newsletter* usually began with letters from readers; *Sister* often devoted at least a full page to letters; and *Distaff* regularly published letters toward the end of an issue. In contrast, the *Valley Women's Center Newsletter, L.A. Women's Liberation Newsletter*, and *Ain't I a Woman?* included fewer letters and printed them less regularly. Letters from readers and editorial policies regarding submissions provide a variety of information about the women's liberation movement, feminism, and the particular publishing collectives studied here. First, based on the range of different kinds of letters and their wide-ranging topics, editors had few preconceived notions about the purposes letters should serve and did not necessarily expect letters to comment on the periodical's content. Second, experience rather than expertise—or experience *as* expertise—became a grounds for authority, blurring the boundaries between amateur and expert and between reader and writer, creating a textual landscape that appeared to value all voices. In this sense, publishing letters was part of the panoply of feminist practices that manifested the ideals of collectivity and efforts to maintain radical egalitarian structures.

All of these periodicals occasionally paired letters with other pieces of writing. *Sister*'s April 1974 issue included a letter in which Robin Sanders wrote, "It's especially important for us in the white women's movement to know and relate to what's coming down in the lives of our 3rd world sisters," as well as Sanders's article about the dynamics of the U.S. labor market, immigration, and the exploitation of Mexican workers.[101] The following month, when *Sister* focused in part on young people's liberation, two poems appeared along with a letter:

> Dear Sisters,
>
> I'm a 12 yr. old feminist and a faithful reader/subscriber to your newspaper, so when I saw the paragraph about the May issue being one devoted to children, I decided to send you some of my poems about women.
>> In Sisterhood,
>> Margaret Talbot[102]

*Ain't I a Woman?* published an article about sexism in the leftist Seattle Liberation Front with letters from Seattle Women's Liberation both preceding and following the article. According to the opening letter, "We are sending you this statement hoping that you will be able to use it in sharing our experience with other women. We acted to strip seven male leaders of their political power and stop them from acting as the spokes*men* of the Left." The postscript then debunked a pamphlet that described the Seattle Liberation Front as supporting women's liberation.[103] A later issue paired a Southwestern Female Rights Union article about racism and sexism in New Mexico with a short letter from union women asking for suggestions and support.[104] And two women identified only as Nan and Mary sent Female Liberation a flyer about an upcoming march on the Pentagon with a note saying that it "would be far out if you could print it up and include it in one Newsletter." The flyer indeed appeared a few pages later.[105] The pairing of a letter and another piece gave women control over their writing, allowing them to explain their intentions and the meaning of their pieces. This practice sent readers a message that their interpretations of and thoughts about others' writing were valid and credible, further disrupting the dominant ideas about whose words merited publication.

The diverse ways in which women self-identified and claimed authorship illustrate the feminist principle of self-empowerment and self-realization and foreground the wide latitude editors permitted in this area. Even when periodicals had explicit editorial policies for letters or other submissions, editors generally left decisions about self-representation in the hands of contributors. This approach reflected the understanding that naming is a political process and project. Female Liberation, for example, criticized the *Boston Globe* for failing to identify Florence Luscomb in a photograph that appeared in that paper. According to the group, Luscomb was "perhaps the best known living veteren of the Women's Suffrage Movement," and "any man of her stature would have been not only named but all his achievements pointed out for us to admire."[106] Several months later, the *Female Liberation Newsletter* published reader Miriam Grezel's account of a visit to the emergency room with her daughter: "The nurse in the emergency room addressed me only as Mother, *no name*, the whole time I was there. Obviously I was not supposed to think of myself in any other terms."[107]

According to an editorial in the February 1974 issue of *Sister*,

> Sister's Staff and contributors are encouraged to use their first and last names in the paper. If you want to use an adopted pen name or feminist name, fine— we understand not wanting to use your husband's or father's surname. But women—like children, servants, and pets—are traditionally called by first name only, to minimize their importance; whereas men are "Mr. A, Dr. B, Professor C." The boss and secretary address each other as "Mr. Twitchell" and "Suzie" respectively. The name game reflects and reinforces their comparative status. As we all know, early women writers and artists had to conceal their identities with male pseudonyms in order to get serious exposure. If you still prefer first name only, or initials when you contribute to Sister, we respect that choice. But, please give our point of view some serious thought.[108]

The editorial note bears a handwritten signature, "Nancy Victoria." Most other contributors to this issue chose to use their first and last names (Susan

Nestor, Cindy Frazier, Gahan Kelley), but others (Carolee, Z. Budapest, Deedee, dell) did not. *Ain't I a Woman?* followed a similar but shorter printing policy: "People keep writing us nice letters and we want to print them. It would save us a lot of time if you would indicate whether or not you want us to print it. We never use anyone's name unless we know she wants us to."[109] Even though a woman writer would be the norm for this publication, the fact that these editors used *she* to refer to a generic writer further illustrates their feminist politics, encourages readers to see themselves as writers, and disrupts existing norms around the publishing industry. Editors therefore linked feminist theory and practice when they let writers have the final say about how they represented themselves, giving each woman the power to determine how she would be named.

After publishing an article, "No More Fun and Games," with no authorial attribution, the editors of *Ain't I a Woman?* explained, "We did, indeed, receive the article unsigned, but we knew who wrote it. It was written by a so-called movement 'star.' The main drawback to the 'star' phenomenon in politics is that groupings develop around or against names, not ideas. We didn't want anyone to prejudge the contents of 'No More Fun and Games,' either negatively or positively on the basis of its authorship."[110] Women's liberation groups struggled with the star system imposed by mainstream media and culture.[111] Held in 1976, the first national Women in Print Conference gathered together printers, bookstore owners and workers, and illustrators but excluded authors because, as organizer Carol Seajay explained, "We didn't put the writers on a pedestal."[112] The visibility of a writer's name could erase the labor of the other women who played vital roles in the publication process—the editors, typists, mimeographers, collators, and distributors. This attitude aligns with the nonhierarchical work ethic that many feminist groups espoused as well as the Marxist belief that the means of production belonged to the collective. In contrast, the publishing industry benefited from supporting the singular best seller or the iconic writer rather than the "multiplicity of women's perspectives and a diversity of feminist interpretations," as Murray explains. Accordingly, she continues, "Definitive pronouncements have a tendency to quash intellectual developments within radical movements.... The publishing industry's publicity motivated star system was thus directly at odds with the non-hierarchical communalism espoused by the women's movement."[113]

These examples highlight the bind women faced: using a pseudonym, no name, first name, or initials might constitute a disavowal of the patriarchal, classist, individualist institutions that gave significance to first and last names, but doing so also reproduced a paradigm in which women did not receive credit for the work they did and the skills they had. Yet claiming authorship by displaying one's name could inadvertently bolster those oppressive institutions and the authorial practices that singled out individuals as the sole creators of a text. Moreover, despite expressing an openness to readers' contributions and self-representations, editors remained curators of the publication and decided what material to include and exclude. Sharon Bas Hannah, for example, asked *Sister*'s editors why they had failed to publish her review of a play and informed them that they had published some of her work without giving her credit.[114] The previous chapter referred to another instance of editorial oversight: the negative experience of a group of high school girls from Springfield, Massachusetts, at the Valley Women's Center did not receive coverage in the center's newsletter, despite center staff's suggestion that the matter be discussed in print.

Feminist periodicals' modes of production resulted from feminist values and politics that gave meaning to the periodicals themselves as well as to feminism, both expressing and embodying feminist politics.[115] A symbolic fit existed between a group's values and the way it represented those values, and periodicals demonstrate this fit.[116] Modes and politics of production, then, are more than material facets of a publication; they are an accumulation of ideas, ideals, feelings, and desires manifested through the materiality of the published text. This finished product, though, reveals moments in its path toward publication, which is shaped by the physical mechanisms editors and printers employed, access to resources such as money and labor, and the different bodies that participated in the process. All together, these different aspects of periodical production contributed to the ways in which feminism existed as a repertoire of practices and social movement identity. In particular, periodicals' seriality meant that readers repeatedly were confronted with the message that certain ideas and practices were feminist ideals.

If identity is what we do, then these periodicals' content about the publishing process told readers how to be feminist. Just as discourses give meaning to the practices among social movement actors, practices sustain an identity by manifesting its ideas and values and by providing models for realizing those values. However, while ideals such as collectivity and the commitment to publishing women's voices predominated, periodicals also show that the individual manifestations of these concepts varied. Through their iteration across multiple issues, collectivity and authorial practices appear in disparate forms and formats. Again, seriality matters, but such variation is an effect of local specificity as well. Each of the five periodicals studied here embodied a collective praxis, but the form of collaborative, nonhierarchical labor differed across the different publications, as did the approach they took to including and naming contributors.

# CHAPTER 4

# Invitations to Women's Liberation

I can't help it: sisterhood has seduced me.

The Chicago Women's Graphics Collective created dozens of images to represent, commemorate, inspire, and complicate feminist activism in the 1970s. One poster depicts an abstract flower with the phrase "Sisterhood Is Blooming" framing the top of the bloom and the words "Springtime Will Never Be the Same" at the bottom, where the roots would be. With a black background and only two bold colors for the image and text, this poster dares you to look away. During the many hours I spent doing research at the Sophia Smith Collection at Smith College, I kept returning to this image, which was among the array of feminist posters that decorated a reading room wall. I later purchased a copy of the poster from the Chicago Women's Liberation Union Herstory project, and it hung by my desk while I worked on my dissertation and now hangs in my office. It still moves me, and my response is, yes, springtime—and summer, autumn, and winter—have never been the same.

The wide appeal of the women's liberation movement and its remarkable growth in the early 1970s coincided with this blooming of feminist sisterhood. Sisterhood was everywhere: in feminist books, pamphlets, periodicals, correspondence, and song lyrics; on bumper stickers, clothing, jewelry and watches, posters, and key chains; and in the names of feminist businesses and organizations. Los Angeles's Sisterhood Bookstore remained in business for twenty-seven years. A Kingston, Ontario, feminist periodical named itself *The Native Sisterhood*; a Tampa, Florida, group published *United Sisters*; and *Sister* was the title not only of the Los Angeles collective's serial but also of a publication by New Haven Women's Liberation. The Amazon Art Works in Berkeley, California, encouraged women to advertise their politics by wearing T-shirts "made by sisters for sisters" and bearing the phrases "Rise up Sisters" and "Sisterlove." Another T-shirt available in a catalog from the Brooklyn, New York–based Liberation Enterprises featured the slogan "Liberté, Egalité, Sororité."[1] And Bronx-based Beahive Enterprises offered matchbooks with covers that read, "Sisterhood Is Powerful."[2] That phrase also served as the title of one of the most visible and widely circulating products of women's liberation print culture, Robin Morgan's edited collection.[3]

Yet my joy in this sentiment is not unfettered. The idea that sisterhood is powerful is not uniformly positive: according to a famous comment attributed to Ti-Grace Atkinson, "Sisterhood is powerful: it kills sisters."[4] Elaborating on what she terms "the dark side of sisterhood," Jo Freeman has described a destructive disciplinary force that prescribed specific norms for which feminists were expected to strive and created unrealistic and unrealizable standards that could be used to exclude women who did not enact or embody "sisterly" characteristics.[5] The issue of *Ain't I a Woman?* dated April 1973 features one long essay, "Academic Feminists and the Women's Movement," that begins with a warning: "This is not a sisterly essay. We believe the women's movement is in danger of co-optation from the right, from small groups of women whose institutional affiliations give them disproportionate power within it."[6] Here, the authors imply that their essay does not embody the ideals of sisterhood, defining sisterly behavior by what it is not: critical and confrontational. Moreover, myriad and invaluable analyses of sisterhood came from those who experienced its exclusions, primarily but not exclusively women of color, poor women, and lesbian women.

I thus find my response to the poster in my office textured with strong ambivalence, aware that sisterhood caused such exclusions and distortions of feminism at the same time that it empowered women to transform oppressive institutions and connected them at the local, regional, national, and international levels. How can we interpret the simultaneous repudiation and idealization of sisterhood? Motivated by this knowledge, this chapter untangles the politics of sisterhood in 1970s feminism, shifting the primary focus of my analysis from the material facets of collective identity (place and modes of production) to the discursive facets (language and imagery).

A social movement cannot exist without boundaries that demarcate Us and Not-Us; however, these boundaries are not monolithic, static, simple, or transparent.[7] An identity's meaning shifts across time and space, so different and potentially contradictory meanings may exist simultaneously. Second-wave feminism includes, for example, liberal feminists, radical feminists, socialist feminists, Marxist feminists, cultural feminists, lesbian feminists, lesbian-separatist feminists, Third World feminists, women of color feminists, Chicana feminists, black feminists, and many others.[8] These subgroups can be further divided and nuanced, and many women also found that their politics blurred these ideological and identitarian boundaries and drew from multiple categories simultaneously.[9] One challenge for social movement actors, then, is to control the meaning of their collective identity, a process that involves clarifying the differences between Us and Not-Us while leaving both categories flexible and fungible in a way that allows a range of people to see themselves as movement insiders. This chapter investigates the way that sisterhood created these boundaries. Similar to the discourse of collectivity, the idea of sisterhood provided an overarching master frame that gave meaning to women's relationships with each other but did not do so by enforcing a singular monolithic meaning. The meaning most often attributed to sisterhood—that all women are sisters because they share a common biological or social situation—instead exists as just one of several possible connotations in feminist periodicals.

I begin by schematizing the ways in which feminist periodicals produced sisterhood as a discourse as well as its limitations and detrimental effects, looking more closely at how sisterhood was used in particular moments. The direct address (for example, "Dear sisters") serves as an interpellative act and rhetorical trope that allows me to analyze the ways in which sisterhood was constitutive of feminism. As in other chapters, I grapple with the tensions between consistency and variety and between privileged and subordinate meanings. Different connotations texture different uses, thus complicating sisterhood's political, identitarian, and affective work in the women's liberation movement.

### Do We Dare to Be Sisters?

Because the concept of sisterhood permeated the movement and because it was used to demarcate an identity, a relationship, and an organizing praxis, it presents a useful lens for analyzing U.S. feminism both in particular locations and as a social movement that spanned national borders, as well as through its discursive and material characteristics. In fact, it is striking that within such a decentralized movement—composed primarily of small collectives that had no official relationship with a national organization or with each other—the terms *sister* and *sisterhood* were used so widely and consistently.

Feminist periodicals not only provide evidence of sisterhood's prevalence but also demonstrate how sisterhood characterized feminism as an identity category, a type of relationship, a value system, and a mode of praxis. This connection was so deep that sisterhood at times came to embody feminism itself. A 1971 article in *Ain't I a Woman?* claimed, "Sisterhood is not just a social gathering, but a political force, that we are willing to use our bodies to free ourselves, to free our sisters from the prisons where men put them."[10] And a 1970 issue of the *L.A. Women's Liberation Newsletter* included an article about collective leadership in which the authors wrote, "At this stage in the growth of the Women's Liberation Movement here in L.A. we face a particular critical turning point—that of fostering unity inside our Movement thereby building collective leadership in order to achieve continuing victory in our overall struggle for the liberation of women.... Unity simply means sisterhood in our common fight for common goals."[11] Here sisterhood and unity coincide in their significance, indicating that this kind of unity is feminist and in turn that feminism exists because of sisterly solidarity. The imbrication of sisterhood and feminism is evident also in the way periodicals characterized feminist spaces. One of the first issues of the *Female Liberation Newsletter* published a full-page flyer that invited readers to the Female Liberation office for "music, refreshments, literature, a film and discussion at 8:00, an opportunity to meet and talk with your sisters."[12] A *Distaff* article about a local women's center art auction held at a church describes the organizers' uncertainty about the event:

> That rainy, gooey Saturday we five women and the spirits of a legion of sisters sat on the benches at the First Unitarian Church on Jefferson.... As we took a quiet moment to look around before the public arrived, we felt good. We thought all the warm surprises there had been—the sympathy of artists, mostly but not entirely women, who were not active feminists, who did not know the terminology of revolution yet who earnestly offered their works to help end oppression [and] the superb and abundant talent among our ranks that we did not know existed in sisters with whom we had worked side by side politically.[13]

Part of what eased anxieties and offered comfort were "the spirits of a legion of sisters," which echoed through the space because of the way in which a community of women had come together to make the auction happen. Constructions of space, place, identity, and community are mutually constitutive; therefore, when sisterhood characterized a space that had already been brought within the feminist fold, it further reinforced the centrality of sisterhood in the women's liberation movement.

The feminist periodicals that I examined deployed the term *sister* in four ways. First, *sister* served as a synonym for woman, a usage that has become the dominant one characterizing feminism in the early 1970s and has come to signify how feminists were supposed to relate to each other. The *L.A. Women's Liberation Newsletter* printed an article about abortion and medical care that ended with the statement, "We shall not be able to secure these freedoms and realize our goal, unless we take the initiative in the abortion movement, to plan a program of care for all women with complete repeal of all birth control laws. Free our sisters; Free ourselves."[14] Here "sisters" refers indiscriminately and universally to women, as the use of "all women" in the first sentence suggests. Along with universality, this usage suggests social/political homogeneity: as a woman, I have something in common with any other woman, so if I work on behalf of her liberation, my liberation will also result. The imperative "Free our sisters, free ourselves," which also suggests a universalized understanding of sisterhood, circulated widely in periodicals. Repeated almost as a mantra, it made a convenient sound bite, and, indeed, it functioned that way for feminists. The *Valley Women's Center Newsletter* published an announcement about a business, Gulch Stickers, that sold feminist ephemera such as stickers and decals, listing two examples of slogans that appeared on these items: "Free Our Sisters/Free Ourselves" and "Sisterhood Is Powerful."[15] The August 1975 issue of *Sister* featured a piece about the campaign to make sexual violence against black women more visible, describing an event at which "across a grassy expanse, another 16 foot banner proclaimed, 'Free Our Sisters, Free Ourselves.'"[16] And the *Female Liberation Newsletter* included a photo of someone holding a poster with the words "Free Our Sisters, Free."[17] Although the bottom of the poster is cut off, readers would likely have been able to complete the thought. Especially without additional context, it contributed to the view that feminism did not exist without sisterhood as well as to the view that sisterhood encompassed all women.

A variation of this usage appears when specific women are named as sisters. It retained an essentialist perspective that sisters were women but did not share the presumption of "Free our sisters, free ourselves." An announcement in *Distaff* explained that the newspaper "is in touch with some of [the] women at the La. Correctional Institute for Women at St. Gabriel, La. Call us ... for information on how you can send a card and/or a gift to a sister behind bars. Your thoughtfulness could make a world of difference to someone."[18] And an editorial in the *Female Liberation Newsletter* elaborated on the organization's decision to march with antiwar protesters in Washington, D.C.: "I would like to try and explain to the sisters who wrote in from Rhode Island why we have backed the United Women's Contingent rather than stage 'our own' march on Washington."[19] Letters published in feminist periodicals frequently began, "Dear Sisters," and writers and editors frequently called readers "sisters." Because such uses refer to a specific group of women, they lack the connotations of "Free our sisters, free ourselves" but instead imply only that the writer and the specific person labeled a sister shared something. Such statements might continue to oversimplify the actual relationships between women but did not posit all women as sisters.

Sisterhood's scope narrowed even further when the term explicitly symbolized an identity produced through feminist activism and struggle. For example, a writer asked the editors of the *Female Liberation Newsletter*, "Do you know you have sisters in Hyannis?" She then described the Hyannis women's activism to desegregate classified ads by gender.[20] *Ain't I a Woman?*'s editors prefaced a reprint from a New York City newspaper, *Rat*, by recognizing that "Ain't I A Woman and many other publications by sisters around the country began as we felt a need for alternative media."[21] In these moments, sisterhood did not constitute an a priori identity based on a common oppression, biology, or psychology but rather emerged from actions and activist commitments characterized by a feminist consciousness. In contrast to utterances in which *sister* becomes synonymous with *woman*, conflating the meanings of these terms does not make sense here.

The third connotation of the term also produces sisterhood as achieved rather than given or as a praxis rather than an ontology. Specifically, this usage produced sisterhood as aspirational, as a potential to be realized. *Distaff*'s inaugural issue urged, "Friends, let us stop talking about sisterhood and make SISTERHOOD A FACT."[22] *Ain't I a Woman?* published a full-page essay from the Women's Counseling Service in Minneapolis that explored the group's ideas about and practices of collectivity: "We find that as each sister risks herself with the collective and finds the response not shock or hostility but sympathy, help and acceptance that comes from realizing our oppression has warped us all, the ugliness and fear of her 'true self' becomes lost in the beauty and strength of the collective. What was before only a phrase becomes a reality— Sisterhood is powerful. Even as we realize this, it is extremely difficult to act out."[23] Posing sisterhood as a challenge for readers to meet, Priscilla J. Warner wrote to the *Valley Women's Center Newsletter* to ask women to take a stand on behalf of a secretary who had been fired from her job: "Do we have the courage? Do we dare take the obvious risks? WE might find ourselves risking our husbands' jobs, our own jobs, and the reemployability of us both. I think that it is worth knowing, in the privacy of our own minds, do we *dare* to be sisters?"[24] Finally, a *Female Liberation Newsletter* article reporting and reflecting on a "Women and Racism" workshop argued that "it is the responsibility of white women to change their tactics within the struggle and concentrate on developing that necessary factor of trust and integrity with their non-white sisters, if there is to be, in fact, a sisterhood. You do not know [black women] as sisters at all, but we know you so very well."[25] These examples challenge the perspectives and actions of feminist women by invoking sisterhood as an ideal toward which women could and should strive.

Finally, sisterhood was invoked through critiques of the concept itself. Although engagement with sisterhood was often unproblematized, these periodicals show that women in the 1970s did not always accept the idea without question. Grappling with the material, practical, and ideological realities of social movement activism, contributors to these periodicals also dispelled the idea that sisterhood was merely a site of rosy utopianism. *Ain't I a Woman?*'s editors reflected deeply on their modes of organizing and relating with other women, as in the July 1971 issue, where they filled four pages with an extended meditation on class and women's liberation.[26] A header running across the first two pages declared, "So far our analysis labels common to all women what is common only to middle-class women." This critique of a middle-class bias in the women's liberation movement as a whole, as well as within the Iowa City group in particular, also involved a critique of sisterhood. According to the editors, "Until middle-class women recognize their place in the class system, really face it and not claim a phony powerlessness by always measuring their power against their male counterparts, sisterhood is a sham."[27] On the next page, the authors described an article from another "midwest women's paper" as

> a good example of the sisterhood conception in that it excludes working or lower class women. That philosophy of "everywoman is our sister" is defined by middle class women, who are blind to anyone but other middle class women, who refuse to see the influence of class. They say "women find themselves in many different roles with many different problems" but refuse to see that women find themselves in many different classes and therefore have different problems. To admit this most women would have to identify with their class which is to admit their own role in oppressing other women. This is hard and painful to do but the only way to begin struggling with sisterhood on any real level. Unless that is done I think we have to realize that any analysis the women's movement comes up with now cannot be trusted.[28]

This fierce self-reflection refuses to rest easily with the dominant definition of sisterhood, recognizing that it erases differences and power differentials between women and can reinforce the dangerous notion that patriarchy is the only or primary force oppressing women. The Valley Women's Center (VWC) voiced its own struggles with unity and solidarity in an August 1972 questionnaire that sought to gauge readers' perspectives on the center's "function and activities": "How do we deal with differences in the women's movement? Pretend there aren't any? Blank them out with the statement 'Sisterhood is Powerful'? Do we bring them out and talk about them, trying to understand each others perspective, or do we smooth them over?"[29] Again sisterhood is invoked as a concept that does not reflect feminist ideals and perhaps could even actively work against them. And again we see feminists from a primarily white community holding themselves accountable for the diverse and complex situations of different women. Yet these problematizations also further enmesh sisterhood and feminism. Even though the *Ain't I a Woman?* piece recognized some incarnations of sisterhood as less than ideal, it still made space for sisterhood to be manifest legitimately or correctly at some future time. Similarly, the members of the VWC staff do not suggest jettisoning sisterhood from their feminist repertoire. And both periodicals' use of the direct address "Dear Sisters" and positive invocations of sisterhood indicate that they found the concept instrumental to feminism.

The feminist world that sisterhood organized developed in relation to the way this discourse characterized other groups. Nuns have for centuries been "sisters," and Christian churches also have conceived of their congregations as sisters and brothers. Civil rights and Black Power activists as well as Third

World revolutionary groups used this language to reflect their communities and political values as in the Chicana/o newspaper, *El Grito del Norte*, which regularly included feminist activist Enriqueta Vasquez's column, "¡Despierten, Hermanos!"[30] Because of their locations and their connections to other social movements, feminists likely drew on these other uses when articulating their social and political bonds. Sisterhood's central role in characterizing feminism, therefore, emerged as part of a genealogy of different sisterhoods (and brotherhoods), specifically building on those committed to horizontal relationships. As Joan Cassell notes, "The term 'sister' uses a kinship model, frequently employed by participants in social movements. It stresses what is perceived as previously neglected female linkages, between sisters, and between mothers and daughters, as opposed to the more frequent emphasis on links with men, with fathers, brothers, and husbands."[31] This observation points to the way that feminists changed the meaning of sisterhood by, for example, challenging familial structures—deconstructing the nuclear family, creating alternative kinship structures, identifying as lesbians, resignifying motherhood—and inflected it with a politicized woman-centered viewpoint that religious groups did not promote.

Despite the various connotations evident in feminist periodicals, the form of sisterhood most often attributed to the women's liberation movement assumes a unity or solidarity premised on the sameness of women.[32] Even when the diversity and complexity of women's experiences are recognized, the essentialized version of sisterhood still seems to underlie its meaning. For example, *Sisterhood Is Powerful* includes pieces about gender oppression from a range of different perspectives, and Morgan offers an astute analysis of the differences among women in her introduction to the anthology, yet she still falls into universalizing sentiments: sharing personal experiences has taught us "that these experiences are *not* our private hang-ups. They are shared by every woman, and are therefore political."[33] Bolstering this view, Morgan continued, "Women in every group must play essentially the same role, albeit with different sets and costumes."[34] Since the shared qualities of women have become emblematic of sisterhood, most critics build their analyses on this foundation, offering valuable insight into the detrimental impact of sisterhood on U.S. feminism. These critiques have explicitly demanded that women recognize and take responsibility for their privileges, highlighted the need for feminists to build coalitions across differences, and argued for the recognition of difference within individuals as well as groups.

An essentialist definition of sisterhood not only homogenizes women's experiences and identities but is based on a particular configuration of femininity. Lynet Uttal observes, "The experiences of Anglo middle class women have defined what these commonalities are in the contemporary women's movement."[35] As a result, according to Pat Alake Rosezelle, "white women forgot what they learned and began using the term 'sister' as if all women were alike; they began to erase Black women."[36] And Elizabeth Fox-Genovese argues that sisterhood is based on a middle-class perspective to such an extent that "the possibilities of even the most generous and inclusive sisterhood cannot extend much beyond the dominant social conditions."[37] These analyses show that sisterhood could be based on the social, identitarian positions of those whose voices most loudly defined this concept. Along with the reductive sound bites that circulated through feminist and mainstream media, white, middle-class women in large cities tended to have the greatest role in shaping what sisterhood was and should be.

When sisterhood reinforces a homogenized, woman-centered collective identity for feminism, it can oversimplify the dynamics of power and privilege and leave them unquestioned, enabling some women to maintain their privilege at the expense of others.[38] This putative sameness at times also universalized women as perpetual victims through the idea that patriarchy has been and continues to be the most fundamental force making women into second-class citizens. Bell hooks notes that building connections through victimization, specifically at the hands of men, meant that "white women liberationists were not required to assume responsibility for confronting the complexity of their own experience," thereby precluding recognition of "their role in the maintenance and perpetuation of sexism, racism, and classism."[39] Similarly calling on white women to account for their privilege, Rosezelle observed that women "came to embrace the racism that they were fighting when they learned to call each other 'sister.'"[40] And Jo Carrillo's poem "And When You Leave, Take Your Pictures with You" suggests that the idea of solidarity with other women is based on a misunderstanding of what creates common bonds:

> And when our white sisters
> radical friends see us
> in the flesh
> not as a picture they own,
> they are not quite as sure
> if
> they like us as much.[41]

Another perceived limitation of the ideology and practice of sisterhood relates to the way that unity is seen as coextensive with unconditional support to such an extent that differences and disagreements may be perceived as personal or political betrayals.[42] María Lugones argues that this principle is more burdensome for women of color because it may ask them to support white women in racist thoughts and actions.[43] And hooks suggests that unconditional support not only suppresses conflicts but reinforces bonding based on homogeneity.[44]

These critics demonstrate that although sisterhood may connote universal inclusion for all women in all places, gender retained primacy. This phenomenon created challenges for feminists in building alliances across difference, in theorizing inclusion, and in formulating an intersectional political praxis. First, the unquestioned centrality of gender effected an either/or bind, forcing women to prioritize one identity over another in their activist commitments: Would they choose their racial identity and align with the Black Panthers, or would they choose their gender identity and align with the women's liberation movement?[45] Beginning with gender also can lead to a narrative of progress from singularity to diversity: feminists were once a monolithic, white, middle-class, heterosexual group but with attention to difference will become more inclusive.[46] In the 1990 anthology *Making Face, Making Soul = Haciendo Caras*, Norma Alarcón points out another flawed politics of inclusion that occurs when gender stays central: the inclusion of writings by women of color in women's studies classrooms did not preclude the "tendency to deny differences if those differences pose a threat to the 'common denominator' category." As a result, others may gain entry only on the terms of those in power.[47] In these circumstances, sisterhood reduces difference to autonomous units that merely need to be added to feminism without interrogating the underlying epistemology or praxis that marginalized these others.[48]

Trenchant critiques of sisterhood, however, did not preclude women of color from using the concept of sisterhood in their activism. In the first issue of the New York City–based *Triple Jeopardy*, the Third World Women's Alliance declared that one of its objectives was to "create a sisterhood of women devoted to the task of developing solidarity among the peoples of the Third World, based on a socialist ideology of struggling for the complete elimination of any and all forms of oppression and exploitation based upon race, economic status, or sex and to use whatever means are necessary to accomplish this task."[49] The mission statement of a Chicana feminist group at California State University, Long Beach, announced, "LAS HIJAS DE CUAUHTÉMOC has manifested their concerns and efforts by adopting as its basic philosophy a most innate and humane concept—HERMANIDAD."[50] And an article about the Pilipino Youth Services sisters group that appeared in the *Asian Women's Center Newsletter* (published in Los Angeles) described the participants: "The sisters, all born in the Philippines, attend Belmont High School and have expressed a need to be together, rap and be involved in constructive experiences."[51] The ubiquity of *sisterhood* and its use by those who also critiqued it indicate that the term was not the sole property of white women and that many women recognized its powerful rhetorical force. However, all groups did not use the term in the same way, and the concept's discursive power does not mitigate the violence it could and did effect.

### Becoming Sisters

One among many instantiations of sisterhood, the imperative "Sisters pick up sisters" encouraged women to pick up female hitchhikers. As the *L.A. Women's Liberation Newsletter* announced to readers in January 1971, "The Center was recently informed that there has been an increase in rape and molestation of female hitch-hikers. To cut down these hideous acts, we ask all sisters to pick up another sister who is hitch-hiking."[52] In December 1972 the VWC reported on a rise in the number of sexual assaults on women hitchhikers, and two issues later, the newsletter announced that the center had begun selling bumper stickers reading, "Stop rape. Sisters stop for sisters."[53] These uses of *sisters* have different connotations. With reference to hitchhikers, *sisters* means all women: drivers are not asked to pick up only feminist women. Here, *sister* is universalized, a biological phenomenon. In contrast, when referring to the driver of a car, the term is politicized. Picking up a hitchhiking woman transforms the driver into a feminist activist: she is keeping her fellow sisters safe, supporting a woman-centered form of community building, and enabling mobility through public space that women could not take for granted. Rona Foster wrote to Female Liberation in June 1971 to suggest that the newsletter include a ride-sharing section because "being a woman its difficult and rather risky to take a ride from a male who you don't know when you're traveling a long distance. I think it would make alot of us feel more secure riding with another female."[54] Warner's question, "Do we *dare* to be sisters?" also shapes the connotations of sisterhood, asking readers whether they were *real* (feminist) sisters. If so, they would manifest their political commitments by assisting other woman in need.

The "Sisters pick up sisters" bumper sticker is striking because it manifests two different versions of sisterhood side-by-side without any apparent sense of discursive contradiction or political tension. Thus, these four words start to show the internal mechanisms of a collective identity and provide an entry point for investigating how that identity can coalesce around certain symbols. As a concept signifying shifts in consciousness, emotional investments, and relationships, sisterhood worked so effectively in the formation of a feminist collective identity because of its plasticity and because it was consistent with broader feminist investments in naming and resignifying *woman* as a category of being and doing.[55]

My sustained attention to the discourse of sisterhood and to the direct address "Dear Sisters" in particular reflects my understanding that in order to better understand how collective identities work we need to look at the creative effects of language. Sociologist Stacey Young argues that texts—which she calls "language acts"—can catalyze political activism by enabling "new forms of subjectivity."[56] And Joan Wallach Scott takes language as "a point of entry, a starting point for understanding how social relations are conceived," a process that also includes the formation of collective identities.[57] In her analytical framework, Butler sets up an even more fundamental relationship between discourse and identity: "Language sustains the body not by bringing it into being or feeding it in a literal way; rather, it is by being interpellated within the terms of language that a certain social existence of the body becomes possible. To understand this, one must imagine an impossible scene, that of a body that has not yet been given social definition, a body that is, strictly speaking, not accessible to us, that nevertheless becomes accessible on the occasion of an address, a call, an interpellation that does not 'discover' this body, but constitutes it fundamentally."[58] Bodies thus exist through and within language, so that if one's body is located "outside of the domain of speakability," one risks "one's status as a subject."[59] Conversely, one must be intelligible within language to be a subject, and part of this intelligibility involves the capacity to be named. Butler elaborates, "The subject is not only founded by the other, requiring an address in order to be, but its power is derived from the structure of address as both linguistic vulnerability and exercise. If one comes to be through address, can we imagine a subject apart from his or her linguistic bearing? We cannot imagine them or they could not be what they are, apart from the constitutive possibility of addressing others and being addressed by others."[60] Butler's subject does not exist prior to the hailing or naming but is produced through it.[61] In other words, a subject must be able to speak and must be speakable within discursive (and social) norms and conventions for its existence to have social meaning.

Because naming sisters creates sisters, imagined communities offer a useful lens for analyzing the effects of sisterhood as a discourse. The proliferation of feminist periodicals in the early 1970s enabled the term *sister* to circulate widely and affirmed the centrality of sisterhood to the women's liberation movement. And certain connotations stuck when *sisterhood* appeared in similar rhetorical contexts, facilitating what we might call a discourse of power because those connotations had greater weight in determining meaning and blocked other meanings from surfacing.

Despite the apparent ubiquity of *sisterhood*, numerous legal, political, psychic, identitarian, and affective factors potentially obstructed its formation.[62] The Valley Women's Center daily log for January 27, 1972, includes an intriguing entry: "celia called to say that a woman was in the other day who had not thought of herself as a woman until someone here turned to someone else here and said, 'this woman has a question. . .'. Had a strong, positive impact on her."[63] An ordinary phrase with an ordinary word—"this woman has a question"—in that moment became something extraordinary. Something shifted this woman's consciousness enough that Celia not only noticed it but called the center to relate the experience. In the 1970s, then, women may not have recognized the identity of *woman* as meaningful. Political and legal structures also worked to erase *woman* as an identity since relationships with men often contained and constrained women's social and familial roles and identities. A fall 1971 issue of the *Female Liberation Newsletter* advised women about how to retain their last names after marrying, demonstrating the challenges of maintaining identities distinct from those of their husbands: "Changing to the husband's name is no problem as that is what is expected, but retaining one's own surname after marriage involves a legal procedure, which is fairly simple even though the idea of it is enraging. First you must obtain a Petition for Change of Name and a 'Request for Information' from the Probate Court in your County. After filling these out you must go to court and your name change will *probably* be approved."[64] The following spring, a letter reminded readers that even women who gained legal approval to retain their names might face social repercussions: "Dear Sisters," Glenys A. Waldman began, "This is just to tell you that there is an informal group of women tentatively calling itself 'Name-Change.' In it are women who have never taken their husbands' names and other women who had, but have changed back to their maiden names or are in the process of doing so. We offer moral support and advice."[65]

*Ain't I a Woman?*, *Distaff*, and *Sister* also reported on this phenomenon, indicating its salience for feminists throughout the country. *Distaff* noted that even married women who had not changed their names had to reregister to vote under their legal names.[66] The July 1974 *Valley Women's Center Newsletter* ran an article about a woman who needed a judge's ruling to register to vote under her maiden name, even though Massachusetts had no law mandating that a wife use her husband's name.[67] And *Sister* explained in a short announcement that "a woman may use her maiden name (or any other, for that matter) regardless of her marital status."[68] This item indicates that some women were prevented from doing so. Women's individual experiences did not uniformly reflect their legal rights, in part because of the idiosyncratic practices of individuals within the political-legal system. The fact that women who sought to retain their surnames had to go through formal legal procedures and sometimes experienced a backlash shows the extent to which a woman's identity was socially and institutionally tied to a man's. (And of course, as one woman pointed out, "Whose name was the maiden one but my father's?")[69] Such constructions of women's identity were not limited to the United States, as a 1971 item in the *Valley Women's Center Newsletter* demonstrated: in Germany a new ruling had replaced "the decree of 1955 whereby unmarried women who wanted to be known as 'Frau' had to state this expressly."[70] These revelations remind us of the many obstacles feminists faced in their efforts to create spaces in which women could identify *as* women and *with* other women, an identification necessary to enable women to align their identities with feminism and see themselves as sisters.

In addition to working with existing linguistic conventions such as keeping their maiden names or insisting on being called *Ms.* rather than *Miss* or *Mrs.*, feminists attempted to break from these conventions in their acts of naming and renaming. *Wimmin, womyn,* and *womon* replaced standard spellings in feminist print as one means of claiming a female identity that was linguistically distinct from *man* and *men*. And the *L.A. Women's Liberation Newsletter* proposed a new symbol for representing women. The writer suggested replacing the commonly used circle atop a cross (♀), the astrological symbol for Venus, with the symbol for Pluto, which adds a semicircle between the cross and below the circle (♀). According to the writer, the Venus symbol "represents the *passive* principle and is also the medieval symbol for women," whereas Pluto "is the symbol for female sexuality and revolution. Pluto is the great transformer and is also the symbol for the deepest forces that move people, especially women."[71] ERA Enterprises, a feminist business in Bellevue, Washington, used the Athena symbol—a triangle atop a cross—in its brand image. A catalog listing their products (which they label a newsletter) explains, "Athena was the original, historical (mythical!) feminist!"[72] These kinds of discursive interventions point to the fundamental levels at which feminist activists were grappling with identity categories and their personal, social, political, and historical significance. However, symbolic analyses of identity can become decontextualized and aspatial, dislocating ideas from their specific local contexts.[73] For example, the *L.A. Women's Liberation Newsletter* used these alternative spellings more frequently than did the other periodicals analyzed here, demonstrating that place matters. And because much feminist activism occurred in small groups disconnected from regional or national organizations, editors and local politics were some of the primary forces influencing a periodical's content.

Social movement literature, particularly that focusing on new social movements, offers rich discursive and symbolic analyses of social movement identities.[74] This field uses framing to demonstrate and analyze processes of constructing, maintaining, adapting, and contesting collective identity.[75] Building on Erving Goffman's use of the *frame* as a "schemata of interpretation," David A. Snow and his coauthors base their argument that "frame alignment is a necessary condition for movement participation" on the premise that frames are what make experiences meaningful.[76] Whether seen as ideology, a set of beliefs, or a cognitive structure, a frame—or, more likely, the interaction of multiple frames—becomes a lens through which individuals interpret and organize their world. Therefore, any identity cannot become recognizable, legitimate, desirable, or distasteful without also being intelligible through some kind of frame.[77] Framing helps activists narrate a movement's identity, draw boundaries around and within a group, locate the movement in relation to other movements, and legitimate a movement's strategies and objectives. Most important for this chapter, framing enables sites of identification, where movement insiders and outsiders can align their values and politics with those of the movement.[78]

To be effective—to persuade outsiders to join and to keep insiders actively working for movement goals—a collective action frame must have consistency. Frame consistency requires regular reiteration of similar messages to affirm a movement's politics, strategies, and identity. As serial publications, periodicals bolstered this symbolic economy. They included a wide variety of contributions from different women, and the regular usage of language in particular ways solidified the structure of the movement's discourse. Just as locational stability was important—a women's center that continually changed locations would have difficulty sustaining an activist community—frame stability aided activists in aligning the movement's message, practices, and objectives with their personal values and experiences.[79] Frame inconsistency can occur in the relationship between theory and practice, a phenomenon experienced by many women active in the New Left. Despite the rhetoric about equality, participatory democracy, the importance of building consensus, and the need to overthrow systems perpetuating inequality, women experienced gendered divisions of labor and read movement publications that marginalized feminism and trivialized sexism. This dissonance led many women to distance themselves from this social movement, some forming women's caucuses within New Left organizations and others breaking away to create autonomous women's liberation groups.

Sisterhood also had material components. In her study of the changes in the Student Nonviolent Coordinating Committee during the 1960s, Belinda Robnett shows how the group became more hierarchical and moved away from its earlier practices of nonviolence and consensus. She concludes that this structure ultimately stifled "the dialectical exchange among participants and between participants and leaders," centralizing and narrowing the cadre of people who controlled the production of the group's collective identity.[80] Jo Reger similarly correlates structure with identity, describing liberal/political feminist organizations such as the National Organization for Women as hierarchical and working within the system to reform it. In contrast, radical/empowerment feminist groups are characterized by a collectivist structure and practices such as consciousness-raising.[81] Both the "liberal/radical" discursive binary and "hierarchical/collectivist" structural binary shape the manifestation and meaning of feminist actions, whether they involve consciousness-raising, publishing a periodical, or running a women's center.[82]

These examples show that structure can draw and reinforce boundaries between different factions within a social movement and by extension shape collective identity. Therefore, organizational forms and practices also require consistency in their expression.

*Sisterhood* provided a measure of consistency as a frame within the women's liberation movement, appearing in a range of feminist media and cultural products across space and time. Periodicals that circulated nationally and internationally used *sisterhood* in similar rhetorical contexts, solidifying the concept's meaning and importance. This frame consistency supported by such repetition was especially important in light of the structure of the women's liberation movement. Alone, *sisterhood*'s ubiquity would merit attention. However, its centrality becomes even more remarkable given the movement's discursive structure, which mirrored its spatial structure: much feminist media was produced by small groups, circulated locally and regionally, and was not accountable to or formally affiliated with a larger organization.

The women's liberation movement was fundamentally grassroots and decentralized, produced and reproduced in locations not always considered places of activism. Many small groups operated in relative geographic isolation, and some women lacked face-to-face connections with other feminists, even within a single city. *Sisterhood* consequently did important work to form and strengthen political and affective connections both on a local scale and across thousands of miles. As an April 1971 announcement in the *Female Liberation Newsletter* exhorted, "WE NEED A CENTER for students, housewives, black and 3rd World women, professional women, gay women, activists, welfare-mothers, young and old, where we can come together informally and BE SISTERS." The following issue included a flyer urging, "Support our Asian sisters in Vietnam."[83] The term *sister*, whether experienced face-to-face or as a felt connection across time and space, provided discursive glue within feminism, allowing individuals and collectives to feel bonds with others in the community and to become part of a much larger entity. The barriers many women faced even to simply identifying as women meant that creating networks was vital not only to facilitate political actions but also to support feminist consciousness-raising. A sense of sisterhood thus created a space in which a woman could name her experiences, start viewing her experiences as the result of structural inequalities rather than individual inadequacies, and know that she was not the only person who saw and questioned the world in a certain way.[84]

Feminism created spaces in which women could understand their identities in new ways, and the connections imagined through *sisterhood* allowed women to manage and analyze these new ways of engaging with and finding meaning in the world. Such a shift often led to reevaluations of bodies, jobs, relationships, and ideas previously considered common sense. As activist Barbara Winslow concisely put it, "The movement changed everything."[85] And as Mary Anderson wrote to the VWC, "Women's liberation is not only assimilated into my whole life, but it has changed the entire way I see my life + the lives of others."[86]

### Dear Sisters

The *Female Liberation Newsletter* began many of its mimeographed issues with a letters section. Below the masthead information, which occupied about a quarter of the front page, and just below the underlined section labeled "Letters" (sometimes in all capital letters, sometimes with only the *L* capitalized), readers would often encounter the salutation, "Dear Sisters," as evidenced in these excerpts from issues published between February and November 1971:

> Dear Sisters, The Newsletter is wonderful.[87]

> Dear Sisters, Working for a temporary job agency in Boston, I get the opportunity to observe many different offices, businessmen, and their secretaries.[88]

> Dear Sisters, There are plenty of Gay Liberationists here, but I haven't seen any sign of Women's Liberation.[89]

> Dear Sisters, A friend and I will be organizing a group of Puerto Rican and American women in San Juan in September.[90]

> Dear Sisters, ... I am a graduate student at Harvard Graduate School of Education, interested in Continuing Education Programs for Adult Women and career development for women—[91]

The explosion of media by feminists and about feminism in the early 1970s meant that the women's liberation movement circulated widely in mainstream and feminist media, including but greatly exceeding print texts. *Sisterhood* features prominently in these artifacts, but feminist newsletters and newspapers were the genre in which *sister* was most often used in the form of a direct address. Despite its ubiquity in periodicals, this rhetorical trope receives little scholarly attention. Though recognized and cited, periodicals remain underanalyzed in general, and scholars most frequently use feminist periodicals as evidence to support an argument about a specific topic (for example, reproductive rights or lesbianism) or as evidence of the richness of feminist publishing rather than reading them intertextually or analyzing them rhetorically on their own terms.

In general, a mode of address offers a narrative about the speaker, the addressee, and their relationship. "Ms. Chatterjee," "Hey you," "Sweetie," and "Your royal highness," for example, reflect identity categories, power differentials, and affective valences as well as provide information about the social and rhetorical situation. The periodicals examined here are social movement publications, created and read primarily by those affiliated with feminism, and the modes of address reflected such an assumption: calling someone a sister hails her as a radical comrade who shared the writer's political vision. The previous chapter elaborated the relational structures editorial collectives attempted to practice, and this sense of kinship was reflected in and reproduced by the discourse of sisterhood. The numerous announcements in which editors asked women to contribute to the publication imagined readers as collaborators, and the variety of voices published in a periodical as well as the frequency with which editorial collective members changed indicates that many readers responded to these hailings.

As with the discourse of sisterhood, a close reading of the direct address shows its appearance in different rhetorical situations. Letters often began with sisterhood. The vast majority of letters printed in the periodicals opened with "Dear sisters," not "Dear editors." "Dear friends," "Dear women," and "Dear [publishing group]" also occasionally appeared, but this epistolary language overwhelmingly reinforces sisterhood as the proper frame for addressing one's audience. Another common mode of address occurred when periodical editors called out to readers, as in, "Sisters, send in your favorite newspaper and magazine clippings to be printed in the Female Liberation Newsletter."[92] In April 1971, the *L.A. Women's Liberation Newsletter* appealed to readers, "Only a small staff is doing ALL the work, for free. We are all going through difficult financial times. Many of us are on welfare or unemployed. It's hard, SISTERS, but we'd be much further behind in the movement if we didn't have a CENTER. Those who have a little more: we're asking you to contribute more for those who have less. No contribution is too small."[93] The fact that one of the words emphasized in this announcement is *sister* illustrates the editors' attempts to cultivate readers' relationship with and stake in the center's existence. The *Valley Women's Center Newsletter* introduced its February 1973 issue, "Hello again sisters, wherever you are; it's that time again—COMMUNICATION. Anyway, it's February, a harbinger of spring, and we're women, and that's nice. All kinds of things have been happening around here which we want to share."[94]

The last form of direct address, a variation on that articulated by editors, appeared less frequently. Many contributors were not editors, and these writers at times seemed to be speaking to other readers, not just to editors. Amy Farrell has noted a similar trend in *Ms.* magazine, where many letters addressed an audience that was "clearly broader than the editor herself. Unlike other magazines, in which readers write to the editor, the readers of *Ms.* wrote to the *Ms.* community—editors, the writers, and, most importantly, other readers."[95] In a *Distaff* article on the revival of a New Orleans women's center, Lynn Miller wrote, "And that, dear sisters, is the beginning of the new beginning for the Women's Center."[96] Theo Kalikow's letter to Female Liberation was clearly directed at a broader audience: "Dear Sisters, I would like to invite women in the Fall River–New Bedford area to come to our weekly discussions about women's roles in life and literature."[97] And in what appears to be an open letter, Pauline Collins offers a scathing critique of the racism and sexism that denies "justice for Black sisters in this country." The statement begins, "Sisters in Alderson [a women's penitentiary], and sisters around the world, this is Pauline Collins speaking. I am now what our decadent system of prison would call a fugitive."[98] Such open letters often manifested multiple rhetorical tropes, drawing from genres such as personal essays, journalistic reporting, manifestos, and persuasive essays. Although the direct address in these cases reflects an epistolary discourse, these pieces are not simply letters to the editor, so their mode of interacting with readers is not the same as the "Dear Sisters" that initiates more conventional letters.

Although the trope of the direct address takes up only a small percentage of space relative to the other text in a periodical, naming matters. To analyze the *I, you,* and *we* produced through the language of the direct address, I turn to interpellation. The direct address, whether spoken or written, hails (interpellates) the reader as a sister. In Louis Althusser's frequently cited example, a police officer shouts, "Hey, you there!" at an individual, who responds by turning around. According to Althusser, "By this mere one-hundred-and-eighty-degree physical conversion, [the individual] becomes a *subject.* Why? Because he has recognized that the hail was 'really' addressed to him, and that 'it was *really him* who was hailed' (and not someone else)."[99] Through this bodily acknowledgment the hailed individual is interpellated and becomes a socially legible subject. Butler does not doubt the power of this process to constitute an individual's subjectivity but offers a different perspective on why it works. For her, the police officer in Althusser's example can hail someone not solely because the officer is in a position of power but because of "the citational dimension of the speech act, the historicity of convention that exceeds and enables the moment of its enunciation."[100] In other words, naming works because of the speaker's and addressee's experiences of the name's historicity, its previous usages, the context of its utterance, and the context of its reception.[101]

The discursive and social effects of interpellation liken it to a speech act (an utterance that does what it says). Butler argues that legal discourses about hate speech rely on the concepts not only that a racist term relays "a message of racial inferiority, but that 'relaying' is the verbal institutionalization of that very subordination."[102] That is, calling someone a faggot is discursively violent because it actually produces that body as a faggot. Similarly, the military's "Don't ask, don't tell" policy assumes that the statement "I am a homosexual" is more than a description: because it constitutes the speaker's sexuality, the words themselves become a form of "homosexual conduct."[103] Butler bases her claims about the performativity of language on the understanding that these statements—simply through their utterance—realize what they say. Part of what contributed to the expansiveness of the women's liberation movement was the ability of the phrase *Dear Sisters* to do what it said. As a specifically interpellative speech act, this phrase called out to readers, and at least in terms of the number of women who identified with feminism, it appeared felicitous.

Phillip Brian Harper shows how a direct address involves at least two parties—the *I* and the *you*—and simultaneously produces both parties grammatically and socially. A *you* is both outside of and dependent on an *I* in that *you* is always *not-I* (and vice versa), and *you* can exist only in a situation that also contains an *I*.[104] In addition, the speaker's identity becomes clarified as that which the addressee is not, thus reinforcing the linguistic distinction with a social/political one. The converse occurs in feminist periodicals. "Dear Sisters" invokes a dyad in which I + you = we, thereby creating a much broader community—a *we* that encompasses potentially all women and revealing the simultaneity of subject and community formation that a collective identity requires. Periodicals emplaced feminism throughout the world; readers encountered sisters through articles, announcements, essays, and letters by and about women in the surrounding community as well as in faraway locales. The direct address therefore connected women who had never met and would never meet to produce an imagined community of feminists. Extending Butler's argument about the way language produces subjects, the use of the term *sister* not only ensured the existence of the individual but also supported the viability of a community.[105]

Building on this imbrication of language, identity, and community, my approach presumes that addressing readers as sisters created and sustained feminism through different rhetorical effects and on different scales. First, a label creates what it names, giving it an ontological and social existence. Regarding sisterhood, this discourse simultaneously produced individuals and a community. A writer's contribution to these publications placed her within the women's liberation movement, a position that her use of sisterly discourse affirms. Since being a sister requires the presence of at least one other "sibling," another individual must also exist. Thus, within the direct address a social and political community forms both between the addresser and the addressee as well as between the addressee and a multitude of other sisters across the world whom interpellation brings into the feminist fold.

However, the community of feminists depended not only on a reader's recognition of herself in a hailing but also on the reader's actions. Periodicals consistently asked women to donate time and money, office supplies, energy, skills, and resources. An announcement in *Sister* reminded readers, "the west-side women's center needs staffers—REMEMBER SISTERS. IT'S YOUR CEN-TER!!!!"[106] And an editor of *Distaff* noted, "Women this is your paper. Mary Gehman and I work seven days a week in order to provide information and coverage of events that you won't find any place else. You need *Distaff*, and *Distaff* needs your support."[107] Seven of the first eleven extant issues of the *Valley Women's Center Newsletter* included appeals for reader assistance. This relationship—between editors and readers, between women's center staff and their local community, between addresser and addressee—required con-stant refueling. The mundane, daily labors of sustaining a social movement indicate both the value and the fragility of a successful direct address or a felicitous speech act. If a reader failed to turn toward the call, the disavowal would not be merely discursive and would not constitute only a refusal to reproduce an ideological system; rather, it could have a tangible, material effect on the women's liberation movement. Without women to physically, materially, and financially support feminism, the movement could not repro-duce itself.

Some women who responded voiced a desire to support feminism despite an inability to do so, showing that a hail does not always succeed and that this breakdown can be both discursive and material. When Female Liberation asked readers, "Why don't the almost 900 of you on our mailing list come to our orientation meetings, business meetings, demonstrations, parties?," one reader who signed her letter "A Sister" explained, "Perhaps you some-times feel that the work is not worth tje effort because you get such little response. . . . You are asking all of us who receive the newsletter why we don't help you. I can't. I am a full-time teacher and this is my first year teaching—I am not free one moment from the enormous work involved in planning good lessons. But I am very much conscious of the women's movement and I try to live in as liberated a way as possible; I also try to communicate tge ideas of the movement in my classes."[108] Similarly, Sue Kirk wrote to *Sister* on behalf of the Center for Women's Studies and Services, "We can only give *moral* support at this time because we are barely making it ourselves. If we can get ahead a little we will be glad to donate some money to SISTER in the future. We are sorry we cannot give you financial support immediately."[109] In these letters, readers turn toward the interpellative call by recognizing themselves as an addressee, but this is primarily a discursive response. Yes, they have taken action to write to the editors and center staff, but they may not be realizing the speech act in the way the editors intended, namely by contributing time, money, or resources.

Though I focus more on periodicals as the source of an interpellative ut-terance and on the need for readers to respond to this hail, the dependence was not unidirectional. Readers reveal the ways in which periodicals nourished them as well. Bobby Darwall wrote to the *Female Liberation Newsletter* in May 1971,

> Dear Sisters,
>
> Yes, please keep sending me your Newsletter, and here's a contribution toward putting it out. It means a great deal to me—and to all the other Feminists on Cape Ann—to be getting news of the Women's Movement. We're so far out in the country, comparatively, that sometimes we feel completely isolated from the movement, and your Newsletter helps us keep going.[110]

When she wrote that the newsletter "helps us keep going," she did not mean that the newsletter ensured her community's linguistic or discursive existence or even its material survival. Rather, she was suggesting that the newsletter provided emotional sustenance, and she connected this emotional well-being to her ability to imagine others producing "news of the Women's Movement." Further affirming the affective power of identifying with other feminists and the role periodicals played in this experience, Sandi Warren wrote to *Sister* in March 1973, "I'm in the middle of reading your February issue of *Sister* which we received today for the Sacramento Women's Center, and I have to stop to write you and tell you how excited I am about this issue."[111] She explains that it addresses many Sacramento women's concerns and questions about women's liberation activism. And another woman began a letter to *Ain't I a Woman?* with, "I just wanted to write you to tell you how important *Ain't I a Woman* has been to me." She explained, "Not only did *Ain't I A Woman* put me in touch with anger and sense of oppression, but more than anything else I read clear headedness, working things out, a sense of commitment, community, joy, even love." While this woman valued the newspaper's analysis of feminist revolution and socioeconomic class, the letter is also heavy with affect, ending "With deep felt thanks and love."[112]

It is by now widely accepted that ontologically, texts may be considered processes as well as products and that readers actively interpret texts rather than passively absorb a singular truth. Texts, then, are always in denotative and connotative motion. Adding to the complexity of meaning making are the generic qualities of periodicals. A textual hailing is not a singularity in the same way as Althusser's "Hey, you there" in terms of both the moment of address and the reader's response. The temporality involved in experiencing a written text gives the reader a chance to negotiate the terms of the address in a way that differs from a response to a singular oral call. Although a reader will have an immediate reaction when reading a text—whether or not she identifies as a sister—she can process the manner and extent to which she embraces that identity over time. She can revisit the text, reexperiencing the direct address, and may respond differently. The seriality of a periodical also ensured that such calls would be repeated, so someone who did not send money after reading one issue might do so after reading the next. Or the next. Furthermore, the speaker of the direct address need not be a singular *I*. Feminist periodicals were almost always the product of collectives, and many collectives explicitly strove for a nonhierarchical editorial process. As a result, any member could be an author, and pieces could be collectively authored or contributed by nonmembers. Many of the newsletters I studied, as well as *Ain't I a Woman?*, frequently lacked bylines, meaning that readers would not have known who the speaker was. The writer of "Dear Sisters," then, could be a known signifier (for a signed piece) or an empty signifier (for an unsigned piece). It could also be a singular *I* or a collective voice.[113]

Interpellation thus is a multifaceted process, producing meaning that is inextricable from a name's previous iterations, the context of its utterance (including its material form), the addressee's affective reception, and how the addressee imagines herself to be similar to, different from, and connected with others who might share the name. Despite the many factors that complicate the production and interpretation of a text, people agree on meanings. To understand this consensus, framing becomes useful. As a master frame, sisterhood gains such strength in part because it can contain contradictory connotations—emerging through a tension between general and specific, between dominant and subjugated meanings—without breaking apart. It contains tracts of semiotic space and myriad points where an addressee can identify as a sister and a subject of feminism.

In addition, the interpellative process invokes a community and a particular world that these subjects inhabit. In Michael Warner's view, "All discourse or performance addressed to a public must characterize the world in which it attempts to circulate, projecting for that world a concrete and livable shape, and attempting to realize that world through address."[114] Looking at iterations of the term *sister* in feminist periodicals demonstrates that it was used both universally and specifically, presenting certain challenges for those employing the word to mobilize women around feminism. On the one hand, its force as a universal term allows a wide variety of addressees to feel included in political, social, and affective ways. But many people perceive this inclusion as superficial and actively reject it. Also working against the term's power to mobilize is the fact that one can feel included without actively supporting or contributing to the movement with their time, labor, money, or expertise. Despite the scale and pace at which feminism in the United States grew, the repeated calls for help suggests that on a grassroots level and on a daily basis, feminist groups were struggling to reproduce the movement in a material way. Therefore, the potential universality of sisterhood created a situation in which any woman who was hailed could figuratively turn around and become part of the community, thereby enabling the discursive or imaginary reproduction of the community without working to ensure the material contexts of its reproduction. Conversely, *sisterhood* connoted a community of women who had already committed their time and energy to change the world in a feminist way, a group that clearly did not include all women.

Investigating the force of interpellation thus points to the importance of the direct address, the challenge of negotiating one's audience, and the obstacles to forming a community whose subjects who are also activists. Attention to the rhetoric of the direct address also demonstrates the tension between the promise or potential of inclusion and how inclusion is practiced and experienced concretely.

Despite its complexity, *sisterhood* has also retained an unproblematized relationship to gender and sex. Whether affirmed or disavowed, *sisterhood* remains stuck to womanhood, making it difficult to dislodge the centrality of gender. As Janet Jakobsen notes, "It makes a difference if you first walk through a door marked gender and then talk about race or if you first walk through a door marked race and then talk about gender."[115] Even if feminist activists recognized the complexity of women's struggles, starting from gender shaped the trajectory of their activism, often resulting in practical exclusions of women of color. I do not seek to measure the success or failure of sisterhood but instead the work it does as a frame that organized women's relationships, practices, politics, and desires. Tracking the circulation and repetition of this concept enables us to piece together the frame and consider how it is made consistent while containing a range of variations. Similarly, images tell a story of collective identity and framing of feminism, also demonstrating this tension between inclusion and exclusion, between what feminism is, what it could be, and what it should be, which is the focus of the next chapter.

CHAPTER 5

# Imaging and Imagining Revolution

The cover of *Sister*'s inaugural issue, published in January 1973, features a hand-drawn graphic of a woman standing next to a bicycle (see figure 4). She is wearing a black garment and what looks like a conical straw hat; her face, in three-quarter profile, does not reveal much, though her gaze is firm, assertive. A large basket filled with items hangs from the horizontal top tube of the bicycle's frame, and a cluster of dense foliage provides the backdrop. Dispelling any ambiguity, this issue's theme appears in prominent typeface along the left edge of the page—"Woman and the War, 50": readers would quickly have identified this person as Vietnamese.

The issue includes a series of articles focusing on different aspects of the Vietnam War. "Why Women and the War," authored by the Women and the War Group, presents an intricate analysis of the way the military-industrial complex and capitalism interact to oppress women in the United States and enact violence against people around the world. The authors highlight the contradiction between the U.S. government's antiabortion rhetoric about a "deep respect for the 'sanctity of human life'" and its brutal use of "chemical defoliants and biological weapons" against the Vietnamese people and their country.[1] Other articles address the role of women in North Vietnamese resistance efforts, critique the U.S. military's recruitment of women for the Women's Army Corps, and characterize the U.S. government's discourse regarding deescalation in Vietnam as empty rhetoric. Although there are moments of universalism, these writers draw out the complexities and breadth of U.S. imperialism and situate sexism, racism, and classism in the United States in relation to, not simply as identical to or analogous to, the cruelties to which Vietnamese people were subjected. The authors also recognize that violence exceeds the impact of bombs and bullets and napalm. The writer of "Amerikan Way of Death" opens by pointing out that "for the Americans attack has not been confined to conventional military targets—it has been directed against the people of Vietnam, against all that is their country and their culture."[2] Altogether, the portion of the issue dedicated to Vietnam belies the homogenizing and essentializing rhetoric of sisterhood that has dominated characterizations of 1970s U.S. feminism. And although *Sister* did not explicitly articulate an intersectional theory of power and privilege, it demonstrated an understanding that multiple forces interacted to shape women's experiences and articulated interconnections between women's liberation and other political activism.

Such an analysis was unique neither to *Sister* nor to this particular issue of the publication. The Iowa City editors proclaimed in the third issue in July 1970, "*Ain't I a Woman* is committed to helping create revolutionary alternatives for women—alternatives to the sexist, racist, imperialist Amerika which defines out-groups as objects, as not quite human. Blacks, Indians, people of the Third World, women—all are out-groups. All are defined as objects."[3] And the author of an article about reproductive rights in *Distaff*'s first issue wrote, "Poor women and women of color with their political grievances cannot be overlooked in a feminist demand for abortion repeal. This is a reason that the only minimal acceptable program a feminist can work for is the demand for: free safe abortions on demand, no forced sterilization, no genocide of poor people and people of color, and free and adequate contraception for all those who desire it, regardless of age. No single part is sufficient in itself—all are closely related to the others." Further, the author recognized, abortion was available only to "the sisters who can *afford* to pay the high fees and have the mobility to travel to states where abortion is legal."[4] In other words, a woman's health needs were based on more than her gender, and reproductive justice involved more than just legalizing abortion. When the *Valley Women's Center Newsletter* reported on a 1976 forum about the state of women's liberation as an autonomous movement, it acknowledged the specificity of race and class oppression and explained that the women's liberation movement needed to provide "a theoretical basis which recognizes the independent existence of women's oppression *and* its connections to other forms of oppression, thereby allowing for a feminist analysis of class and race."[5] The *Female Liberation Newsletter* similarly articulated a complex sense of interconnectivity between sexism in the United States and U.S. imperialism in reprinting a speech given at the 1971 National Peace Action Committee conference: "We see that the same government which denies the people of Southeast Asia the right to self-determination also denies women the right to control over our own bodies and lives. [President Richard Nixon] declared that his reverence for 'the sanctity of life' extended even to the unborn in womb—that is of course, as long as it isn't the womb of a Vietnamese Woman."[6] A June 1973 *Sister* piece reflecting on the state of feminism in Los Angeles concluded with a call to action: "We have formed a Women's Union because these and the many other forms of women's oppression make us angry—because we wanted to fight against them as effectively as possible. This can only be done by acknowledging the many forms that the oppression takes. We will not win if our analysis deals only with our own personal oppression and not with that of our sisters around the world. The Women of L.A. will not be free until the women and men of Wounded Knee and Vietnam are free. None of us are free until all of us are free."[7]

Feminists challenged racial divides beyond the essays, articles, and creative writing published in periodicals. Between September 1974 and July 1975, *Distaff* was coedited by Mary Gehman, who was white, and Donna Swanson, who was black. A May 1974 special issue of *Ain't I a Woman?* on race was edited by a "white-oriented halfbreed" with the assistance of "her mulatto friend."[8] And Female Liberation reported on a teach-in in Seattle, Washington, at which "many Chicanas were present indicating a new interest on the part of Third World Women in Feminism [and] Mariana Hernandez from Austin, Texas spoke on the need for the women's movement to support the movement of Black and Brown sisters."[9] These examples do not necessarily mirror the whole of women's liberation, nor do they show the extent to which women used the richness of their differences to build social and political coalitions. The special issue of *Ain't I a Woman?* exemplifies some of these tensions and contradictions in its opening editorial: "I have tried to get different women of color to work on this issue. Two of them said they didn't want to work on a white women's paper, but I have been given full control of copy and layout." On the one hand, these two women had free rein to curate this issue, signaling that the Iowa City feminist community recognized race as an important issue; on the other hand, labeling it the "Issue on Race" clearly marked it as an exception from *Ain't I a Woman?*'s regular existence, which, by default becomes "a white women's paper." As a result, this kind of special issue may not only marginalize women of color but erase whiteness as a racialized category. In addition, Gehman and Swanson's unusual collaboration lasted less than a year (although Gehman wrote that it ended as a consequence of their commitments to family and their lack of financial resources and labor power rather than for reasons related to race or racism).[10] Feminist communities clearly grappled with the complexities of race and racism, both locally and within feminism more generally, showing that race mattered to the women writing and editing these periodicals.[11]

Offering another narrative of U.S. feminism, women of color, poor and working-class women, lesbians, women from other countries, and antiracist white women have forcefully demonstrated the limitations of dominant 1970s feminist theories and practices. Feminism homogenized the category *woman* and allowed women to avoid confronting their power and privilege. *Triple Jeopardy*, published by the Third World Women's Alliance, addressed both of these concerns in a 1973 article about International Women's Day: "The feminist movement and those middle-class white women who acknowledge that 'the struggle for third world and white women is not the same' should be criticized because they show no willingness to overcome the gap between their own class background and ethnic privileges and the needs of all women and the society as a whole."[12] The discursive awareness of difference that is evident in feminist periodicals did not necessarily translate into activism and alliance building across these differences. As Elizabeth Lapovsky Kennedy has pointed out, the women's liberation movement suffered from a "commitment to antiracist work [that] was mainly abstract, rooted in interracial work of the past and in a universalist understanding of the concrete differences in women's lives."[13] Such a gap is evident in the *Valley Women's Center Newsletter*'s report on a showing of a documentary, *Angela Davis: Portrait of a Revolutionary*, for which Florynce Kennedy and Jill Johnson traveled from New York City. The piece ends with an admonition: "The relationships between racism, sexism and the capitalist society were explored at length with reference to the films. Too bad *only eight of us* showed up!"[14] Though the event created a space in which the aims and practices of women's liberation could be complicated specifically with regard to race and class, feminists in that community seemed uninterested in being a part of it.

Created in part as "a reaction to the racism of white feminists," *This Bridge Called My Back: Writings by Radical Women of Color*, a landmark 1981 anthology, responded boldly to the exclusions of and myopia in the U.S. women's liberation movement.[15] Contributions overwhelmingly demonstrate that women of color continued to be perceived as Other, that white women remained unaware of their race privilege, that single-issue politics persisted, that white women had been slow to self-educate about racism, and that white women's attempts to build alliances with other women often involved merely tokenizing forms of inclusion.[16] Such practices allowed some feminists to reproduce their privileges at the expense of others and reinforce a narrative of progress in which women of color start outside of and then gradually are included within the movement.[17] Although the volume's poetry and prose frequently and insightfully address racism, it is not the anthology's only subject. The writers also focus on how feminists' political and identitarian practices keep gender, whiteness, heterosexuality, the United States, and the middle class central to the foundation and origins of feminism.

The version of the women's liberation movement (and the field of women's studies, which is often narrated as the movement's academic arm) presented in *This Bridge Called My Back* differs considerably from the one represented in the pages of the feminist periodicals I examined. Confronted with these two versions of feminism I began to wonder to whose blindness Mitsuye Yamada referred when she wrote that "our white sisters should be able to see how tenuous our position in this country is."[18] What accounts for these disparate versions and visions of the women's liberation movement? What do the particular ways in which feminist periodicals grappled with race and racism tell us about feminism as an identity, political practice, value system, and mode of relationality? I address these questions by analyzing women of color in feminist periodicals, focusing specifically on visual portrayals—photographs, hand-drawn graphics, and clip art—and their significance in relation to the surrounding text and to each other. Like *sisterhood*, the bodies of women of color were a site of semiotic struggle: different meanings rose and submerged, patterns and exceptions to those patterns appeared, specificities clashed with generalizations, and views that reflected racism appeared side-by-side with those that astutely analyzed individual and structural dimensions of racism.

Continuing the thread woven through previous chapters, I analyze feminist collective identity formation, using portrayals of women of color in feminist periodicals to unpack the women's liberation movement's uneasy relationship with race and racism. Specifically, I argue that in feminist periodicals, women of color reinforced the idea that feminism was a serious revolutionary movement. Reading dozens of different feminist periodicals and hundreds of different issues made certain patterns visible, one of which was the wide circulation of images of Sojourner Truth and Indochinese women.[19] The frequency and visual consistency of these portrayals demonstrate the significance and power of these figures. For this chapter I thus venture beyond the five periodicals on which I primarily focus, bringing patterns in the depictions of women of color into sharper relief. Once again, repetition is a mechanism that solidifies meaning and allows us to see how this meaning goes beyond denotation: images not only represent the world but also instruct readers in how the world should be interpreted and do so through an interplay of denotations and connotations with affective and cognitive impact.[20] According to Maylei Blackwell, "Yo Soy Joaquín," a foundational text in the Chicano liberation movement, signified "revolutionary male prototypes . . . over and over until they became archetypes of Chicano nationalism, visually encoding the political subjectivity of the movement as male."[21] In the same way, repetition reveals the markers that produce a dominant—perhaps even hegemonic—feminist discourse about revolution.[22]

Periodical editors can be seen as appropriating women of color when imaging and imagining them in the pages of a newsletter or newspaper, using the connection between nonwhite women and revolutionary struggle to boost feminism's apparent radicalism. Especially in relation to the manifold examples of white women's racism and ethnocentrism, we must grapple with this claim, but I offer another perspective on the significance of these representations by contextualizing them within a discursive field consisting of mainstream media, New Left rhetoric, and the self-representations of people involved in U.S. and Third World revolutionary movements. Periodicals cultivated a feminist sisterhood not only by including diverse groups of women within the scope of women's liberation but also by pushing back against the way mainstream media and the New Left portrayed feminism and feminists. Just as *sisterhood* becomes more nuanced when we situate it within and as a response to cultural manifestations of sexism (for example, the difficulties married women faced in retaining their maiden names), we can better understand feminists' engagements with race when we attend to the racialized dimensions of cultural discourses about feminism from other media. These sites frequently trivialized and caricatured the women's liberation movement, so feminists pushed back. Scholars and activists tend to explore the sexism in this dialectic, but less often foregrounded is how these depictions implicitly and explicitly racialize feminists and female activists.

Such an investigation involves not only resituating images of women of color but also examining constructions of whiteness. Victoria Hesford has analyzed feminist ideas and rhetoric to see how they produced "an economy of emotion that marked the movement as white" and that contrasted with the forceful, angry, confrontational representations of Black Power.[23] Focusing particularly on mainstream and mass-produced media, she explores why and how "the whiteness of women's liberation is remembered as an inevitable, or naturalized, historical effect."[24] I, too, consider the racialization of 1970s feminism to be a product of media—feminist, mainstream, and leftist—but whereas she analyzes nationally circulating texts such as Erica Jong's *Fear of Flying* and "Women's Lib: A Second Look" (a *Time* magazine article on Kate Millett), I approach the question through grassroots feminist ephemera.

This method integrates history, sociology, and semiotics to place the images and language in feminist periodicals within a broader social, political, and historical context. I also employ an intertextual analysis, considering words and imagery together. My approach, though, relies less on tracing the genealogy and origin of particular images and instead on placing them within a discursive structure: How and where is an image placed in a periodical and on the page? What kinds of text does it modify? How and when do tropes associated with the image appear elsewhere? Who might be their silent interlocutors? In answering these questions, I presume that the meanings of words and imagery mutually constitute each other through a messy and overdetermined process. Images are not simply supplementary components of the text proper, illustrating "a text in a literal way," and the text proper does not simply instruct readers about how to interpret an image, guaranteeing that all will come away with the same understanding.[25] Furthermore, some scholars argue that a visual image has an impact on us before we process it cognitively and thus that it exceeds verbal description and our ability to articulate its full meaning.[26] I cannot know how individual readers interpreted an image, but the patterns in language and imagery, when considered as part of a larger conversation about feminism and race, point to likely and preferred connotations.

Beyond these cognitive and affective processes of interpretation, the materiality and genre-specific components of these periodicals have an impact. First, these periodicals contain different types of images and use images for a range of different functions: they accompany articles, essays, and creative writing; they are part of advertisements; they are examples of women's art; they are decorative; they are informative; and sometimes, no clear function is apparent. Because of the different rhetorical situations in which images were used, images in some instances appeared auxiliary to the written text and in other cases were the "proper text" rather than paratextual.

Covers, for example, greeted readers with an image that could lack context. The image of the Vietnamese woman with a bicycle gains meaning from the issue's theme as well as from readers' knowledge about *Sister* and its purview. Because *Sister*'s issues often had themes, the cover art was situated as part of this theme, giving readers some interpretive guidance. *Ain't I a Woman?*, however, used cover art much more ambiguously: in the November 19, 1971, issue, for example, the cover is horizontal across a full page, with the newspaper information on the right and a graphic of a face—probably a woman's—filling almost half the page. Two clenched fists are stacked in the middle of the page, each a little larger than life-size. Although disconnected from the body, they are drawn in the same style as the face, implying that the two are corporeally and symbolically related.[27] Even in fragments, this body has a strong presence. It is composed almost as a collage of solid black irregular shapes that do not fit neatly together and are surrounded by uneven amounts of white space. Who is being depicted? Does she symbolize women's power and resistance to a patriarchal ruling order? Is the message about violence? Is the woman's fragmented visage a manifestation of the way culture has fragmented her psyche? Neither the cover nor the content of the issue— primarily long pieces that analyze and reflect on lesbianism and middle-class privilege as well as a four-page supplement about women's health—provide any definite answers.

Among the periodicals I studied most closely, Indochinese and black women repeatedly signified women fighting a revolution and through this association came to stand in for the idea of revolution more generally. Since many feminists had ties to the antiwar movement, Indochinese women, especially those from South Vietnam, were prominent in feminist media. North American women also cultivated ties with their Indochinese comrades, most prominently in the 1971 Indochinese women's conferences in Vancouver and Toronto.[28] Because of U.S. feminism's temporal and cultural proximity to the civil rights and Black Power movements, the activism of and symbolism used by black men and women were significant. Panther women such as Angela Davis, Ericka Huggins, and Assata Shakur shaped white women's visions of a feminist revolution and contributed to the ways that white feminists engaged with women's struggles more broadly. The resistance efforts of Vietnamese people merged with Black Panther and Black Power activism in the feminist imagination. A 1970 flyer from Bread and Roses invited sisters to "Join the Fight!," which encompasses two areas: "U.S. get out of Vietnam, Cambodia, & Laos," and "Free the Panthers & all political prisoners."[29] The cover of a New England Free Press flyer about women's revolutionary actions around the globe tells readers that "women all over the world are part of revolutionary struggles to tear down oppressive institutions and build more just societies. Black women in this country, and women in other countries, in revolutionary countries like Vietnam and Cuba, are doing more than speaking out: they are working and fighting."[30] Such juxtapositions turn bodies of women of color into radical Others and, through repetition, into signifiers to which certain meanings and affects stick. Although white women participated in radical—and sometimes violent—acts, these women were rarely used to explicitly exemplify a discourse of revolution in the periodicals I studied. *Ain't I a Woman?* was the most likely of the five publications to offer this alternative narrative of whiteness—for example, in a four-page 1973 piece by Jane Alpert, a Weather Underground activist who went into hiding to avoid prosecution.[31] Other women of color appeared in these periodicals but did not embody revolution as fully or frequently as black and Indochinese women. Coverage of Chicanas' struggles against U.S. imperialism received coverage, but it was often framed in relation to class and labor issues.[32] American Indian women received even less attention, although some feminists perceived indigenous women as symbolizing an important connection to the environment, motherhood, warriorhood, and spirituality.

These representational patterns reflect not only the local contexts of a publication and the perspectives of writers and editors but also the ways in which groups accessed information, including a dependence on existing media sources and services. Editorial collectives exchanged periodicals with other publishing groups, and women's centers often had literature racks and libraries that included ephemeral publications. As with other networks in the women's liberation movement at this time, the feminist mediascape emerged through idiosyncratic lines of connection. For example, in addition to requests from local women for information about local feminist events and locations, the *Valley Women's Center Newsletter* published an announcement about French feminists who sought to organize "an International Collective to find ways that women throughout the world can work together and exchange information."[33] But the Northampton women did not regularly publish updates about women's liberation in France, nor did they explain how or from whom they received this update. *Ain't I a Woman?* ran a 1970 article about racial discrimination in hiring at an Oscar Mayer packing plant in Davenport, Iowa, that disproportionately affected Chicanas. None of the other periodicals I studied picked up the story.[34] Feminist periodicals also drew information from various leftist media and media clearinghouses, including the New England Free Press, the Liberation News Service, and Pittsburgh-based KNOW, Inc. Given the finite and often scarce resources that most feminist editors could access, their choices—particularly regarding nonlocal stories—were to a significant extent limited by what these other institutions chose to cover. To recognize these structural factors is not to excuse editors from doing the labor of researching and writing about the myriad struggles women faced but rather to recognize some of the external forces that shaped periodicals' content and to explain why African American and Indochinese women provide the basis for my analysis.

### Radical Others, Revolutionary Women

A growing number of scholars are analyzing the complexity of identity politics within feminist activism as well as the gendered activism of women of color.[35] Judy Tzu-Chun Wu's powerful conception of "radical orientalism" has been particularly useful for exposing the romanticized lens through which North American activists viewed women from Vietnam, Laos, and Cambodia.[36] For Wu, figures of Indochinese women served as "exemplars of revolutionary womanhood," acting as a kind of mirror for the West and "representing a contrasting image of revolutionary hope to oppressive gender roles in North American societies."[37] Building on her work, I have adopted the term *radical Other*, widening the scope of this romanticization to include black women and potentially other women of color. This chapter thus contributes to the rich body of literature that examines, deconstructs, and challenges the stereotype that gendered activism in the 1970s was the province of white, middle-class, heterosexual women and that these women were concerned only with their own liberation.

Images of revolutionary women in periodicals appeared in basically two forms: photographs and hand-drawn graphics. Photographs of Indochinese women reflect four main representational tropes. First, they are visible as women of color, and most often their Asianness is marked by the presence of a rifle. While a gun is not a specifically Indochinese accessory, the presence of the Vietnam War in the national imaginary linked Vietnamese women with guns, and the wide circulation of such imagery solidified this connection. Even when not pictured, a gun could become present through the surrounding text. A short pamphlet distributed by the New England Free Press included a photograph of a young North Vietnamese woman taken with the camera angled upward to give her an aura of dignity and courage. Although the photo does not clearly foreground a gun, the caption does: "This girl is a North Vietnamese freedom fighter. She helped to shoot down planes that

FIGURE 9. *Sister*, March 1973, 8. Woman's Collection, Texas Woman's University Libraries, Denton.

were supposed to drop bombs on her country.... She knows that no one is too young to help build a revolution, or to help defend it. In Vietnam there is no such thing as a woman's 'place.' A woman is a person and all people join in the revolution."[38] The connotations of a gun formed an important component of these images. Resting on a shoulder or possibly in the next room, a firearm became semiotically, politically, and affectively interconnected with the signifier *Vietnamese woman*.

Second, captions and articles rarely gave women's names or specific locations. The March 1973 issue of *Sister* featured a full-page image of four women with the caption, "We Salute with Love Our Sisters of Vietnam" (figure 9).[39] Without the caption, readers might have difficulty understanding what they are seeing: the image lacks signs of place and identity, clothing such as a conical hat that denotes a certain cultural context, or markers that would indicate where it was taken. Another photograph appeared on the cover of a spring 1972 issue of a Louisville, Kentucky, publication, *Womankind*; in the *Los Angeles Woman Worker* in May 1970; and in the November 1970 edition of a Cambridge, Massachusetts, periodical, *Battle Acts*. The photograph shows a smiling woman at the front of a line of soldiers; a gun rests horizontally on her left shoulder. The group is walking through a clearing, surrounded by waist-high grass, and trees fill the background. An editorial on page 2 of *Womankind* tells readers that this is a "Special Indochina Issue" but offers no additional information about the cover image. Written content in both *Woman Worker* and *Battle Acts* suggests that the woman is Vietnamese but gives no specific biographical or geographical information.[40] *Womankind* further abstracts the woman by cropping the image so that only her face and the gun are visible; the other people and the scenery have been removed. The only information regarding the image's provenance comes from *Battle Acts*, which credits the

Liberation News Service (LNS).[41] But the LNS generally provided little context for the subjects of photographs, such as "From a non-liberated area in South Vietnam. Credit Paul Temple/LNS."[42] Feminist editors did not arbitrarily delink Vietnamese women from their specific geographies and histories but rather were constrained by available resources.

Third, the figures in photographs are most often shown outdoors, surrounded by rural and pastoral scenery. The photographs discussed previously reflect this trope, as does an International Women's Day publication from the Cambridge Women's Center.[43] The back page features a photograph of four young women surrounded by grass that reaches their torsos. What they are doing is unclear, but they look toward the ground, two appear to be smiling, and two have rifles strung over their shoulders. The image is accompanied by a quotation from "a Vietnamese woman," Trieu Thi Trunh (often spelled Trieu Thi Trinh), a third-century Vietnamese warrior renowned for her resistance to Chinese imperialism: "My wish is to ride the tempest, tame the waves, kill the sharks, I want to drive the enemy away, to save our people. I will not resign myself to the usual lot of women." This text clarifies any ambiguity about who is being depicted and how the editors wished them to be perceived. The first article in *Sister*'s "Women and the War" issue depicts another woman with a gun over her shoulder; the caption explains that she is pulling a section of a U.S. warplane shot down over North Vietnam.[44] Because the photo is a high-angle shot, the only backdrop is the ankle-deep water through which she walks. Although the content of feminist periodicals recognized a greater complexity in the lives of these women and situated them in varied locations, these visual portrayals repeatedly place them in the countryside, and the primary marker of their identity as Indochinese women is a gun.

Some photographs included Vietnamese children alongside women. *Sister*'s "Women and the War" issue, for example, placed a close-up shot of an elder holding a young child in the middle of a page containing an article about women's roles in North and South Vietnam.[45] The November 1971 *L.A. Women's Liberation Newsletter* captured a moment when three (presumably) U.S. soldiers surrounded a (presumably) Vietnamese woman holding a child with the jungle in the background. The accompanying article, "There Are No Neutrals in the War in Southeast Asia," notes that a "grenade stuffed into the wombs of women is a frequently practiced information-gathering technique" and that chemical warfare in Vietnam was increasing the rate of birth defects.[46] This page powerfully indicated that the act of parenting could be a form of resistance to imperialism. Because Vietnamese people could not take survival for granted, the work of caring for a family—the myriad daily practices involved in social reproduction—are part of a repertoire of resistance that can indeed be revolutionary.

These photographs thus created Vietnamese women as radical because of this revolutionary struggle. And they are Other in their physical distance from the U.S. women who created this feminist ephemera as well as in their semiotic distance—feminist activism and Vietnamese resistance against U.S. imperialism differed greatly in portrayals by mainstream media and the New Left. An issue of *Ain't I a Woman?* reinforced this logic in its juxtaposition of text and imagery. An untitled, unattributed free-form poem whose content wrestles with existentialist and political issues such as love, imperialism, and the values of the women's liberation movement spreads across the page, its stanzas interspersed with two photographs and two drawings.[47] One photograph shows a woman (presumably Vietnamese) walking away from the camera with her head turned toward the right, carrying a rifle on her shoulder and wearing a conical hat. She has been placed near a stanza that reads,

> And when I realize that while I'm occupied
> with these thoughts [about romance]
> This country is continuing its
> extermination of the Third World.

The photograph modifies the text by constructing the Vietnam War as one site of this extermination, and the text emphasizes a distinction between the writer and this Third World woman.[48] The writer was concerned about "a physical gesture / of affection being taken / as some carnal advance" by another woman while Vietnamese women were fighting the threat of genocide posed by U.S. imperialism. The focus on relationships and intimacy situates the writer's life and bodily integrity in stark contrast to what Vietnamese— and other Third World women—faced. This poem also potentially characterizes feminism as trivial through a transitive logic: If feminists were concerned with such frivolous matters, could the feminist movement be revolutionary?

The frequent location of Vietnamese women outdoors and in rural areas reinforced this distance between U.S. feminists and the Third World, putting them out of place and time with the West. On the one hand, these images could situate Vietnamese women in a premodern past, in a place/time outside the mechanized, technologized, urban culture of the West. Even though South Vietnam's largest city, Saigon (now Ho Chi Minh City), had a population of about three million in 1970, urban culture did not characterize these revolutionary freedom fighters.

When markers of the West appear, they are an invasive species. They do not belong, symbolizing a lethal force that the accompanying text often reinforces. In *Sister*'s photograph of the woman pulling part of a warplane, the fact that the plane originated in the United States creates the West as a site of modern technology and adds weight to an East/West, premodern/ modern binary. The article on the following page explains that because of the destruction of the countryside by U.S. militarism, "peasants were forced into the cities, into a money-based society completely alien to them. There a conscious attempt has been made to replace the traditional values of the village with new values—those of a consumer society."[49] The piece concludes that "American-sponsored death" has caused "the destruction of Vietnamese culture" and "the corruption of Vietnamese values." These examples formed part of a national antiwar discourse that brought attention to atrocities committed by the U.S. government and military in Vietnam and more specifically highlight the binary logic that structured American feminists' visions of Vietnamese women, revolutionary activism, and the feminist movement.[50]

Graphics and hand-drawn representations of Indochinese women added another dimension to the symbolic value of revolutionary activism and struggle by gendering it. Because they are not beholden to verisimilitude, artists can create graphics that diverge from the way women appeared in photographs. Therefore graphics are particularly useful for their insight into the ideological investments of U.S. feminists in revolutionary women and women of color. They reflect how artists and activists imagined Other women and which visual tropes most strongly signified the concept of revolution. In these graphics, the gun remains integral to the image, and artists often include the conical hat. Graphics, though, add another component to represent revolutionary womanhood: a young child. On the cover of the September 1971 *L.A. Women's Liberation Newsletter*, a figure cradles a baby in one arm and a rifle in the other (see figure 3). Kneeling, she appears prepared to jump up to defend or attack as needed. Another graphic depicting this combination of tropes appeared on a 1970 Bread and Roses Mother's Day flyer and on a booklet chronicling the women's liberation movement written by Washington, D.C., activists, likely in the late 1960s.[51] The woman also cradles the infant and the rifle rests on her lap. Her cultural, racial, and ethnic features are a little more ambiguous, but in the Bread and Roses flyer, Indochina is foregrounded. Below the image is a list of incidents of U.S. imperialist violence: the top three items are "U.S. invades Cambodia," "U.S. shoots to kill students in Ohio and California," and "U.S. bombs Vietnam." While the flyer encompasses a range of communities damaged by the U.S. government (Black Panthers, Greeks, Haitians, South Africans, American Indians, Mexican Americans, and Puerto Ricans), the text about Indochina would likely be more strongly connected to the image of the woman because of its proximity.

Another image that appeared in multiple publications depicted a woman with a large gun in her right hand and a small child held in a cloth against her back.[52] The April 1969 inaugural issue of the *Los Angeles Women's Newsletter* featured the image on the cover, and it subsequently appeared on 1970 International Women's Day flyers and pamphlets from Seattle, Washington, and Urbana, Illinois, and on a poster created by the Chicago Women's Graphics Collective. A similar image was also published in a September 1969 issue of *The Movement*, a New Left newspaper.[53] Unlike the portrayal of a woman with an ambiguous racial, ethnic, and national identity, the woman in the Los Angeles periodical is either African or African American. The style of her clothes and head cover suggest traditional African garb, and, emphasizing this connection, she carries a book with *Black Studies* on the cover. Although deterioration of the ink makes it difficult to discern some details, the artist's name, "Emory," appears by the woman's feet, signaling that the artist was likely Emory Douglas, minister of culture for the Black Panther Party.

Regardless of her geopolitical origin, the connotations of the woman's body are clear. The headline in the Urbana publication, "Revolutionary Women," appears just above her, so they inflect each other: the image emphasizes the revolutionary nature of the article, while the article solidifies the meaning of the image.[54] However, the women mentioned in the article are not Black Panthers or women from Angola, Guinea Bissau, Mozambique, or other African countries where decolonization struggles were being fought. Instead, the authors focus on Vietnam:

> We must reject the individualistic ethic that society forces on us and replace it with a collective effort to change those institutions into ones which encourage a revolution in personal fulfillment and human relationships.
>
> The women of Vietnam, for example, realize that their personal and political liberation are inseparable. While fighting for self-determination of their country they are also fighting for their own self-determination within that country. These women have broken out of their traditional "feminine" roles and now assume significant political, economic, and military positions. . . . The Vietnamese people realize that a democratic, socialist, humanist society can only be achieved through the active equal participation of all the people. They see the vital connection between democratic socialism and the liberation of women.[55]

This moment reflects the interconnections of the Black Power movement and other Third World struggles in Western feminists' imaginations, showing that the concept of *revolutionary woman* is not an effect of being from a specific place or being involved in a specific struggle. Instead, it formed from an amalgamation of ideas and ideals about those fighting imperialist forces and was manifest in specific visual and textual tropes that could accompany a range of bodies (primarily those of women of color).

Incorporating a child in these graphics recognizes that social reproduction involves fighting imperialism both by carrying guns and by raising children. She is not just a warrior but a *woman* warrior. However, the graphic possesses a semiotic ambivalence by both challenging and reinforcing the scope of sex and gender categories. On the one hand, these women are portrayed outside of the private sphere and in roles that do not conform to the traditional Western ideals or to the lot of women that Betty Friedan elaborates in *The Feminine Mystique*. On the other hand, these images leave un-questioned the biological and social facets of *woman*—particularly women's roles as mothers—reflecting U.S. feminists' attachments to gender. Feminist activists had invested not in transforming the mechanisms that formed iden-tity categories but in expanding the scope of available roles that women could or should be able to occupy.

Another feminist vision of a radical Other featured Sojourner Truth. Depic-tions of her likeness in feminist periodicals allow me to further contextualize the way feminists collaged different iconography to imagine revolutionary women, although in this case, we travel through time instead of across the globe. Between 1863 and 1875, Truth commissioned a number of photographs that she sold as *cartes de visite* to provide income to support her traveling and speaking.[56] One of these *cartes* served as the basis of a graphic that ap-peared in feminist periodicals and other ephemera across the nation as clip art (figure 10). The image's popularity almost a century earlier likely led to its use in the 1970s: it served as the frontispiece for the 1875 edition of her biography, *Narrative of Sojourner Truth*, and according to Nell Irvin Painter, it was one of Truth's favorite *cartes*, suggesting that Truth herself played a role in promoting this image.[57] In the original version, Truth sits with a table at her left. She holds an unfinished knitting project; a vase with flowers and an opened book rest on the table. Her dress and the other props in the pho-tograph, which carried meanings related to gender, class, religion, and race, highlight her ties to middle-class respectability, a radical claim for an illiter-ate former slave.[58] The meaning of these objects and her clothing would likely not be common knowledge to the generic mid-twentieth-century feminist periodical consumer, but the garments became signifiers that marked her as Sojourner Truth, for these items—especially the head covering and shawl—appeared in almost all of Truth's *cartes*.[59] The clip art version that appeared in feminist periodicals places Truth in the left half and shows her from the waist up, with her head cover, white shawl and collar, and spectacles as the primary visual symbols of her identity. The caption reads, "Sojourner Truth, 'The Libyan Sibyl.'" The right half of the graphic consists of an excerpt from her famous "Ain't I a Woman?" speech at the 1851 Women's Rights Convention in Akron, Ohio.[60]

Other representations of Truth echo the formula in the clip art. *Distaff*'s November 1979 issue embedded a hand-drawn graphic of Truth in an article, "Our Very Own Bureau in Baton Rouge."[61] According to the piece, the Bureau for Women in the Louisiana Department of Health and Human Services pro-vided training programs for women; assistance in finding emergency shel-ter; programs for Native American women and incarcerated women; support for pregnant teens; and other services. This image of Truth features the head cover, spectacles, and shawl, but her arm is angled outward, with her hand

# No More Radical Sabbaticals

## FEMALE PERSPECTIVES

The Southwestern Female Rights Union is a small collective of women interested in establishing a strong women's movement based on the struggle of the most oppressed in the Southwest. At this point we are primarily an informational office.

Because of the problems we have talked about it is especially difficult to organize here. We are in the process of developing ideas for various positive programs.

We are interested in any suggestions and help people have to offer. Some of us live together in a house where we also have our office. We are desperately in need of contributions for our rent and the first issue of our journal. Some of us are going to Cuba and so our staff will be severely depleted. We are in the process of trying to catch up with correspondence. We ask that all be patient.

Struggle,

(Nancy Adair, Martha, Mary Maxine)

## THE SITUATION IN NEW MEXICO

The situation in New Mexico, in the South, in the ghetto, demands special attention from the white Women's Movement and the Movement as a whole; it demands analysis and sensitivity on the part of all white (anglo) people. We have studied, and are still studying and reading about the problems and the oppression of the Black in her ghetto. Movement papers have analyzed the problems and establishment press, television, and films have inundated us with propaganda concerning the Black's situation. The Movement in centers like New York and Berkeley is just beginning to understand the situation and deal effectively with its racism. In New Mexico, however, we are just beginning to understand our chauvinism and racism because the situation demands a different analysis. Most of us were educated in "heavy" Eastern and West Coast politics. Most of the communication and information we have with other groups comes from both these areas. It is time now for the analysis of the problems of this area, by the women of this area, to reach the rest of the country. (For the beginnings of the analysis of Chicana problems we suggest you read Enriqueta Longauex y Vasquez' articles in "El Grito Del Norte").

Racism thrives here in the form of imperialism and supremacy. New Mexico is a colony as is the South. The government can test its bombs and missiles at White Sands and Los Alamos because it does not have to put up with the objections of an urban white middle class whose good-will it has to nurture. They build their bombs in a third world area and drop them on third world people. The atomic bomb, developed and tested in New Mexico was dropped on Japan. The government which did this continues to send missiles over New Mexico to land at White Sands. Could anyone imagine their sending it over Chicago to land in Lake Michigan?

The government comes to the Southwest and offers good, well-paying jobs to anglos. The Chicano remains unemployed - except in the low-paying menial jobs - his land is legally 'stolen' in quit-claim deeds - he moves to the ghetto of the city with his family where he can be easily contained and constantly harrassed by the police. (We use he in this instance because the plight of the Chicana is much worse - she usually owned no land, her jobs are worth less money, welfare is ridiculously low.

The Chicano and Indian are people raised on the land. A hundred years before the Pilgrims landed the Chicano and Indian were fighting the harsh elements, growing their crops, and herding their sheep. They built irrigation systems to tap the precious water supply. They fought droughts and flash floods, they fought for their freedom - from Spain - the frontiersman - and the United States government. When the railroad came the land became valuable for raising cattle to supply beef for the East. The anglo raped the mountains for minerals and stole the range lands, overgrazing them, turning the plains into a desert. With the help of "heroes" like Kit Carson they raped and massacred the Indian. They destroyed the buffalo and the deer. Worst of all they brought their capitalistic, imperialist system; the economy that turns people into leeches, parasites who live off the misery of others, that creates the Vendido and Uncle Tomahawk.

A second migration is inundating the Southwest... the cult of the commune, the freak, the longhair. Hollywood and Dennis Hopper have discovered a cheaper way to make "authentic" movies. The "richey" comes to escape the noise and smog of the city, the artist comes because this is truly "the land of enchantment" and the people are so "real", so "genuine". They live in dirt houses, attend dirt churches, eat tortillas, chile, and beans. Tourists don't have to deal with the expense and language of a foreign country when they can visit the quaint mountain villages of the Sangre de Cristo and the "sublime" pueblos of the Rio Grande. The beauty of New Mexico has created a mask unlike Harlem that covers reality of extreme poverty. The tourist, imperialist representative in his own country, does not see that there are no hospitals for thousands, that the mountain streams - the very subsistence of the people - are polluted by mines, lumber mills and "hippies orgies". They do not see into the schools where children are forbidden to speak their own language, that the history which is taught is not their history but that of the Pilgrim... Kit Carson, a genocidal murderer, who led their forefathers on a death march, is acclaimed a great American hero. The media tells them how lucky they are that the anglos came to build them good highways to the ski resort and the nearest McDonalds - the former they could not afford and at the latter they would not eat.

Movement people come through on their way to California, light up a joint, and stay because it is so beautiful...when they travel from Berkeley to San Francisco they do not stay in Oakland because it is so beautiful. New Mexico is becoming the land of the Radical Sabbatical. The Mesa has a way of suspending our sense of humanity. How can hunger, disease, despair exist in such beauty? It does. We call for a boycott on travel and Tourism in New Mexico. If you come -- come as a true revolutionary, come with the consciousness that we have to work together and to fight together -- when asked-- against the oppression of the most oppressed.

Anglo women who were planning to come to the workcamp had not been invited by Chicanas. They were coming to work and learn, but we who planned the camp did not have sufficient insight or knowledge to understand the position we would be in. Instead of arriving as sisters we would be seeing the loveliness which brings tourists; instead of achieving unity we might be splitting the ranks of the Chicanos. Rather than be guilty of any of these errors in judgement we called off the workcamp. We offer our apology to our sisters in California who helped us but who did not participate in the decision. We, in New Mexico, were solely responsible for our ignorance and insensitivity to the problems. We feel that we have learned something from this experience and we have wanted to share it with you. Our further apology for the delay in this analysis reaching you. Sometime in the future it may be possible to have a camp when we are invited. The Cuban people have asked many North Americans to join the Venceremos Brigade and participate in the sugar harvest. When and if a group of Chicanas find it opportune to educate a group of white middle-class Female Liberationists then, perhaps, we can have a workcamp. We feel that women should get together in workcamps next summer. We must learn to work together after we have learned to talk together. We support the efforts of any who are interested in holding such camps. We welcome any correspondence, critical anaysis.

"That man over there say that a woman needs to be helped into carriages and lifted over ditches, and to have the best place everywhere. Nobody ever helped me into carriages, or over mud puddles, or gives me a best place... And ain't I a woman? Look at me. Look at my arm! I have plowed and planted and gathered into barns, and no man could head me... And ain't I a woman? I could as much and eat as much as a man when I could get it, and bear the lash as well... And ain't I a woman? I have borned thirteen children and seen them most all sold off into slavery. And when I cried out with a mother's grief, none but Jesus heard... And ain't I a woman?"

SOJOURNER TRUTH. "THE LIBYAN SIBYL."

Sojourner Truth: Speech before the Woman's Rights Convention at Akron, Ohio in 1851.

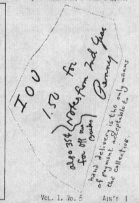

12

VOL. 1, No. 5        AIN'T I

FIGURE 10. *Ain't I a Woman?*, September 11, 1970, 12. Woman's Collection, Texas Woman's University Libraries, Denton.

resting on her hip, and she almost seems to be smiling. The excerpt from her speech is framed by her arm: "I have done a great deal of work, as much as a man, but did not get so much pay. We do as much, we eat as much, we want as much." Her name and the year *1853* appear below.[62] This portrayal suggests that the artist was familiar with the formula—Truth = image (including the shawl, spectacles, and cap) + excerpt from her speech + name and date. In a practice that reflects the portrayals of Indochinese women, Truth's image appears with content not directly related to black women's struggles. *Ain't I a Woman?* used the graphic of Truth in multiple issues in this way. The October 1970 issue, for example, places the graphic amid a scattering of letters from readers and announcements; in May 1972, it appeared next to an ad for a lesbian publication, *The Ladder*, and text from an article on the extent to which the *Ain't I a Woman?* collective was revolutionary.[63] In these cases, it seems unlikely that the editors intended the graphic to serve primarily as an illustration for the other text on the page. Yet the piece also does not seem to be meant to stand on its own. This ambiguity is reinforced by the repetition of Truth's image as clip art in the newspaper: it appears with a wide range of different texts, and these varying discursive contexts allow it to become semiotically spacious. Repetition clarifies the power of her image while refusing to dictate only one denotation.

The Los Angeles women also found the symbolism of Truth compelling, carrying a statue of her through the streets during the 1971 Los Angeles International Women's Day march, renaming the destination in her honor, and reading the "Ain't I a Woman?" speech aloud at the concluding rally.[64] Truth's status as a revolutionary figure—rather than some specific tie to International Women's Day—seems to have been the reason she was chosen to symbolize the march, and the article about the event emphasized this symbolism: "Renee Harding from the L.A. Committee to Free Angela Davis, told of Sojourner Truth's life and the hardships and degradation she endured as a black woman slave. After gaining her freedom, Sojourner committed herself to fighting for the rights of women and blacks just as, today, Angela Davis has made that same commitment." By linking Truth to a contemporary freedom fighter, the Los Angeles women demonstrated that they saw Truth as revolutionary.

As a migratory subject, Truth "transgressed borders of race, class, gender, literacy, geography, and religion."[65] With this characterization, Patricia Hill Collins refers specifically to Truth's remarkable ability to move among different communities during her lifetime, but the concept also reflects the circulation of Truth's textual and graphic representations nearly a century after her death. The way her image infused feminist print culture reflects a continued mobility both in the way she traveled through time and in the prevalence of her likeness in different publications. Such an identitarian positioning gave

Truth authority in multiple registers, showing that she had become a symbol whose cultural capital extended beyond issues specifically related to the intersections of race, gender, and slavery. Feminists incorporated her name into their activism outside print culture, as well: Cambridge, Massachusetts, activists published a journal, *Sojourner*; Atlanta had the Sojourner Truth Press; in Los Angeles, Sojourner was a feminist store that sold "books, gifts, cards by, for, and about women"; a Philadelphia group called themselves Sojourner Truth's Disciples; and New Orleans women created a Sojourner Truth Award.

The Iowa City feminists demonstrated Truth's legacy not only by taking the title of their newspaper, *Ain't I a Woman?*, from her words but also by using a striking image of her on the cover of the first issue (see figure 1).[66] Truth retains the iconic white head cover and collar as well as her spectacles, but the artist has taken great liberty with Truth's left arm. It has a life of its own—it is muscular and substantially out of proportion to the rest of her body, and her hand is raised and clenched in a fist as large as her head. Reaching nearly the top right corner of the page, the arm frames the commonly cited excerpt from her speech. This image was not reproduced in any other periodical, and it appeared again in *Ain't I a Woman?* only once, when the editors celebrated the newspaper's two-year anniversary. But it clearly affected other feminists, since someone at the Valley Women's Center posted the *Ain't I a Woman?* cover on the wall there.

This cover also points to another visual mashup that manifests feminists' vision of radical Others. It puts nineteenth-century markers of class and gender into conversation with mid-twentieth-century markers of revolutionary liberation movements, indicating another way feminists sought power and claimed revolutionary status. Departing drastically from the photographic basis of the clip art, the Iowa City women let imagination take over, guided by the iconography of the Black Power movement and informed by the version of Truth presented by Frances Dana Gage, an abolitionist and feminist who attended the Ohio Women's Rights Convention. Gage's account of Truth's "Ain't I a Woman?" speech was published in the New York–based *Independent* in 1863. Gage used dialect that the editors of *Ain't I a Woman?* did not reproduce, but Gage's description of Truth could have been a template for the Iowa City image. According to Gage, Truth said, "'Nobody eber helps me into carriages, or ober mud-puddles, or gives me any best place;' and, raising herself to her full height, and her voice to pitch like rolling thunder, she asked, 'And ar'n't I a woman? Look at me. Look at my arm,' and she bared her right arm to the shoulder, showing its tremendous muscular power. 'I have plowed and planted and gathered into barns, and no man could head me—and ar'n't I a woman?'"[67] The voluptuous language not only refuses to ascribe a victim status to Truth but embodies Truth as almost superhuman. The Iowa City artist adds exclamation points in the speech that point to a voice like "rolling thunder": "Look at my arm!" and "I could work as much and eat as much as a man—when I could get it—and bear the lash as well!" And without a doubt, the "tremendous muscular power" of Truth's arm dominates this particular representation.

Just as the figures of Indochinese women could help feminists draw an affective line connecting their fight for justice with the lives of Vietnamese, Laotian, and Cambodian revolutionaries, the figure of Sojourner Truth linked the women's liberation movement to black women's struggle, which was, among other things, a praxis of resistance against gender, racial, economic, and sexual dehumanization and genocide. Speaking from her position as a "Black woman warrior poet," Audre Lorde observes that "to survive in the mouth of this dragon we call america, we have had to learn this first and most vital lesson—that we were never meant to survive. Not as human beings."[68] The lives of black women, black men, and other people of color in the United States have been precarious for centuries, so they, like Indochinese freedom fighters, cannot take survival for granted. Abolitionist and civil rights movements succeeded (at least within certain legal, political, and social spheres) in part because black activists spoke from these experiences and gave word to the horror and violence of slavery and racism. This brutality—so clearly a violation of someone's right to be human—gave ethical and affective power to antiracist struggles for justice: as Patricia Hill Collins explains, "When feelings are involved—when individuals *feel* as opposed to *think* they are committed—and when those feelings are infused with self-reflective truths as well as some sort of moral authority, actions become fully politicized."[69]

There is no concrete evidence of a connection between Gage's chronicle and the cover of *Ain't I a Woman?*, but the image certainly suggests that Gage struck a cultural chord. Painter recognizes the broad application of this effect: "Today Americans who love Sojourner Truth cherish her for what they need her to have and buy her images to invest in the idea of strong women, whether or not they are black."[70] This symbolism involves a kind of stickiness, or semiotic consistency, in which a dominant meaning—in this case the strong black woman—seems inherent.[71] *Strength* sticks to *Sojourner Truth* in a way that allowed her to become a symbol for a range of different activist projects and political moments. The fist in the Iowa City vision of Truth, however, provides compelling visual evidence of the Black Power movement in the feminist conscious—and unconscious.[72] The fist can be seen as another protagonist on the cover of *Ain't I a Woman?*: although Truth's head and shoulders, her words, and the newspaper's title take up the majority of the page, Truth's arm makes the fist a destination for our gaze. Its sheer mass imposes its presence, daring us to look away.

The fist's prevalence in feminist media demonstrates its status as a potent visual marker for the women's liberation movement. In some cases, the fist reconfigured the woman symbol of a circle atop a cross. Some feminist versions extended the vertical line of the cross to end in a clenched fist within the circle. The *L.A. Women's Liberation Newsletter* and its successor publications used versions of this symbol. Sometimes it is hand-drawn and sometimes clip art, the latter of which indicates that the editors saw the image as integral enough to their identity that they wanted a version that they could easily reuse. Moreover, the "Certificate of Sisterhood" created for the Women's Day march contained only one graphic—the woman symbol with a fist. This reformulation of the symbol, like the discourse of sisterhood, appeared in feminist cultural products as well: catalogs of feminist accessories show it on T-shirts, bumper stickers, patches, jewelry, and buttons, and it appears in red on the cover of the 1970 Vintage edition of Robin Morgan's *Sisterhood Is Powerful*. Shirley Weber connects the fist iconography specifically to the desire for power shared by the women's liberation and Black Power movements to a desire not merely for social, political, and economic inclusion, citing the incident at the 1968 Olympic Games in Mexico City when Tommie Smith and John Carlos raised black-gloved fists in protest during the playing of the U.S. national anthem during their medal ceremony.[73]

One last image illuminates the power of these revolutionary tropes and suggests that this power is intertwined with their ability to move, to attach to a range of bodies and to circulate through time. In May 1980, *Distaff* published a full-page article, "Interview with a Sandinista," that featured the words of Olga Aviles, a prominent actor in the 1979 Nicaraguan Revolution. According to the interviewer, Aviles's "experiences are foreign to most of us, who are not part of the Third World struggles, but her courage, strength, and fierce belief in her ideals cross the borders of experience and touch us all."[74] Just below the headline, a hand-drawn woman in a dress holds a child with one arm and raises a gun with the other. The unknown artist and the editors evidence an understanding of the symbolic value of the image. Rather than a lifelike portrayal of Aviles or a Nicaraguan female rebel, they illustrated the article with an archetypal image to convey the larger connection to an ideal. Readers might well have failed to recognize a lifelike portrayal of Aviles, but the woman-child-gun trope would almost certainly have been familiar and thus would have hailed Aviles as a radical Other.[75]

The portrayals of radical Others in feminist periodicals reflect geographical and temporal contours of feminism as a collective identity. Recuperating figures like Truth as part of feminism's history and depicting contemporary radicals narrates them as part of feminism's present, particularly through the language of sisterhood. In April 1971, the *Female Liberation Newsletter* published a flyer for an antiwar march in Washington, D.C., that has the phrase "Support Our Asian Sisters in Vietnam" above a collage that includes the Statue of Liberty, a black woman, and two other women of unclear racial or ethnic identities (though the text seems to indicate that one is white and from

the West and the other is Asian).[76] The flyer's language draws a connection between the war in Vietnam and the United States through the rhetoric of self-
determination, and the figures overlap in the collage, two features that work
to show radical Others as part of feminism. Furthermore, the lack of explanation that accompanies many of the references to and depictions of Indochinese women and Sojourner Truth suggests that editors did not feel the need
to justify the use of these images as icons for feminism. Even though they are
not explicitly labeled as feminist, their presence in feminist periodicals and
their physical placement on a page include them within feminism's circum-
ference. Conversely, the ways in which women of color and women outside
the United States disproportionately bear the weight of revolution narrate
U.S. feminism as Other to these women—as always already lacking. U.S. feminism is not revolutionary enough, not inclusive enough, not transgressive
enough. In this sense, radical Others embody what Rachel Lee describes as
a "pure space" and a "triumphal end point," existing outside of feminism and
constituting a place toward which feminism attempts to move.[77]

So far, my analysis of radical Others has focused on discursive components—how images and text are juxtaposed, the significance of a photograph
versus a graphic, what tropes are repeated. Bringing in history of the book
allows us to see another factor that shaped the representation and construction of radical Others. Periodical editors did not have unlimited access to images and depended on distribution services (the Associated Press, LNS, and
Underground Press Syndicate), other feminist media, and activists' personal
collections. The LNS distributed packets twice a week to subscribers, and
even though underground papers paid only fifteen dollars a month (in contrast to the one thousand dollars per month the LNS charged mainstream media), even such a tiny fee could be prohibitive for perpetually cash-strapped
feminist periodicals. Editors also took from mainstream newspapers and
magazines—both to report on events covered and to show examples of
sexism—and borrowed heavily from other women's liberation and alternative
media. Examples of borrowing abound, demonstrating how these feminist
periodicals circulated across the country and the movement's ideology about
intellectual property.[78] Sources often were not cited, complicating efforts to
trace the provenance of articles and images and to determine whether they
came from the editors, directly from contributors, or from other publications.

These publishing practices give additional context for the use of Sojourner
Truth clip art. Because periodical publishing was relatively cheap, so was
space in the periodicals themselves. Mimeographing an additional newsletter page was inexpensive, especially when volunteer labor was used. Although
groups that edited newspapers had to be more mindful about space—a single
page could not be added, since one sheet of newsprint holds four newspaper
pages—that form, too, was much less resource- and capital-intensive than

book publishing. Further, the prevailing citation conventions for feminist periodicals meant that groups could easily use, reuse, and reprint items or images without getting permission, paying money, or even obtaining information about where the material had originated. Moreover, clip art could be reproduced almost indefinitely, providing a continually renewable source of feminist iconography. In some instances, therefore, editors likely inserted whatever clip art they had that would fit the available space on a page. The small rectangular image of Sojourner Truth could quickly and easily be placed into white space next to articles or essays on different topics. I do not intend to trivialize editors' decisions or the historical realities of Truth's life, and I am not arguing that the seemingly random placement of clip art had no meaning. But recognizing the opportunities and obstacles that accompanied these modes of production allows us to better understand the seemingly incongruous juxtaposition of text and imagery in feminist periodicals.

The kind of printing technologies to which feminist collectives had access thus enabled and constrained the content of their publications. Offset-printed newspapers proved more hospitable to photography, while mimeographed newsletters were better equipped to reproduce simpler graphics with little nuance in shading. Newspapers, conversely, could accommodate more complicated content but lack of access to feminist presses meant that editors had to deal with outside publishers and their politics, which could lead to refusals to print certain content. In 1973, for example, *Sister* had difficulty publishing an issue that contained photographs of a woman conducting a vaginal self-examination, and in November 1971, *Ain't I a Woman?* announced, "This was to be a twelve page paper, with four pages of medical self-help material on menstrual extraction. However, we couldn't get them printed."[79] Without editorials or organizational records, we cannot know why something was included or excluded. Yet this instance shows that a periodical's content resulted not only from editors and writers projecting their fantasies of feminism—or revolutionary women—but also from material constraints. Editors had to make choices based on the resources they could access and on constraints imposed by the publishing process.

## Feminism Is a Revolutionary Movement

The 1968 Miss America Pageant protest served as a flashpoint for some of the strongest archetypes of U.S. feminism produced by mainstream media. On September 7 of that year, a group of women traveled to Atlantic City, New Jersey, where they marched on the boardwalk with posters before disrupting the pageant itself. The photographs associated with this event, which have become iconic in histories of U.S. feminism, reveal groups of white women civilly occupying the boardwalk. Media reporting shows no raised fists, no weapons, no imagery that resembles the photographs or graphics of women of color. Underestimating the radical impact of this action, the images that circulated most widely did not construct women's liberation as a threat. For example, one photograph appears in Sara Evans's national history of U.S. feminism, *Tidal Wave*, and Bonnie J. Dow's book about feminism in the mainstream media; it also accompanies two articles published in the early 2000s, suggesting both that it is easily accessible and (likely a result of this accessibility) that it has become broadly symbolic of the U.S. women's liberation movement.[80] Attributed to the Associated Press, this photograph depicts two white women, each of whom holds a poster: one states in all capital letters, "Welcome to the Miss America Cattle Auction"; the other depicts a woman whose unclothed body is divided into different cuts of meat—rib, loin, rump—and captioned, "Break the Dull Steak Habit." The second poster certainly disrupts norms of respectable, middle-class white femininity, but it does so in a very different way than the image of a Vietnamese woman wielding a gun to protect her child's life.

Similarly, the phrase *bra burning* started appearing in popular media after the Atlantic City protest and has since become inextricable from the collective identity of U.S. feminism in the 1970s.[81] It has stuck despite the fact that no bras were burned at the event (they and such other items of patriarchal femininity as girdles, high heels, and issues of *Ladies' Home Journal* were deposited into a "freedom trashcan"). The ubiquity of this characterization is, according to Ruth Rosen, "a symbolic way of sexualizing—and thereby trivializing—women's struggle for emancipation."[82] Affirming this interpretation, Dow points out the contrast between the characterizations of draft card burning and bra burning. The latter "became less a symbolic act of political defiance—as other burnings had been—and was used more to symbolize feminists' personal disdain for conventional femininity." Instead of viewing bra burning as a serious critique of gender norms, "dominant media used [it] as evidence that feminists had so little of substance to complain about that they were concerned with undergarments."[83] The analogy with draft cards uses the Vietnam War as a counterpoint to minimize feminist activism, but U.S. racial politics also reiterated this logic. Dow analyzes the *New York Times* coverage of the radical feminist protest and the Miss Black America Pageant planned by grassroots activists based in Philadelphia, two events that occurred at the same time as the Miss America Pageant. While the *Times* depicted the Miss Black America Pageant as a political event, it failed to recognize the Miss America pageant as a legitimate object of political dissent, thereby delegitimizing feminist activism.[84]

Highlighting the *ad feminem* perception of women's liberation, the fall 1970 issue of the *Female Liberation Newsletter* asked readers to weigh in on one topic in particular: "The question for this week is as follows: 'I'm all in favor of women's liberation, but why are all the women in the movement so ugly?' (and why don't you have any sense of humor?).''[85] And Joan Cassell has described the 1960s stereotype of feminists as "hysterical, shrill-voiced, physically blemished sexual and societal rejects."[86] By focusing on women's appearance and behavior, such characterizations resist—at least explicitly—granting the women's liberation even a shred of political importance. Opponents would not have demeaned feminism if the movement had not disrupted the status quo, so ridicule likely reflected anxieties about the social and political challenges posed by women's liberation. Yet it is difficult to imagine Angela Davis or Madame Nguyen Thi Binh of the South Vietnamese Provisional Revolutionary Government being questioned about their sense of humor. Of course, women activists of color faced forms of epistemic and material violence that reflected centuries-old legacies of imperialism, and these women were also caricatured—often in demeaning ways—through representations of their hair, clothing, and other bodily features. Nevertheless, the trivialization of feminists drew on particular gendered and racialized tropes that were distinct from popular treatment of other revolutionary movements, a phenomenon that manifested particularly clearly in the politics of the New Left.[87]

Because *revolutionary* refused to stick to *feminist*, the radical Otherness of the struggles for social justice of women of color and of the Third World could provide a kind of cultural capital for women's liberation.[88] The *Female Liberation Newsletter* told readers in 1970, "The word liberation signifies to us freedom from oppressive social relations, sexual humiliation, fear and the daily outrages and indignities which are our lives. The word liberation, because of its reference to all oppressed peoples, Blacks, Orientals, Chicano and other Third World and Working Class people, constantly relates our movement to these others. It shows lack of respect and seriousness about the Female Movement not to use this word in all its strength and dignity."[89] A comment in *Distaff* cited the phrase *women's lib* as "one of those semantic put downs" used by a "hostile male press."[90] An early issue of the *L.A. Women's Liberation Newsletter* echoed this sentiment: "Using the diminutive 'Lib' for Women's Liberation serves to make the movement smaller, less important, perhaps more palatable.... Let's not demean our movement by shortening liberation to LIB. Have you ever heard of Black Lib? Or Chicano Lib?"[91] In an editorial following this statement, Joan Hoffman called on readers to write to the *Los Angeles Times* to explain how the paper's use of lib robbed feminism of its power. Cassell offers a similar provocation when she asks, "To give but one small example, would the people who so glibly discuss 'women's lib' ever talk about 'black pow'?"[92] These revolutionary movements not only imbue the term *liberation* with certain connotations but also evoke potent affective claims, as the editors of *Ain't I a Woman?* indicate when they explain the need for feminists to create their own media instead of "working through the pig media. We work in other ways, through local [women's liberation] groups, through our own media, until the pigs like [Hugh] Hefner and [Dick] Cavett are afraid to enter the same room with [women's liberation] women in the same way pig racists fear the very presence of Black Panthers."[93] This statement acknowledges the Black Panthers' power to command attention through fear, an emotion women's liberation rarely evoked, and thus articulates an affective and discursive connection (or disconnection) between feminism and other revolutionary movements. In addition to its connotative stickiness, *liberation* evokes potent affective claims. Thus, as periodicals use language and imagery to correlate women's, Third World, and Black Power movements as comparable in their revolutionary potential, for feminists this correlation often appears to be a goal rather than a reality.[94]

Feminists not only responded to the mainstream media's representations of revolutionary struggles but also found women's activism the object of New Left derision. Robin Morgan explained that feminists took over *Rat*, a New York–based alternative newspaper, in 1970 because of its "token 'pussy power' or 'clit militancy' articles. The snide descriptions of women staffers on the masthead" and "the porny photos, the sexist comic strips, the 'nudie-chickie' covers (along with their patronizing rhetoric about being in favor of women's liberation)."[95] Further reinforcing the gap between New Left and women's liberation activism was the location of women within the antiwar movement. Although visible on the front lines of protests against the war, women nonetheless were relegated to an ancillary place in the movement's structure.[96] A widely circulated slogan, "Girls say yes to guys who say no!," encapsulated one facet of the gendered division of activist labor: men were the activists, while women comprised a (sexualized) support staff.[97] These views directly discredited gender as a legitimate site of struggle, but this message could be conveyed obliquely as well. Another leftist newspaper, the *Old Mole*, published a section of a late-1960s U.S. Army manual, that explained how to disassemble and reassemble an M16A1 rifle. Titled *How to Strip Your Baby* and accompanying an image of a woman with long blond hair and a stereotypical hourglass figure holding the rifle, the title's double entendre diminishes any strength or revolutionary fervor the woman holding a gun might otherwise have presented.[98] Even though *Old Mole* appeared to be critiquing this image, it nonetheless conveyed the message that a woman with a gun served mainly as a sexual object for the men looking at her.

This treatment of women by some men in the New Left paints a picture of sexism; however, these sentiments also provide a more nuanced way of understanding the depictions of women of color in feminist periodicals. According to Ellen Willis, "White male politicos recognized the race issue as morally legitimate, while dismissing feminism as 'a bunch of chicks with personal problems.'"[99] Reflecting this attitude, Morgan poses a rhetorical question:

"*How*, [women] are asked, *can you talk about the comparatively insignificant oppression of women, when set beside the issues of racism and imperialism?*" She answers, "This is a male-supremacist question."[100] Winifred Breines also documents the glorification and romanticization of revolutionary freedom fighters by the New Left and the contrasting perception that women's liberation was frivolous and bourgeois. She quotes a white socialist feminist's description of a stereotypical sexist New Left male: "Such a man will sit at his desk with his feet up and point to the poster on his wall of a Vietnamese woman with her rifle on her back, telling you, 'Now that is a truly liberated woman. When I see you in that role, I'll believe you're a revolutionary.'"[101] These visions of revolutionary activism not only reify and glorify Third World women as ideal freedom fighters but also contain an implicit class component: women who began organizing autonomously "were accused of fragmenting and weakening the New Left by being selfishly self-indulgent (bourgeois) in their (middle-class) concerns."[102] *White* and *middle-class* thus became signifiers that stuck to feminism, determining perceptions of women's liberation politics of the 1970s.

These portrayals reflect and reproduce a discursive paradigm in which racism and sexism parallel each other as social justice issues. Mainstream media often situated gender and race as separate and competing political agendas, with feminism carrying less validity.[103] At the same time, feminists often relied on a race-sex analogy to legitimize their attacks on patriarchal institutions. Though it reflected awareness of the extraordinary injustices that racism and imperialism effected, the analogy nonetheless tended to oversimplify and homogenize the varied initiatives undertaken by people and communities of color.[104] Regardless of its characterization of feminism, this framework failed to articulate an intersectional understanding of identity and erased the ways in which groups such as the Black Panthers and feminist activists articulated their struggles in ways that recognized oppression as multiple and interlocking.

### The Semiotics of Revolution

White feminists struggled to shed the sticky stereotypes and caricatures of women's liberation that were repeated in mainstream media and New Left imagery and discourse. Because of their involvement in revolutionary struggles, Indochinese women and other women of color "assisted American activists in imagining the possibilities of new political identities and new ways of organizing society" and became part of a discourse through which U.S. feminists could produce their activism as revolutionary.[105] On the one hand, positioning women of color as radical Others acknowledges that institutionalized racism and imperialism has produced different realities for women. The lives of women of color are crucially distinct from the lives of white women (and women perceived as white) in the United States. On the other hand, this approach may produce women of color as a homogenous radical Other: any female body with certain visual markers can invoke revolution. The characteristics that might locate a woman in a specific time, place, and community become less important than the ways in which she produces the idea of revolution itself. This reification is an effect not only of a denotative repetition but also of an affective repetition, one that produces certain women of color as a revolutionary ideal through their suffering and courage. In fact, the way affect moves and sticks allows these bodies to become textually interchangeable as radical Others, as *Distaff*'s interview with Olga Aviles demonstrates. The wide circulation of the woman-gun-child trope allows a somewhat abstract representation of a woman to signify revolutionary struggle.

In light of these stereotypes of revolutionary womanhood, the writers and editors in the periodicals I examine arguably appropriated the bodies of radical Others, romanticizing and exoticizing women's lives and struggles. However, such a narrative removes these representations from the media and political discursive field within which they emerged and limits the possibilities for understanding race and racism in the U.S. women's liberation movement. Feminists sought to create a movement that was taken seriously as a force for revolutionary change, and their vision of revolution built on existing discourses and imagery. Mainstream media and New Left ideologies existed primarily as a counterdiscourse, and the images and narratives about Indochinese and other women of color provided an ideal. Moreover, feminists were not the only activists inspired by revolutionary struggles. A radical Asian group, the Red Guards, adopted Black Panther aesthetics and militant political tactics, and Mao Tse-tung's writings influenced the Panthers, some of whom also wore clothes that resembled those of Chinese peasants.[106] According to Jane Rhodes, the Panthers also contributed to a kind of radical Other discourse: another Douglas illustration, "Revolutionary Sister," depicted "beautiful black women in African garb toting a rifle," illustrating that "women could be simultaneously alluring, true to African traditions, and modern-day warriors."[107] Therefore, the symbolic power of these Third World freedom fighters appealed to U.S. radicals as well.

The self-representations of revolutionary women and men comprised another component of this framework. As Teresa C. Zackodnik has demonstrated, black people in the United States have a long history of working to control how they are represented in images and language. In the early twentieth century, African American periodicals such as *Voice of the New Negro* and *Colored American Magazine* used photography in particular to frame the qualities of the "New Negro" in the cover photographs.[108] Closer to the women's liberation movement, Angela Davis, Huey P. Newton, and Bobby Seale published political and autobiographical works about their lives and activism. Extending the power of self-representation to public events, the Black Panthers actively cultivated their revolutionary authority, using mainstream media as well as their own cultural productions—public performances and publications such as the *Black Panther* newspaper, first published in 1967.[109] The Panthers understood the power of the press and capitalized on the U.S. media's attraction to the spectacular. Before entering the California State Capitol in Sacramento with loaded rifles and shotguns in May 1967 to protest the Mulford Act, the Panthers first notified the media. According to Seale, "Those hungry newspaper reporters, who are going to be shook up, are going to be blasting that news faster than they could be stopped."[110] These purposeful, highly visible, and staged performances were critical in constructing the stereotype of the Panthers as "beret-wearing, gun-toting, angry young black men" whose "mission was essentially to scare white people about armed revolution in retaliation for discrimination." The Panthers' actions contributed to J. Edgar Hoover's declaration that they constituted "the greatest threat to American national security."[111] What could white feminists have done that would have aroused such reactions from the FBI or the press?[112]

As Wu argues in her work on the Indochinese Women's Conferences held in Canada in 1971, the women who attended from Vietnam and Laos presented different versions of their revolutionary struggle to different audiences. The U.S. activists from older, established organizations such as the Women's International League for Peace and Freedom could identify with Indochinese women's emphasis on the family, motherhood, and more traditional gender roles; the women associated with liberal feminism could find inspiration in the equal roles Indochinese women appeared to play alongside men in planning and implementing policy; for those aligned with the more radical facets of feminism, the ways in which Indochinese women were transforming social and political systems evidenced their revolutionary characters; and U.S. and Canadian Third World women could find solidarity with Indochinese women through the intersections of their anti-imperialist, anti-capitalist, and antipatriarchal struggles.[113]

Moreover, U.S. women of color explicitly aligned their struggles with those of women across the world. In *Triple Jeopardy*, a newspaper published by the Third World Women's Alliance, Pat Sumi wrote in 1972,

> What is our common enemy? Is it not the exploitation of women's labor, Third World labor, and all labor? Is it not racism which reduces Vietnamese people to a pile of "gooks" in a ditch at My Lai and us into degraded peoples of color? Is it not an ideology of women which reduces Angela Davis to blind animal driven by sex instead of a proud revolutionary Black woman? . . . The history of women's struggles throughout the world and in the U.S. shows us the way. The

example of the Indochinese and Vietnamese women shows us the way. They have shown us the oppression of women stems directly from an oppressive system called capitalism and imperialism.[114]

Accompanying this article is a graphic of a Vietnamese woman from the waist up. In one hand is the muzzle of a rifle (with the butt of the gun presumably on the ground), while the other hand holds a book—likely *Quotations from Chairman Mao Tse-tung*—over her head. Also juxtaposing image and text, a drawing depicting the female delegates from Southeast Asia who attended the 1971 Indochinese Women's Conference is titled "Solidarity with Our Indochinese Sisters and Brothers." It first appeared in the periodical *Gidra* in May 1971, and the *Asian Women's Journal* then reprinted it.[115] These intertextual moments resemble the visions of revolution that appeared in the five periodicals on which I focus, creating discursive overlap among women in Third World struggles. And Enriqueta Longeaux y Vasquez writes about the place of women in Chicano activism in *El Cuaderno*, a publication from La Academia de la Nueva Raza, an activist institute in northern New Mexico. Her 1971 essay invokes Vietnamese women in response to the stereotype that feminism causes a woman to lose her femininity: "This question as to our femininity doesn't make much sense. After all, we have seen the Vietnamese woman fight for survival with a gun in one hand and a child sucking on her breast on the other arm. She is certainly feminine. Our own mothers and grandmothers still recall how many of them fought with the men in the revolution and they were brave and beautiful, perhaps more human because of the struggle they fought for."[116] Here Longeaux y Vasquez explicitly names the woman-gun-child trope as evidence that women can be activists without compromising the movement or their gender identity. I am not arguing that *Triple Jeopardy*'s editors and writers and Longeaux y Vasquez had the same intentions as U.S. feminist editors and writers or that pieces such as these had the same effects as those in *Sister* or *Ain't I a Woman?* These examples, however, expand the mediascape that gave significance to portrayals of women of color in U.S. activist print culture and point to the ways in which women of color and others in Third World revolutionary movements actively represented themselves as revolutionary.

Despite the repetition of similar tropes in the construction of revolution, the meaning of *revolutionary* is never fully stable and fixed: instead of leading definitively to one single meaning, a signifier refers to another signifier, which refers to another signifier, ad infinitum. Because chains of signifiers will not be identical for all viewers, their interpretations will not produce identical meanings.[117] Repetition is an important force in countering this instability; it can prefer, privilege, and limit the range of possible meanings of images and language, an important process in social movements. If a social movement needs some consistency in its message, framing, identity, and politics, then exploring the denotative, affective, and political facets of repetition can illuminate how and why certain messages appear more frequently and seemed to have a greater impact on collective identity formation.[118]

My analysis speaks to the field of contemporary gender history as well, adding another perspective to the scholarship that disrupts the oft-cited portrayal of U.S. feminism in the early 1970s as concerned only with white, middle-class, U.S. women's lives. U.S. feminists articulated their theories and politics as part of a conversation that was much broader than the women's liberation movement itself. The trivialization of feminism, sexism, and the valorization of heterosexism by the New Left and U.S. culture more generally resulted in a climate in which the existence of autonomous feminist organizing did not guarantee that movement outsiders would take it seriously. Moreover, the Third World uprisings—both in the United States and around the world—inspired U.S. feminists and gave them language and imagery that symbolized revolutionary struggle.

In addition to linking affect, politics, and collective identity, repetition lets us interrogate the narratives used to explicate the U.S. women's liberation movement's relation to race and racial formations and to media and the culture more generally. Such an analysis does not absolve white feminists of responsibility for their representations of women of color, nor does it deny that these representations involve appropriating an Other to one's own ends. Instead, this analysis adds nuance to our understanding of the logic by which women of color became icons of revolutionary possibility for white women bent on liberation and aids in the development of methodologies for examining the politics of representation in a range of social movements.

Sara Ahmed's claim that repetition both enables and blocks the production of meaning allows us to place competing discourses in relation to feminism. New Left and mainstream media were discursive blockages: they prevented the women's liberation movement from being seen as revolutionary by depicting feminism as middle-class, bourgeois, and white, and thus as antithetical to the characteristics associated with revolutionary movements. Juxtaposing these different sets of discourses also makes visible the way whiteness served as an often unspoken modifier for feminism, pushing us to confront the ways in which feminism formed not only as a gendered identity but also as a racialized one.

## CONCLUSION

# Feminism Redux

The University of Arizona Library, the Lesbian Herstory Archives, and the Sophia Smith Collection have all become moments of reflection on the path I've carved through U.S. feminism in the 1970s. Each of these archival encounters between 2002 and 2009 marks a shift in my perception of feminist periodicals, and together they anchor my research narrative and shape this book's story of the women's liberation movement. Embedded in this genealogy, however, is (at least) one more coordinate. It became visible in 2015, when I had lunch with a colleague and her niece, who was attending the same small liberal arts college where I did my undergraduate work. The niece mentioned her interest in reviving a student zine from the 1990s, and I realized that she was referring to *Breaking Ground*, a periodical on which I had worked for three years.

When I joined the editorial collective for *Breaking Ground*, the statement that introduced each issue described it as a "radical feminist journal."[1] At that time in my life, I had only a vague sense of what this phrase meant. Looking back, I can see that one facet commonly ascribed to radical feminism—separatism—manifested in the practice of limiting editorial collective membership to women (transgender persons were not part of our conversation at the time), and from my current vantage point, I have a different understanding of one particularly heated discussion about whether to accept a submission from a cisgender man. I remember experiencing some unease about the contours of this woman-only framework but lacked the language to articulate my feelings. Instead, when discussing the journal, I verbally inserted a comma, telling people that *Breaking Ground* was a "radical, feminist journal." I don't know if anyone noticed, but it tempered my concerns. The comma created enough distance between the two adjectives that *radical* no longer modified *feminist*, and *Breaking Ground* became a feminist publication that also happened to be radical.

When reading about more contemporary versions of feminism, I found writers expressing a similar discomfort. Feminists of the 1990s, who often self-identify as part of the third wave, have typified 1970s feminism as white, ethnocentric, heterosexist, racist, woman centered, and without a sense of intersectionality in both theory and practice. In addition to these political-theoretical limitations, 1970s feminists also appeared rigid and dogmatic about their values. These characterizations stood in stark contrast to what I encountered in the University of Arizona Library where I first read *off our backs*, *Ain't I a Woman?*, *Rat*, and *It Ain't Me, Babe*. While gender had a salient and dominating presence, the writers and artists in these publications show that feminists were thinking about it in relation to an almost inexhaustible array of political, cultural, historical, legal, and economic realms: imperialism, labor issues, capitalism and classism, race and racism, the medical-industrial complex, other revolutionary movements, sexuality, day care, ageism, art, family, beauty, and spirituality—just to name a few. What, I wondered, had tamed the "cacophony of ideas" that Kathryn Thoms Flannery attributes to feminist periodicals of the 1970s and turned this era of feminism into what Walker wrote to introduce her 1992 collection of essays, *To Be Real*: second-wave feminism "will dictate and regulate our lives, instantaneously pitting us against someone, forcing us to choose inflexible and unchanging sides, female against male, black against white, oppressed against oppressor, good against bad"?[2]

Although feminists in the 1970s were not immune to racism, homophobia, classism, and U.S.-centrism, individuals and groups also did not simply and uniformly reflect these stereotypes. Nevertheless, this portrayal entrenches 1970s feminism in binary logic, tying it to either/or thinking that obscures the interlocking facets of oppression and that promotes activism based on only one identity category. It also reflects and reinforces the narrative most commonly used to frame U.S. feminist history. The first wave generally begins with the 1848 Women's Rights Convention in Seneca Falls, New York, and ends with the passage of the Nineteenth Amendment, which granted suffrage to (white) women. Then, after a four-decade lull, feminism began to regerminate during the 1960s: John F. Kennedy created the Presidential Commission on the Status of Women in 1961, *The Feminine Mystique* appeared in 1963, in 1965 Casey Hayden and Mary King circulated "Sex and Caste: A Kind of Memo," and the National Organization for Women formed in 1966. While these moments laid a foundation for the second wave of feminism, the 1968 Miss America Pageant Protest is often cited as the act that initiated it. Twenty-four years later, Rebecca Walker's now-famous utterance, "I am the third wave," in an article in *Ms.* magazine, has come to mark the start of a new generation of feminism.[3] And some people now argue that we are in the midst of a fourth wave.[4] The linearity of this model enables a narrative that at best depicts different waves as mutually exclusive (one wave follows the other, each signaling the end of the previous one) and at worst paints them as actively hostile toward each other (those in the current wave articulate their feminist identity in opposition to previous versions of feminism).[5]

A growing body of literature has demonstrated the epistemological effects of the wave model. Critics most commonly address the ways that waves misrepresent feminism and engender oppositionality.[6] Becky Thompson's pathbreaking 2002 article, "Multiracial Feminism: Recasting the Chronology of Second Wave Feminism," was one of the first to analyze the 1970s in this way, elaborating how the wave model has excluded the organizing of women of color and antiracist white women. Nancy Hewitt reaches similar conclusions with regard to the late nineteenth and early twentieth centuries.[7] While Hewitt and Thompson illuminate the heterogeneity of activism within the purported waves, Amber Kinser questions the boundaries distinguishing one wave from another. Declaring "I am the Mid Wave," she signals that she does not find a home in either the second or third wave but rather identifies with different aspects of each.[8] Together, these analyses of feminism question the utility of the waves to represent the range and complexity of theories and practices that have challenged gender oppression.[9]

Other scholars have worked to deconstruct waves by looking for continuities across time periods. Alison Piepmeier offers one such analysis, articulating a genealogy of what she calls feminist participatory media by comparing zines, late nineteenth- and early twentieth-century scrapbooks, and the women's health pamphlets published by Margaret Sanger and Mary Ware Dennett in the early twentieth century.[10] And Whitney Peoples argues that hip-hop feminism in the 1990s carried on the activist work of first- and second-wave black feminists through "themes such as empowerment, the importance of images and representation, and black women's involvement in coalitional politics."[11] Ednie Kaeh Garrison further notes the benefits of seeing third-wave feminism as a product of and not solely antithetical to previous feminist activism.[12] These interventions demonstrate that although feminist activists have developed different pathways to reach their goals, they drew on similar values and repertoires of praxis.

Despite the critiques of the wave model, the 1970s remain fixed as part of the second wave. Even after allowing for the heterogeneity, contradictions, multiplicity, and local idiosyncrasies of the decade, I have yet to see an analysis suggesting that a new wave of feminism might have begun prior to Walker's 1992 declaration.[13] Why not? What, instead, made Walker and 1992 the pivotal moment? This chapter does not offer a response to these questions but rather takes them as a starting point and explores how evidence might be used to answer them. Specifically, how does print culture as a type of evidence enable and constrain the kinds of histories we can tell about U.S. feminism?

The third wave is commonly considered to have begun in the early 1990s. But scholars and activists have noted a shift in the structure and politics of U.S. feminism significantly earlier. In the mid-1970s, feminist activists recognized that they were living in a moment of flux and transition. Ann Hunter Popkin's 1978 sociology dissertation explored the women's liberation movement through Bread and Roses, a Cambridge, Massachusetts, socialist feminist group that she helped form in 1969.[14] The questionnaire she used in 1975–76 to gather data from women participants asked, "How would you describe the women's movement today?" Eighteen of the seventy-six respondents indicated that feminism had become less coherent and cohesive since the 1960s, describing the current moment with words such as *disorganized, dissipated, diffuse,* and *divided.* And eleven of the eighteen used some form of the term *fragmented.* Of course, these activists spoke from their personal identities and experiences and from a feminist hub that would be expected to feature multiple strands of feminism and, consequently, splintering.

Other voices, however, have affirmed that the Cambridge women's perceptions were not unique, that the mid-1970s was a transitional time for feminist organizing and organizations. In her dissertation on Iowa City feminism, Linda Yanney explains that although her decision to focus on the 1965–75 period is "somewhat arbitrary," "by 1973, the key institutions and organizations necessary to carry the momentum of feminist organizing forward in Iowa City were in place. By 1975, they were well-established, with institutional lives of their own, hence the closing date."[15] For her, 1975 marks a time when feminism in the city became more stable, finding ways to occupy proper space and relying less on tactical activism to achieve its goals. Los Angeles saw a change at this time as well. Only one edition of *Sister* was published in the last half of 1976. Dated December 1976–January 1977 and taking as its theme "The Women's Movement in L.A.," the issue featured an editorial describing the movement as "crumbling" and groups as "collapsing," while *Sister* "staggers to her feet."[16] The following issue (February–March 1977) contains another editorial that elaborated on the shift, explicitly connecting the way space had shaped the movement: "The past two years have seen a decline and dispersal in radical feminist organizing to the extent that the Women's Center no longer houses any radical groups. All such groups (except *Sister* and the Fat Underground . . .) have either disbanded or moved to other quarters."[17] And Barbara Ryan labels 1975 "a watershed year" in her monograph about late twentieth-century feminism, emphasizing the significance of this moment with her only chapter title that includes dates, "Social Movement Transformation: The Women's Movement from 1975 to 1982." Within this chapter, she offers section headings that reflect this turmoil: "The End of the Original Radical Feminist Groups," "Fragmentation on the Left," and "Internal Challenge in NOW."[18]

Other scholar-activists bring attention to theories and theorizing as a way to track different threads of feminist activism. Joan Cassell, for example, has bridged theory and practice with her observation that "early, influential revolutionary women's liberation groups are dissolving at the same time that the movement spreads in widening circles, reaching a new constituency. By 1973 many early women's liberation groups that created and defined women's liberation theory, analysis, and tactics had dissolved or appeared to be losing focus and direction."[19] Jean Curthoys has correlated the disappearance of radical liberation theory from academic feminism by the late 1970s and "the emergence of a powerful and bureaucratically connected women's studies movement," suggesting that the trend had begun mid-decade.[20] Providing a historian's perspective, *Daring to Be Bad* is subtitled *Radical Feminism in America, 1967–1975* because, as author Alice Echols wrote, "by 1975 radical feminism virtually ceased to exist as a movement. Once radical feminism was superseded by cultural feminism, activism became largely the province of liberal feminists."[21] Sara Evans has dated radical feminism comparably, though she extends it to 1976.[22] Patricia Bradley ended her study in 1975, when "the initial energy of the movement was over, at least as far as mass media was concerned."[23] And Elizabeth Lapovsky Kennedy has articulated a distinction between the socialist feminist theories of the 1960s and 1970s and those of the late 1970s and early 1980s.[24] While these scholars have varying reasons for selecting a particular time span, a consensus nonetheless emerges: something happened to feminism in the mid-1970s, and whatever happened related to the presence (or absence) of radical feminism.

Three of the archival collections in which I conducted my research further bolster a renarration of feminism in the 1970s. The Valley Women's Center records span 1971–77, Female Liberation's papers are dated 1968–74, and the Los Angeles Women's Liberation Movement Collection runs from 1970 to 1976. The first two date ranges very closely reflect the life span of the group's periodical; although *Sister* continued until 1979, 1976 still served as an end point within Los Angeles feminism. Formal organizational records for *Distaff* and *Ain't I a Woman?* have not been archived, but the latter ceased publication in 1974, while the former experienced a four-year hiatus in the mid-1970s, offering additional evidence of a shift in feminism across the country at this time.

These ephemeral publications become evidence of a transition in feminism for other studies of print culture. Introducing their anthology of primary source texts from the women's liberation movement, Rosalyn Baxandall and Linda Gordon write, "The documents collected here are the flesh, bones, and spirit of the women's movement and they carried its dispatches across the country and all over the world. We feature the earliest years of the movement, from the mid-1960s to about 1977, because this was the period of the most yeasty ferment, creativity, and mass participation."[25] Flannery foregrounds a similar time frame in *Feminist Literacies, 1968–1975* because, "in this brief moment... feminists attempted the potentially radical task of addressing a wide audience."[26] According to Flannery, the period stretched from "the first flush of identifiably separate feminist periodicals in 1968 to what one might call the 'mainstreaming' of feminism in the midseventies."[27] *Feminist Literacies* concludes with a chapter about women's studies as a site of feminist pedagogy, indicating that the institutionalization of feminism in academia constituted part of this mainstreaming. At least temporally, then, a decline in "yeasty" and "radical" feminist publishing correlated with the growth of academic publishing, an enterprise that gained momentum with the first issues of *Feminist Studies, Women's Studies Quarterly,* and *Women's Studies: An Interdisciplinary Journal* in 1972 and became more established over the next few years. Both *Signs: Journal of Women in Culture and Society* and *Frontiers: A Journal of Women's Studies* appeared in 1975, followed by an array of journals explicitly committed to feminist content: *Camera Obscura* (1976), *Psychology of Women Quarterly* (1976), *Women's Studies International Quarterly* (1978; now *Women's Studies International Forum*), *Feminist Review* (1979), and *Feminist Collections* (1980).[28]

Sustaining a scholarly journal requires a greater commitment than newsletters and newspapers and, unlike publishing a monograph or anthology, requires constant infusions of money and labor. To meet conventional academic standards, these publications also needed a steady stream of quality articles and an ever-shifting pool of potential contributors and reviewers. Readers for such texts would also expect high-quality copy editing and production values, so this form of feminist publishing depended on access to people trained in the industry, a significant change from the women who had put out ephemeral periodicals. These journals have undoubtedly made radical interventions, but they are nonetheless very much a part of established institutions and signal the ways in which feminism became more intertwined with and welcome in political and intellectual sites of power. Given this broad consensus that the mid-1970s constituted a time of transition in U.S. feminism and in feminist print culture, why have scholars and activists not seen 1975, 1976, or 1977 as the start of a new wave or generation of activists?

Before I can answer this question, I must take care to avoid uncritically reproducing the limitations that waves effect. In challenging the construction of the second wave as a monolithic phase of U.S. feminism, am I simply creating smaller units of homogeneity, placing them within a linear chronological narrative, and presuming their mutual exclusivity? Even though evidence from primary and secondary sources marks the mid-1970s as a time of flux, there are exceptions. First, despite *Distaff*'s and *Sister*'s disruptions in publishing, both persisted through the decade, other periodicals had much shorter life spans, and *off our backs* had a remarkable thirty-eight-year print run. Furthermore, not all studies of feminist print culture highlight a shift around 1975 or 1976. Martha Allen's dissertation about feminist periodicals has chapters for 1968–72 and 1973–83.[29] Julie R. Enszer situates her study of lesbian-feminist publishing between 1969 and 1989; however, instead of setting up each of these two decades as unique, she argues that this era represented but "one example of lesbian, feminist, and queer publishing in a long history."[30] Even though 1975–76 saw the growth of outlets for feminist scholarship, scholarly articles also appeared in journals published at the start of the decade, such as *No More Fun and Games* (Cambridge, Massachusetts), described as "a theoretical journal of female liberation" by one of its founders.[31] Its second issue, appearing in February 1969, includes a Marxist analysis of the family as a site of patriarchy as well as a deconstruction of sexism in social science approaches to studying human behavior. Since there were not yet many venues for scholarly analyses of gender, feminist journals in the late 1960s and early 1970s were critical sites for the circulation of such pieces. These articles were not peer reviewed, but their publication provides a reminder that the appearance of academic journals in 1972, while groundbreaking, did not initiate such work.[32]

Nancy Whittier's cohort model posits another approach to exploring flux and stability in the women's liberation movement. A political cohort comprises people who first encountered a movement in the same time and place, and based on this understanding of collective identity Whittier demarcates four different feminist political cohorts between 1970 and 1984 in Columbus, Ohio (1969–71, late 1970–78, 1973–78, and 1978–84).[33] Although her study retains a linear generational model, it nonetheless disrupts the homogeneity of 1970s feminism and allows us to see different cohorts coexisting simultaneously. Because shifts in local conditions and local protest cycles can produce a new political cohort while a previous cohort remains active, Whitter, like Popkin, reminds us that place and scale matter. Whittier's decision to analyze feminist activism at the organizational scale (as opposed to an individual scale) and her choices about which organizations to study affected the cohorts that became visible.[34] And the particular conditions in Columbus shaped the moments at which generations emerged, peaked, and waned. Moreover, whereas Popkin found that women's liberation in Cambridge in 1975 and 1976 was more fragmented and divided, Whittier's assessment leads her to describe 1974–78 as "the feminist heyday" in Columbus.[35]

Difference abounds, as Popkin's and Whittier's seemingly antithetical descriptions of feminism in the mid-1970s indicate, so the phrase *a movement of movements*, which has been used to label the civil rights struggle, is apt for women's liberation as well.[36] It is almost too obvious, too facile, to point out that any model of any movement—whether drawing on waves or on another metaphor—would be inaccurate. Something will always refuse to fit—an exception, a contradiction, excess, messiness, different interpretations of the same evidence. Therefore, the more challenging, and perhaps more important, task involves presenting a new way of understanding how we know what we know about U.S. feminism.

I start this work by returning to history of the book and the communications circuit developed by Robert Darnton.[37] In their revision of Darnton's circuit, Thomas Adams and Nicolas Barker add survival as a stage in a text's life cycle. A text survives when it is stored in complete form in personal or public libraries or even in boxes in a closet. Survival also occurs when we reuse and recycle parts of a text: newspapers can be wadded up and turned into packing material; photos can be cut from magazines for elementary school art projects and to decorate teens' bedroom walls; writers cite other texts in their books and essays. A book-history conception of survival foregrounds not only the imbrication of matter and what matters but also the weight that different evidence carries. Peter McDonald notes that Darnton's communications circuit only implicitly recognizes power differentials. While Darnton recognizes that social, legal, economic, and political contexts affect a text's production and consumption, his communications circuit does not consider forces such as status and principles of value.[38] Some authors have more literary and cultural capital, some publishers are more esteemed than others, and some publications have wider circulation, and all of these factors affect whether a text ends up with a consumer, how it will be read, and whether it is preserved.

Survival therefore brings up questions about what as well as why, and such questions, when applied to an event such as the 1968 Miss America Pageant Protest or to a statement like Rebecca Walker's announcement that she is the third wave, point to the impact of media on histories of U.S. feminism. Widespread coverage of the 1968 protest in mainstream media solidified that moment in the popular imagination, and because this coverage has remained more accessible and available than a text such as Popkin's dissertation, the event is likely to carry more power in shaping the dominant narrative of the women's liberation movement. Even though Popkin's dissertation has survived—I can download it through a Proquest subscription—it is not likely to circulate outside the small audience of gender historians or social movement scholars interested in this particular topic. Therefore, the perceptions of Popkin's survey respondents are muted, both by Popkin's decisions about what evidence from the survey to use and by its material manifestation.

In contrast, Walker's *Ms.* article rapidly gained traction among feminists. Although *Ms.* magazine has a smaller circulation than a newspaper such as the *New York Times*, it nevertheless carries significant cultural capital and maintains one of the largest readerships of any feminist periodical. The wide accessibility of *Ms.* and the convenient sound-bite length of "I am the third wave" are textual and material factors that have shaped the article's prominence in the history of contemporary feminism. In other words, it not only survived, it thrived. If someone proclaimed the start of a new wave in the mid-1970s, that proclamation is not visible, and so, from a practical viewpoint, it did not survive. Social and political factors undoubtedly facilitated such a receptive audience for Walker's pronouncement that a new wave had arrived, suggesting the absence of a critical mass of feminists in the mid-1970s looking for ways to distance themselves from a particular feminist formation.

So: What matter? And what matters?

When I ask how and why certain frameworks (for example, the wave model) create space for certain histories of feminism, the history of the book gives me not only another way to answer it but also other questions to ask: How is the survival of feminism related to the things of feminism that survive? What archival evidence is most likely to travel through time from the 1970s to the historian's or sociologist's manuscript? Alana Wingfoot has written that second-wave feminists wanted to secure "the right to an abortion" whereas "maintaining that right, and learning how to use it properly" is the province of the third wave. But what evidence informs this distinction?[39] Such queries extend beyond print culture to the myriad materials that constitute a social movement—mailing lists and T-shirts, photographs and video recordings.

Regardless of the particular object, the beginnings and endings of waves have formed because of certain evidence, and while scholars and activists have not arbitrarily chosen this evidence, my work with feminist print culture has pushed me to reflect more purposefully on the types of evidence that mark these moments. While this approach helps renarrate the history of U.S. feminism through feminist print communications, it also makes an argument for analyzing the relationship between evidence and argument, between primary sources and historical narratives. It demands that we consider how we select evidence to tell our histories and how this evidence shapes the narratives we produce. Such an approach can open up and complicate our taxonomies and histories of feminism. Understanding feminism's trajectories specifically through print helps make sense of the movements within and across this social movement by illuminating local idiosyncrasies and national trends. Feminist publications tell these stories in their content and material forms, altering the genealogies we produce about feminism and about what feminism matters.

# NOTES

## ABBREVIATIONS

| | |
|---|---|
| AESL | Arthur and Elizabeth Schlesinger Library on the History of Women in America, Radcliffe Institute, Harvard University |
| *AIW* | *Ain't I a Woman?* |
| FL Records | Female Liberation: A Radical Feminist Organization Records, Archives and Special Collections Department, Northeastern University Libraries. |
| *FLN* | *Female Liberation Newsletter* |
| *LAWLN* | *L.A. Women's Liberation Newsletter*, Los Angeles Women's Liberation Movement Collection, box 1, folder 1, Southern California Library |
| SCL | Southern California Library |
| SSC | Sophia Smith Collection, Smith College |
| VWC Records | Valley Women's Center Records, Sophia Smith Collection, Smith College |
| *VWCN* | *Valley Women's Center Newsletter* |

## INTRODUCTION. ORIGINS AND REPRODUCTIONS

1. Pamela Hafner, "The Valley Women's Center," *Valley Review*, February–March 1971, 6.

2. Polly Ormsby Longsworth, "The Valley Women's Center," *Smith Alumnae Quarterly*, April 1971, 16–18.

3. Negatives and eight-by-ten-inch prints of these photographs can be found in Valley Women's Center Records, folder 5, box 1, SSC.

4. Feminist groups tended to be small, informal, and uninstitutionalized, and even groups that incorporated or gained nonprofit status were not guaranteed access to or inclusion in preexisting organizational networks. Therefore, the movement consisted primarily of "scattered organizations and groups of women all over the country" (Pamela Allen, *Free Space*, 41).

5. Morgan, "Introduction," xxxvi.

6. Lee Walker to *Sister*, March 1974, 9.

7. Jo Sullivan to *FLN*, November 1, 1971, 1.

8. Nancy Savage to *Distaff*, December 1981, 2.

9. I draw from Martha Allen's use of the term *multiissue* in "Development of Communication Networks."

10. "Sisters Smash Sexism, Technology, and Planned Obsolescence," *AIW*, March 12, 1971, 10–11. See Beins, "Revolution in Ephemera."

11. Blanchard, "Speaking the Plural."

12. Scott, *Fantasy of Feminist History*, 48.

13. Ahmed, *Cultural Politics*, 91.

14. Ibid., 91–92.

15. Ibid., 45.

16. Hesford, *Feeling Women's Liberation*, 32.

17. Butler, *Gender Trouble*, 179. See also Butler, *Bodies That Matter*, chapter 7.

18. Somers, "Narrative Construction of Identity," 607.

19. See Morgan, *Saturday's Child*, 263. For the media implications of the Miss America Pageant protest, see Dow, *Watching Women's Liberation*, chapter 1. For alternative narratives of U.S. feminist history see Evans, "Women's Liberation"; Gilmore, *Feminist Coalitions*. On the impact of media coverage of the Miss America Pageant protest on one of the main organizing groups, New York Radical Women, see Kelly, "Whatever Happened to Women's Liberation?," 168–69; Hanisch, "Struggles over Leadership," 83–84.

20. See Martha Allen, "Development of Communication Networks," chapter 3.

21. Dow, *Watching Women's Liberation*, 3; Hesford, *Feeling Women's Liberation*, 3.

22. Dismore, "When Women Went on Strike." See also Dow, *Watching Women's Liberation*, 146.

23. "Feminist Chronicles"; Gilmore and Kaminski, "A Part and Apart." Freeman puts the number of NOW chapters at seven hundred by 1974 (*Politics of Women's Liberation*, 87).

24. Cassell, *Group Called Women*, 109–10.

25. Freeman, *Politics of Women's Liberation*, 103–4.

26. *Women: A Journal of Liberation*, February 26, 1971, 10, Women's Liberation Collection, box 7, folder 12, SSC. See also Suzanne Pharr interview, 37–38, Voices of Feminism Oral History Project, SSC, http://www.smith.edu/library/libs/ssc/vof/transcripts/Pharr.pdf.

27. Anderson, *Imagined Communities*.

28. Martha Allen, "Development of Communication Networks," 68. See also Mather, "History of Feminist Periodicals," 82.

29. Godard, "Feminist Periodicals," 212.

30. Cadman, Chester, and Pivot, *Rolling Our Own*, 72.

31. *FLN*, February 21, 1972, 4.

32. Bunch, *Passionate Politics*, 218.

33. While feminist presses worked to make their services available widely and provided an important resource for activists and writers, the costs involved would have been prohibitive for most local feminist groups.

34. Bunch, *Passionate Politics*, 217–18; Onosaka, *Feminist Revolution in Literacy*, 15.

35. See Kate Adams, "Built Out of Books."

36. See, for example, Beins and Enszer, "'We Couldn't Get Them Printed'"; Davis, *Making of "Our Bodies, Ourselves"*; Enszer, "Whole Naked Truth"; Harker and Farr, *This Book Is an Action*; Hogan, *Feminist Bookstore Movement*; Hogan, "Women's Studies"; Meeker, *Contacts Desired*; Murray, *Mixed Media*; Onosaka, *Feminist*

*Revolution in Literacy*; Travis, "Women in Print Movement"; Young, *Changing the Wor(l)d*.

37. Springer, *Living for the Revolution*, 90–93.

38. Third World Women's Alliance Records, box 2, folders 5, 6, 8, SSC.

39. Roth, *Separate Roads*, 139–43.

40. *Asian Women's Center Newsletter*, Women's Center—CSU Dominguez Hills Collection, folder "Asian Women," SCL. When I conducted research in the fall of 2008, this collection was uncataloged. On the journal *Asian Women's Journal*, see Chu, "Asian American Women's Studies Courses," 100.

41. Havlin, "'To Live a Humanity.'" For more on women's contributions to Chicano print culture, see Rodriguez, "Covering the Chicano Movement."

42. Gray, *Watching with the Simpsons*, 33.

43. Flannery, *Feminist Literacies*, 41.

44. Blackwell, *¡Chicana Power!*, 10.

45. I did not conduct interviews for this study and instead focus on textual analysis. Memory is an interpretation of an experience, so asking about a writer's or editor's intentions or the meaning of particular content would not necessarily lead to a more accurate truth about feminism than I would find in the periodicals themselves.

46. On the way written texts convey tone and emotion, see Laflen and Fiorenza, "'Okay, My Rant Is Over.'"

47. Blackwell, *¡Chicana Power!*, 39.

48. The nonprofessional production process also resulted in many other sorts of "errata"—crooked text, inconsistent formatting, the use of different types of paper within an issue, handwritten text apparently added after a stencil was typed or art was pasted on, and misnumbered pages. I do not explore these sorts of errors in depth in this volume.

49. Chartier, "Introduction," vii.

50. Darnton, "What Is the History of Books?," 68.

51. Adams and Barker, "New Model." For other critiques, see McDonald, "Implicit Structures"; Atton, *Alternative Media*, 27. See also Murray, *Mixed Media*, 15–17.

52. Melucci, *Nomads of the Present*, 35.

53. Polletta and Jasper, "Collective Identity," 285. See also Young's discussion of different social movement theories (*Changing the Wor(l)d*, chapter 5); Melucci, "Process of Collective Identity."

54. Holland, Fox, and Daro, "Social Movements and Collective Identity," 97.

55. Steward, Shriver, and Chasteen, "Participant Narratives."

56. Holland, Fox, and Daro, "Social Movements and Collective Identity," 97; Melucci, *Nomads of the Present*, 60; Ferguson, "Sharing without Knowing," 39.

57. Berezin, "Emotions and Political Identity"; Tarrow, *Power in Movement*, 111–12.

58. Polletta and Jasper, "Collective Identity and Social Movements," 290. See also Jasper, "Emotions of Protest," 415.

59. Farrell, *Yours in Sisterhood*, 161–62; Morgan, *Saturday's Child*, 296.

60. Kathy to *LAWLN*, October 2, 1970, 6.

1. "Freep Take-Over," *LAWLN* [ca. August 1971], 1.

2. "Even a Woman Can Do It: Bird Women's Caucus," *Great Speckled Bird*, October 11, 1970, 3.

3. Morgan, "Goodbye to All That," 6.

4. Martha Allen, "Development of Communication Networks," 23.

5. For the ways mainstream media published about and represented well-known feminists, see Hesford, *Feeling Women's Liberation*.

6. Los Angeles Feminist Women's Health Center to *VWCN*, December 1972, 2.

7. Brenda Davillier, "It Doesn't Hurt to Try," *Distaff*, January 1973, 3.

8. "Want to Communicate?," *Female Liberation* [Minneapolis], March 1971, Ann Hunter Popkin Papers, box 3, folder 46, AESL.

9. See Flannery, *Feminist Literacies*, 26–30.

10. Bradley, *Mass Media*, 56.

11. On the *Ladies' Home Journal* sit-in, see Lichtenstein, "Feminists Demand 'Liberation,'" 51; Hole and Levine, *Rebirth of Feminism*, 255–58; Morgan, "Introduction," xxix–xxx. McDermott refers to "dildo journalism" (*Politics and Scholarship*, 2).

12. Newton, "Intercommunalism," 197.

13. Glessing, *Underground Press in America*, xiv–xv.

14. See Rhodes, *Framing the Black Panthers*; Rodriguez, "Covering the Chicano Movement," chapter 2; Ogbar, "Yellow Power."

15. McMillan, "'Our Founder,'" 85.

16. Ibid., 86.

17. Martha Allen, "Development of Communication Networks," 50.

18. Pearson, "Mapping Rhetorical Interventions," 159. See also Whittier, "Turning It Over," 184.

19. DuPlessis and Snitow, "Preface," xvii. One contribution focuses on both New York and Cambridge, while another focuses on New York and New Jersey.

20. Though Los Angeles has been featured in local studies or studies about specific areas of feminism. See, for example, Gerhard, *Dinner Party*; Pomerleau, *Califia Women*; Broude and Garrard, *Power of Feminist Art*.

21. Evans, *Tidal Wave*, 31.

22. Ibid., 108.

23. These demarcations, however, oversimplify the landscape of feminist periodical publishing. *Heresies*, for example, focused on feminist art, but each issue had a theme (for example, Third World women, sex, or food), and some NOW chapter newsletters resembled the newsletters in my sample.

24. In an interview, an editor of *Women: A Journal of Liberation* explained that in the editorial collective's vision, the journal would be "more professional than the mimeographed publications" (Zanoni, "'Working on Many Levels,'" 84).

25. Farrell, *Yours in Sisterhood*, 24; "Budget—9/24/70 to 11/28/70," FL Records, box 1, folder 7.

26. Farrell, *Yours in Sisterhood*, 28; Frontani, "Alternative Press," 15.

27. However, as Farrell notes, by the end of the 1970s, the Ms. Foundation (pub-

lisher of the magazine) incorporated as a nonprofit organization (*Yours in Sisterhood*, 111).

28. This distribution structure reflected feminist publishing more generally. *Feminist Bulletin*, a publication of the San Diego Center for Women's Studies and Services, noted that "the lack of presses in different geographical regions is unfortunate because even while there now exists a large distributor for women's presses, the reality remains that small publishers distribute their books primarily to local audiences" (Cobbs, "State of the Press," 15).

29. "Important," *LAWLN*, September 11, 1970, 1; "A Note from the VWC Workers," *VWCN*, April 1972, 11; "The Newsletter," *VWCN*, April 8, 1971, [4]; "Budget—9/24/70 to 11/28/70," FL Records, box 1, folder 7.

30. *Distaff*, February 1973, 1, November 1979, 1; Mary Gehman, conversation with author, November 10, 2009.

31. "The Speakers Bureau of Female Liberation," [ca. 1972–73], box 1, folder 14, FL Records.

32. "The Second Wave: A Magazine of New Feminism," *FLN*, January 21, 1971, 4; "Feminutes," *FLN*, August 30, 1971, 5.

33. *FLN*, April 10, 1972, 1. The newsletter's editors had frequently asked readers for donations for the newsletter. In February 1972, for example, they explained, "Right now, the Newsletter is Female Liberation's biggest expense. Over $250.00 a month. We're asking our readers to consider the dire financial situation that we now face. We don't want to charge a subscription rate for the Newsletter. Please send any donations you can, no matter how small, to us to help defray some of the costs" (*FLN*, February 21, 1972, 4).

34. *VWCN*, October 1975, 1.

35. See Kesselman, "Women's Liberation"; Ezekiel, *Feminism in the Heartland*; Gilmore and Kaminski, "A Part and Apart"; Hogan, "Women's Studies"; Valk, *Radical Sisters*; Gilmore, *Groundswell*; Pomerleau, *Califia Women*.

36. See, for example, "International News Flashes," *Sister*, April 1975, 5; "Les Femmes en Marche," *Distaff*, August 1973, 9 (described as "a selection of quotes and news items from recent issues of feminist journals, magazines and newspapers that reach our office").

37. Bunch, *Passionate Politics*, 221.

38. "We Must Have Money to Keep Going," *FLN*, May 23, 1971, 8.

39. "Distaff Goes on a Diet," *Distaff*, January 1974, 2.

40. Pat Sackrey and Gayle LeTourneau, interview transcript, n.d., 2–3, Women's Liberation Collection, box 9, folder 1, "Women's Liberation—Massachusetts: Amherst Women's Liberation," SSC.

41. "Big City, Little City," *AIW*, July 24, 1970, 10.

42. Liebling, "Wayward Press," 109.

43. For a survey of the local political climate, see Yanney, "Practical Revolution," chapter 2.

44. Ibid., 49–50.

45. The Iowa City feminists used the language of "cells" to categorize the special-interest groups connected to the Women's Liberation Front.

46. See Silander, "Emerging Women's Voices"; Jo Rabenold Papers, Iowa Women's Archives, University of Iowa; http://www.emmagoldman.com/; http://wrac.uiowa.edu/.

47. *AIW*, September 11, 1970, 3, March 12, 1971, 12, January 7, 1972, 12.

48. For example, the Furies collective in Washington, D.C., also shared housing while publishing a newspaper (Valk, "Living a Feminist Lifestyle").

49. *AIW*, August 8, 1972, 12.

50. In April 1971, the editors explained, "We occasionally request that articles be written, we request that people subscribe or buy issues but we don't need steady volunteers like a daycare group needs or women to show up in large numbers for a public action" ("Who We Are: Carol, Trudy, Linda, Dale, Pat, Jeannie, Vickie, Ann," *AIW*, April 30, 1971, 2).

51. "Self-Criticism and Direction," *AIW*, February 11, 1972, 8.

52. "Lest We Begin to Oink," *AIW*, September 25, 1970, 4. See also "More Thoughts on Structuring a Revolution," *AIW*, May 19, 1972, 2. The cryptic notes by one of the editors, Dale McCormick, reveal the ways that issues related to collectivity dominated their meetings (Dale McCormick Papers, box 2, folder "Dale McCormick; 1970s; Notebook, 1971–1973," Iowa Women's Archives, University of Iowa).

53. *AIW*, June 26, 1970, 2.

54. Ibid., September 11, 1970, 3.

55. Every issue except for one was published as a newspaper. The issue dated April 1973 differed in appearance, in content, and apparently in process of production. It contains a single essay and was published as a small booklet, *Academic Feminists and the Women's Movement*. The masthead lists Ann Leffler, Dair L. Gillespie, and Elinor Lerner Ratner as authors.

56. *AIW*, October 30, 1970, 2.

57. Mary Gehman, "*DISTAFF* Marks Special Anniversary: One Year of Publication," *Distaff*, November 1980, 9.

58. Mary Gehman, "Distaff Is Back," *Distaff*, September 1974, 2.

59. Voices from the Louisiana Women's Movement: First-Hand Accounts from People Who Made It Happen (videotapes), Newcomb Archives and Vorhoff Library Special Collections, Newcomb College Institute, Tulane University.

60. "Why a New Distaff?," *Distaff*, November 1979, 2.

61. Gehman has continued her work as a publisher and remains committed to giving voice to underrepresented and marginalized communities. She started Margaret Media in 1981 (http://margaretmedia.com/index.php) and gives women's history tours of New Orleans.

62. *Distaff*, September 1973, 12.

63. Ibid., May 1980, 2.

64. Other more formally published periodicals, among them *Ms.* and *Quest*, also attempted to realize collectivity in their editorial practices.

65. *Distaff*, February 1973, 12.

66. Despite assumptions that the U.S. South lacked feminist communities, this region hosted a range of activist projects. Though I am surely omitting groups, in my research I came across feminist periodicals published in Durham and Chapel Hill,

North Carolina; Atlanta; Austin, Texas; and Tampa, Florida. Additionally, founded by women from the Chapel Hill women's liberation group, Lollipop Press published nonsexist and nonracist children's books. See also Giardina, *Freedom for Women*; Zajicek, Lord, and Holyfield, "Emergence and First Years"; Stokes, "Constituting Southern Feminists."

67. Louisiana was the last state to repeal the Head and Master Laws, which gave a husband legal authority over household matters and all jointly owned property. Diana Bajoie, who in 1976 became the first woman elected to the Louisiana State Senate, made a statement when she entered the bathroom in the state capitol building marked "Senators" (Kim Gandy, in Voices from the Louisiana Women's Movement: First-Hand Accounts from People Who Made It Happen [videotapes], Newcomb Archives and Vorhoff Library Special Collections, Newcomb College Institute, Tulane University).

68. "Women's Center Policy," *LAWLN*, [October–November] 1970, 1.

69. Joan Robins, interview by Dara Robinson, February 11, 1984, http://symposia .library.csulb.edu/iii/cpro/DigitalItemViewPage.external?lang=&sp=1001664&sp =T&sp=1&suite=def. For information about the Crenshaw Women's Center, see "Los Angeles Women's Center," n.d., Los Angeles Women's Liberation Movement Collection, box 1, folder 3, SCL, which describes the center's history from the initial planning in 1969 through the March 1971 International Women's Day march.

70. Joan, Sherry, [Janet?], big donna, Barbara, Stephanie, diane, Sue, Z.B. [Z Budapest], "wow: Look at Us," *Women's Center Newsletter*, June 1972, 7, Oral History Collection: Los Angeles Women's Movement, folder "Women's Union," California State University, Long Beach, Special Collections and University Archives.

71. Joan Robins-Hoffman Ghia, "There Must Be Some Way Out of Here," *Sister*, February 1973, 1. One announcement reads, "Sisters—Hawk the newspaper! Keep 15¢ on each copy you sell. See Donna Cassyd and/or pick up a bunch at the Westside Center" and the other is, "Newsletter general meetings are the first Thursday of every month, at the Westside Center, 218 So. Venice Blvd., at 7:30 P.M." Robins refers to a tension between the Crenshaw and Westside centers, describing the latter as "siphon[ing] off some energy" from the former (Joan Robins, interview by Dara Robinson, February 11, 1984, http://symposia.library.csulb.edu/iii/cpro /DigitalItemViewPage.external?lang=&sp=1001664&sp=T&sp=1&suite=def).

72. The Virtual Oral/Aural History Archive at California State University, Long Beach, which includes a series of interviews with Los Angeles feminists, notes that Robins and Robinson "began the [Crenshaw] Center Newsletter, which eventually became *Sister* newspaper" (http://symposia.library.csulb.edu/iii/cpro /CollectionViewPage.external;jsessionid=73C0254F310F7EEC2A9E81DACE317710 ?lang=&sp=1000071&suite=def). See also "Workshops," n.d., Joan Robins Papers, Organizations Section, box 2, SCL: "Come and learn how we put our newspaper together. How *Sister* grew out of the Crenshaw Women's Center newsletter, how *Sister* relates to the Women's Union. Join us and be a part of the newsletter staff."

73. See "Victory!," *Sister*, January 1973, 6, 8.

74. The Feminist Women's Health Clinic was mentioned in the five periodicals examined here, indicating the extent to which the clinic and its work was known.

75. The records of the Comisión Femenil de Los Angeles, which published the *Chicana Service Action Center Newsletter*, are held at the Chicano Studies Research Center at UCLA. The records of Hijas de Cuauhtémoc, which published *Encuentro Femenil*, are held at the California State University, Long Beach, University Archives.

76. The valley to which the newsletter and center refer is the Pioneer Valley. Made up of Franklin, Hampshire, and Hampden Counties in western Massachusetts, the valley is bisected by the Connecticut River (so sometimes it is referred to at the Connecticut Valley) and is home to Amherst College, Hampshire College, Mt. Holyoke College, Smith College, and the University of Massachusetts, Amherst.

77. *Amherst Women's Liberation Newsletter*, October 16, 1970, 1, Women's Liberation Collection, box 9, folder 1, SSC.

78. *VWCN*, July 1972, 1. The June 1972 newsletter begins with "The next General Meeting of the Amherst Women's Liberation will be on July 2 at 8 p.m." whereas the August 1972 issue states, "The next general meeting of the area women's liberation movement will be September 10, 8:00."

79. "HELP!!!," *VWCN*, January 1972, 5.

80. *VWCN*, January 1974, 1.

81. Ibid. See also "Structural History of the Valley Women's Union," VWC Records, box 2, folder 12.

82. "A Working Structure for the Valley Women's Union," *VWCN*, January 1974, 7.

83. *Valley Women's Union Newsletter*, October 1975, 1, Valley Women's Union Records, folder "Newsletters and Publicity," W. E. B. Du Bois Library, Special Collections and University Archives, University of Massachusetts, Amherst. Because of the ambiguities in the publication's name, I refer to it as the *Valley Women's Center Newsletter* throughout the book except when citing particular issues published after the name change.

84. For an overview of the valley's political activism, see Cline, *Creating Choice*; Patric A. Whitcomb, "Forging a New Political and Cultural Identity: Socialist Feminism in the Valley Women's Union, Northampton, Massachusetts," May 11, 1998, VWC Records, box 5, folder 18.

85. *VWCN*, April 8, 1971.

86. Cline, *Creating Choice*.

87. The Female Liberation Office hosted meetings and events; curated a library, bookstore, and archives; offered space to other women's groups; established a speaker's bureau, and published the *FLN* and *The Second Wave*. Even though the space functioned as a women's center in many ways, the group did not identify it as a women's center.

88. "The Speaker's Bureau of Female Liberation," n.d., FL Records, box 1, folder 14.

89. *FLN*, February 28, 1972, 6.

90. The October 1973 issue refers to the potential dissolution of Female Liberation (Marge Fentin to *Female Liberation*, October 22, [1973], 1–2, FL Records, box 2, folder 1).

91. *FLN*, March 4, 1974, 1.

92. "Female Liberation Press Release," *FLN*, March 4, 1974, 3.

93. Statement, July 29, 1969, Ann Hunter Popkin Papers, box 3, folder 50, AESL.

94. Dana Densmore, Lisa Leghorn, Abby Rockefeller, Betsy Warrior, and Jayne West, Cell 16 Statement, November 25, 1970, Ann Hunter Popkin Papers, box 3, folder 50, AESL. Cell 16's statement appeared in *AIW*, December 11, 1970. See also FL Records, box 1, folders 5–7; Rochelle Ruthchild Papers, box 1, folder 8, AESL.

95. Statement approved at the November 30 business meeting, *FLN*, [December] 1970, 2.

96. Northeastern University's Archives and Special Collections Department has an online exhibit of local feminist activism with a number of primary documents: http://www.lib.neu.edu/archives/voices/w-intro.htm.

97. See Hole and Levine, *Rebirth of Feminism*, 164–65; Echols, *Daring to Be Bad*, 158–66; Evans, *Tidal Wave*, 105–8.

98. DuPlessis and Snitow, "Feminist Memoir Project," 11.


CHAPTER 2. LOCATING FEMINISM

1. Marge Piercy to Female Liberation, June 26, 1972, FL Records, box 1, folder 10, Archives and Special Collections Department, Northeastern University Libraries.

2. Rena Szajman to Female Liberation, August 23, 1970, FL Records, box 1, folder 9.

3. Adamson, "Feminists, Libbers, Lefties, and Radicals," 255; Angus, Dineen, and Robertson, "Toronto Women's Caucus." The Toronto Women's Collective began publishing a newspaper, *The Velvet Fist*, in September 1970, shortly after Szajman wrote her letter.

4. Sandy Baird to *FLN*, February 6, 1971, 1.

5. Bobby Darwall to *FLN*, May 23, 1971, 1.

6. Diana Charles-Huppert to *FLN*, November 8, 1971, 1.

7. *FLN*, September 6, 1971, 7.

8. *VWCN*, April 8, 1971, [2].

9. Mary Gehman, "Analysis: N.O. Women's Movement: A Comprehensive Herstory," *Distaff*, October 1973, 8. See also Elaine Fiedler to the Atlanta Lesbian Feminist Alliance, n.d., Atlanta Lesbian Feminist Alliance Archives, box 3, folder 2, "1973–1974 Correspondence 3.2," Sallie Bingham Center for Women's History and Culture, David M. Rubenstein Rare Book and Manuscript Library, Duke University: "For some time now, ever since I first heard about your group when I came to Atlanta, I've wanted to find out more about you. And for the last few weeks, I've had a kind of desperate need to talk to somebody, and the more I thought about it, the clearer it became it was you people I should be talking to. After a lot of hesitation, I finally tried calling you yesterday, but the number I rang, which I got from THE BIRD [*The Great Speckled Bird*], was out of order. So would you please contact me some way and tell me where your place is and what your phone number is and when is a good time I can come and who I can talk to. I feel lost and I think I need help."

10. Mary Gehman, "Analysis: N.O. Women's Movement: A Comprehensive Herstory," *Distaff*, October 1973, 8.

11. Quoted in Enke, *Finding the Movement*, 1.

12. Ibid., 2.

13. Freeman, *Politics of Women's Liberation*, 231.

14. Annie to Valley Women's Center, December 28, 1971, box 2, folder 5, VWC Records.

15. Arnold, "Feminist Presses," 18.

16. Cassell, *Group Called Women*, 181.

17. Roth, *Separate Roads*, 18.

18. Enke, *Finding the Movement*, 257.

19. For a chronicle of the feminist occupation of a Harvard University Building in 1971, see Spain, "Women's Rights and Gendered Spaces," 165–67.

20. Spain, *Constructive Feminism*, 16–17.

21. Longhurst, "Introduction," 284.

22. James Martin, "Identity," 98.

23. Brown and Pickerill, "Space for Emotion." On feminist bookstores as a place of identity formation, see Liddle, "More Than a Bookstore"; on churches as places for civil rights organizing, see Reed, *Art of Protest*, 12.

24. Merrifield, "Place and Space," 522. See also Abarca, *Voices in the Kitchen*, chapter 1.

25. Ahmed, *Cultural Politics*, 148–49.

26. See Hubbard, "Place/Space," 42.

27. Nicholls, "Place, Networks, Space."

28. Anderson, *Imagined Communities*, 44.

29. Ibid., 45.

30. On the relationship between place and time, see Massey, "Places and Their Past," 186.

31. Some feminist radio and television programs appeared on a regular basis, but such media were less widespread, accessible, and long-lived than were periodicals.

32. Flannery explains that tables of contents in feminist anthologies can serve as "'roadmaps' to the movement" that outline categories related to identity and politics (*Feminist Literacies*, 37).

33. *VWCN*, November 1972, 7.

34. "New Women's Liberation Group in Orange County," *LAWLN*, Summer 1970, 1.

35. "Guide to Women's Organizations," *Distaff*, January 1974, 12.

36. *AIW*, February 1973.

37. *VWCN*, September 1972, 4.

38. *Sister*, September 1974, 18–19.

39. Friday, "Prague 1968."

40. *AIW*, September 11, 1970, 3.

41. Sidonie Cassirer to *FLN*, August 30, 1971, 2. *Distaff* presents a similar perspective in an editorial responding to readers' comments that the newspaper "should have more national and international news on women" ("Local News," *Distaff*, June 1975, 2).

42. *VWCN*, November 10, 1971, 3.

43. See, for example, *Sister*, March 1973, 8.

44. "What I Did Last Summer, Part 1," *AIW*, October 15, 1971, 6; "What I Did Last Summer, Part 2," *AIW*, October 15, 1971, 7.

45. "Vaginal Politics, Menstrual Extraction," *AIW*, November 1971, 2–3.

46. Olive Schreiner, "I Saw a Woman Sleeping," *Distaff*, August 1973, 3.

47. Audrey Brown to *FLN*, August 23, 1971, 1.

48. A Sister to *FLN*, January 10, 1972, 4.

49. Maria Schachter to *FLN*, February 12, 1973, 4.

50. "Communications and Outreach (Staffing) Work Group," *VWCN*, January 1976, 3.

51. *AIW*, April 2, 1971, 10. See also Beins and Enszer, "'We Couldn't Get Them Printed,'" 197.

52. Cover, "Engaging Sexualities," 114.

53. Ibid., 115.

54. For example, Cell 16's statement was reprinted in *AIW*, December 11, 1970, 11.

55. Dana Densmore, Lisa Leghorn, Abby Rockefeller, Betsy Warrior, and Jayne West, "Cell 16 Statement," November 25, 1970, 2, Ann Hunter Popkin Papers, box 3, folder 50, AESL. For additional materials detailing this split, see FL Records, box 1, folders 5–7. For business meeting minutes for Cell 16 preceding this split, see Rochelle Ruthchild Papers, box 1, folder 8, AESL.

56. Dana Densmore, Lisa Leghorn, Abby Rockefeller, Betsy Warrior, and Jayne West, Cell 16 Statement, November 25, 1970, 1, Ann Hunter Popkin Papers, box 3, folder 50, AESL.

57. Diana Diamond and Omie (?) E. West to VWC, September [8], 1972, VWC Records, box 1, folder 4.

58. Ahmed, *Cultural Politics*, 148.

59. Lee Porter to VWC,[August 1972], and attached handwritten note by Michelle Aldrich, VWC Records, box 1, folder 4.

60. Daily log entry, August 26, 1972, VWC Records, box 1, folder 9.

61. "Certificate of Sisterhood," n.d., Los Angeles Women's Liberation Movement Collection, box 1, folder 4, SCL.

62. "Songs and Chants Information Sheet for March 8, 1971 International Women's Day," n.d., Los Angeles Women's Liberation Movement Collection, box 1, folder 4, SCL.

63. Ethel H., "March 8th International Women's Day Celebration Rousing Success," *LAWLN*, April 1971, 3.

64. See Third, "'Shooting from the Hip,'" 108; Hole and Levine, *Rebirth of Feminism*, 294–98; Carden, *New Feminist Movement*, 74; Freeman, *Politics of Women's Liberation*, 126. On repertoires of action, see Tilly, "Getting It Together in Burgundy."

65. Echols, *Daring to Be Bad*, chapter 2; Third, "'Shooting from the Hip.'"

66. Dow, *Watching Women's Liberation*, 5.

67. On moral shock, see Jasper and Poulson, "Recruiting Strangers and Friends"; on the way a group is perceived by others, see Sewall, "Space in Contentious Politics," 58. Alice Echols describes the 1968 Miss America Pageant protest in Atlantic City, New Jersey, as marking "the end of the movement's obscurity because the protest— the movement's first national action—received extensive press coverage" (*Daring to Be Bad*, 93).

68. On the tension between tactical and strategic media activism, see Dieter, "Becoming Environmental of Power."

69. Certeau, *Practice of Everyday Life*, xix.

70. Ibid., 107.

71. Ibid., 34, 37.

72. Bakhtin, *Rabelais and His World*, 10.

73. Rossiter, *Organized Networks*, 23.

74. Withers, "Feminist Performance Art," 160–61.

75. Ethel H., "March 8th International Women's Day Celebration Rousing Success," *LAWLN*, April 1971, 3.

76. Quoted in Enke, *Finding the Movement*, 178. See also Certeau, *Practice of Everyday Life*, 66.

77. Nancy Robinson, "Support the Center," *LAWLN*, October 2, 1970, 1.

78. "Urgent Message from the Fund Raising Committee," *LAWLN*, [October–November] 1970, 4.

79. *LAWLN*, December 1970, 6.

80. See also Joan Robins, interview by Dara Robinson, February 11, 1984, http://symposia.library.csulb.edu/iii/cpro/DigitalItemViewPage.external?lang=&sp=1001664&sp=T&sp=1&suite=def.

81. Certeau, *Practice of Everyday Life*, 36.

82. Ibid., xix.

83. Ibid., 37; see also 36.

84. For an analysis of this claim, see Massey, *For Space*, 25–26.

85. Certeau, *Practice of Everyday Life*, 89.

86. Andres, "Differential Spaces," 764.

87. Staggenborg, "Social Movement Communities," 183.

88. Ethel H., "March 8th International Women's Day Celebration Rousing Success," *LAWLN*, April 1971, 2.

89. Mary to *FLN*, July 26, 1971, 1.

90. Mary McDermott to *FLN*, August 2, 1971, 1.

91. Sandy Kent to *FLN*, August 9, 1971, 1; Karen Lindsey to *FLN*, August 9, 1971, 2. Excerpts from these letters also appeared as "Notes on Sterilization," *VWCN*, August 20, 1971, 1.

92. Louise to *FLN*, August 16, 1971, 2.

93. Mary to *FLN*, September 20, 1971, 1.

94. *FLN*, September 6, 1971, 2.

95. Mary McDermott to *FLN*, January 17, 1972, 5.

96. "Late Notices," *FLN*, June 19, 1972, 6.

97. Karen Lindsey to *FLN*, August 14, 1972, 1–2.

98. "New Distaff," *Distaff*, January 1982, 12.

99. Mary Gehman went on to collaborate with Brad Ott, editor of an antinuclear paper, *Dialogue*, to continue publishing *Distaff* as a newsletter (Mary Gehman, "Notes from the Editor," *Distaff*, March 15, 1982, 1). I located only one issue of this later iteration of *Distaff*, and I am not sure how long it continued to publish.

100. *Valley Women's Union Newsletter*, January 1977, 1, VWC Records, box 4, folder 2.

101. I found no records to indicate that the center relocated after the eviction.

102. See, for example, Colebrook, "Certeau and Foucault"; Dieter, "Becoming Environmental of Power"; Gayle, "History in Multiplicity"; Wood, "Crafted within Liminal Spaces," 339.

103. Cassell, *Group Called Women*, 117.

104. "SPEAKOUTRAGE: A Woman's Right to Choose," *FLN*, August 28, 1972, 4, 5.

105. Coralee Webb, Marie Colaneri, and Heidi Chrissos, "How, Then, Shall We Lead?," *LAWLN*, October 1970, 2.

106. Mary An, "A Question of Leadership," *LAWLN*, December 1970, 5.

107. "Resources and Services," *Sister*, December 1975, 8.

108. *LAWLN*, October 2, 1970, 6.

109. "Archives," *VWCN*, April 8, 1971, 4.

110. "More Material in Female Liberation Bookstore," *FLN*, June 19, 1972, 1.

111. Meeker, *Contacts Desired*, 125. Meeker also examines the genre of gay guidebooks, such as *The Gay Girls Guide* and *Le Guide Gris* (The Gray Guide) for the ways they produced knowledge about and thus changed the space of cities.

112. Barale, "Queer Urbanities," 207–8.

113. Crampton, "Cartography."

114. See, for example, Reed, *Art of Protest*, 88; Lorde, "Poetry Is Not a Luxury."

## CHAPTER 3. DOING FEMINISM

1. *VWCN*, [April–May] 1972, 4.

2. See Flannery, *Feminist Literacies*, 50–59.

3. Reed, *Art of Protest*, 4.

4. I borrow this phrase from ibid., 3.

5. Ferguson, "Sharing without Knowing," 38.

6. See Cadman, Chester, and Pivot, *Rolling Our Own*, chapter 3; Murray, *Mixed Media*; Sjoholm, "She Who Owns the Press."

7. Bunch, *Passionate Politics*, 219.

8. "Lest We Begin to Oink," *AIW*, September 25, 1970, 4. For a wonderful overview of the tension between mainstream and feminist publishing, see Gilley, "Feminist Publishing/Publishing Feminism," 24–31.

9. Travis, "Women in Print Movement," 280.

10. On the relationship between feminist values and feminist praxis in relation to print culture, see also Gilley, "Feminist Publishing/Publishing Feminism"; Enszer, "'What Made Us Think.'"

11. Genette, *Paratexts*; McCoy, "Race and the (Para)Textual Condition," 156. See also Santana, *Foreigners in the Homeland*, chapter 3.

12. Koedt's and Mainardi's essays were published as pamphlets by the New England Free Press and KNOW, Inc., respectively, but individuals also mimeographed and distributed the pieces.

13. Connie Dorval-Bernal, "*DISTAFF*: A Labor of Love," *Distaff*, November 1980, 7.

14. Mary Gehman, "DISTAFF Marks Special Anniversary: One Year of Publication," *Distaff*, November 1980, 8–9.

15. Darnton, "What Is the History of Books?" 68.

16. Renee Cowhig and Jo Hyacinthe, "Sister Process," *Sister*, December–January 1976, 1.

17. "To Our Readers," *AIW*, October 30, 1970, 2.

18. "Distaff Goes on a Diet," *Distaff*, January 1974, 2.

19. Jeanne Katz, "Hawking the Newspaper (Some Hints by Jeanne Katz)," *Sister*, February 1973, 10.

20. *LAWLN*, Summer 1970, 3.

21. *FLN*, October 28–November 1, 1970, [4].

22. *FLN*, February 7, 1972, 5.

23. *VWCN*, June 1972, 2.

24. *Sister*, July 1973, 13.

25. *Distaff*, January 1982, 6.

26. Quoted in Beins and Enszer, "'We Couldn't Get Them Printed,'" 204.

27. *LAWLN*, October 1971, 3.

28. *Sister*, February 1973, 5.

29. Ibid., July 1973, 13.

30. *AIW*, September 11, 1970, 3.

31. Ibid., March 12, 1971, 12.

32. *Valley Women's Union Newsletter*, January 1975, 2. *And 6* was crossed out by hand, and the page number for Daphne's essay was handwritten next to a crossed-out number.

33. *FLN*, August 30, 1971, 7.

34. *Distaff*, June 1980, 1.

35. *AIW*, March 30, 1972, back page.

36. "We Are Not Newsweek," *Sister*, December [1976]–January [1977], 2.

37. *AIW*, June 26, 1970, 2.

38. Ibid., July 19, 1970, 8.

39. Joslyn McGuire, "Editorial Reply," *Distaff*, January 1974, 4.

40. Firestone and Koedt, "Editorial," 2.

41. See Martha Allen, "Women's Media," 14. Other feminist print projects were committed to a feminist praxis, so this characteristic is not unique to periodicals. See, for example, Cadman, Chester, and Pivot, *Rolling Our Own*; Murray, *Mixed Media*; Beins and Enszer, "'We Couldn't Get Them Printed.'"

42. "Sister Staff Notes," *Sister*, August 1973, 2.

43. Self-Help Clinic One, "How to Do Self Examination Using the Plastic Speculum," *Sister*, July 1973, 8.

44. Donna Cassyd, "Will *Sister*'s Santa Monica Newsracks Be Threatened?," *Sister*, January 1974, 4.

45. Donna Swanson, "Editorial," *Distaff*, December 1974, 2. In April 1971, *FLN* published an announcement from editors of *The New Broadside* indicating that Swanson and Gehman's experience was not unique: "MOST NEWS DEALERS ARE NOT FEMINISTS The fact is, most news dealers don't give a damn whether the new Broadside is displayed on their stands or not. There are dealers who take copies and keep them hidden under everything else. HERE'S YOUR CHANCE TO OUTWIT A SEXIST NEWS

DEALER TODAY! SEND IN YOUR SUBSCRIPTIONS ON THE FORM BELOW AND LAUGH THE NEXT TIME YOU PASS A NEWSSTAND!" (*FLN*, April [5], 1971, 2).

46. Deborah Turney to *Sister*, December 1978–January 1979, 9.

47. "The Mail," *FLN*, October 4, 1971, 2.

48. *Distaff*, January–February 1975, 6.

49. Sandra Kent to *FLN*, March 4, 1971, 1.

50. Susan Thees to *LAWLN*, October 1971, 2.

51. Murray, *Mixed Media*, 16.

52. Polletta, *Freedom Is an Endless Meeting*, 22; Martha Allen, "Development of Communication Networks," chapter 4.

53. Ezekiel, *Feminism in the Heartland*, 61–63.

54. Ibid., 61–62.

55. *VWCN*, June 1972, 4.

56. Flannery, *Feminist Literacies*, 54.

57. Cadman, Chester, and Pivot, *Rolling Our Own*, 5.

58. Blanchard, "Speaking the Plural," 87.

59. Farrell, *Yours in Sisterhood*, 36–40, 154–57.

60. Murray, *Mixed Media*, 132.

61. Ibid., 153. For the struggles of lesbian feminist publishers in the United States, see Enszer, "Whole Naked Truth."

62. *Distaff*, January 1973, 10.

63. Ibid., February 1973, 12.

64. *LAWLN*, [Summer] 1970, 3.

65. *VWCN*, March 1972, 3.

66. "More Thoughts on Structuring a Revolution," *AIW*, May 19, 1972, 2.

67. The editors' inward focus is also apparent in the absence of such items as calendars and announcements of upcoming events and reports on events mentioned in earlier issues.

68. "Notes from the Newsletter," *FLN*, October 18, 1971, 2.

69. "Feminutes (October 25, 1971)," *FLN*, November 1, 1971, 7.

70. "Mother Jones Press," *VWCN*, May 1974, 3.

71. Ibid., 3–4.

72. "Summer Workshops," *VWCN*, May 1974, 5.

73. Ibid., 3; the announcement appears verbatim on 7.

74. "Graphics," *VWCN*, May 1974, [6].

75. Ibid., [7].

76. *Distaff*, February 1973, 12, March 1974, 2.

77. Ibid., February 1973, 12.

78. Ibid., October 1973, 2.

79. *LAWLN*, [Fall] 1970, 3.

80. "Who We Are: Carol, Trudy, Linda, Dale, Pat, Jeannie, Vickie, Ann," *AIW*, April 30, 1971, 2.

81. "Female Liberation Press Release," *FLN*, March 4, 1974, 2.

82. Murray, *Mixed Media*, 16.

83. Freeman, "Tyranny of Structurelessness."

84. Daily log entry, July 5, 1972, VWC Records, box 1, folder 15.

85. Ibid., April 5, 1973, box 2, folder 7.

86. Ibid., April 9, 1973.

87. Freeman's movement contemporaries found her analysis salient. See Zoe Tafoya, Terry, Lorey, Sue, Janie, and Karen, "The Feminist Woman's Health Center—'The Tyranny of Structurelessness,'" *Sister*, May 1974, 11. Freeman's article was also reprinted in *AIW*, June 26, 1972.

88. Freeman, "Tyranny of Structurelessness," 20.

89. See also Evans, *Tidal Wave*, 123–24.

90. Polletta, *Freedom Is an Endless Meeting*, 165–70.

91. *Sister*, August 1974, 6.

92. Cheryl Diehm, "News Writing Workshop," *Sister*, August 1974, 4.

93. Because most requests for contributions sought written texts, I simplify this discussion by using the terms *writer* and *author* to refer to reader-contributors. Nevertheless, some visual artists contributed works as well.

94. Flannery, *Feminist Literacies*, 51.

95. Ibid. Feminist periodicals supported this ethic in other ways as well. Donna Cassyd's "Car-Nal Knowledge," for example, instructed readers how to fix a burned-out automobile light (*Sister*, October–November 1977, 3). Similarly, a piece in *Ain't I a Woman?* explained to readers how to deal with fuses and understand amperage ("How Not to Blow Your Fuse," *AIW*, August 27, 1971, 9).

96. "Hang Ups," *AIW*, June 26, 1970, 2.

97. Cadman, Chester, and Pivot, *Rolling Our Own*, 6–8.

98. Lorde, *Sister Outsider*, 116.

99. McClellan, "'Unpaid-for Education,'" 17.

100. Trinh, *Woman, Native, Other*, especially chapter 3.

101. Robin Sanders, "Mexican Mothers Starved by Welfare," *Sister*, April 1974, 2.

102. "Woman Thoughts," "Transformations," and letter from Margaret Talbot, *Sister*, May 1974, 4.

103. Anna Louise Strong Brigade, Fanshen, and "Many Independent Women" to *AIW*, October 9, 1970, 3; "Gang Rape in Seattle," *AIW*, October 9, 1970, 3.

104. Nancy Adair, Martha, Mary, Maxine, "More Perspectives," and "The Situation in New Mexico," *AIW*, September 11, 1970, 12.

105. Nan and Mary to *FLN*, [March] 1971, 3.

106. "Nameless," *FLN*, [October] 1970, 1.

107. Miriam Grezel to *FLN*, February 26, 1971, 1.

108. Nancy Victoria, editorial, *Sister*, February 1974, 14. For a similar analysis, see Laura, "Report on the July 3 Collective Newsletter Meeting," *Feminist Newsletter* [Chapel Hill, North Carolina], July 8, 1973, 1, AESL.

109. "Our Printing Policy . . ." *AIW*, May 19, 1972, 12.

110. "Self-Criticism and Direction," *AIW*, February 11, 1972, 8.

111. Valk, "Living a Feminist Lifestyle," 319; Murray, *Mixed Media*, 179, 196–97.

112. Sullivan, "Carol Seajay."

113. Murray, *Mixed Media*, 179.

114. Sharon Bas Hannah to *Sister*, January 1974, 13.

115. On the way a text reflects publishing politics, see Atton, *Alternative Media*, 23–24.

116. On symbolic fit, see Hebdige, *Subculture*, 113.


CHAPTER 4. INVITATIONS TO WOMEN'S LIBERATION

1. These catalogs were part of the Women's Center—CSU Dominguez Hills Collection (SCL), which was uncataloged at the time of my research in fall 2008. The Liberation Enterprises catalog is hand-dated November 1973, and the Amazon Art Works catalog is undated.

2. Beahive Enterprises Catalog (Autumn 1972–Winter 1973), Vertical File Collection, Feminist Products, AESL.

3. Gilley, "Feminist Publishing/Publishing Feminism," 31.

4. Quoted in Norman, "Consciousness-Raising Document," 39.

5. Freeman, "Trashing."

6. Ann Leffler, Dair L. Gillespie, and Elinor Lerner Ratner, "Academic Feminists and the Women's Movement," *AIW*, April 1973, 1. This piece also appears in a scholarly journal, *Critical Sociology*.

7. Reger, "Drawing Identity Boundaries," 104.

8. In addition to moments in the archive that have become points of origin, this project developed in relation to the discourses about the second wave of U.S. feminism. Despite the contestation around the wave metaphor, I use the term "second wave" purposefully here, for it gets invoked often to produce a very specific kind of feminism, one that often comes to stand in for feminism as a whole.

9. See Beins and Enszer, "'We Couldn't Get Them Printed.'"

10. "Sisterhood Is," *AIW*, January 29, 1971, 3.

11. Francine Parker and Nancy Robinson, "Getting It Together: On Collective Leadership," *LAWLN*, Summer 1970, 3.

12. *FLN*, September [20], 1970.

13. Kris Pottharst, "Women's Center Art Auction," *Distaff*, March 1973, 1.

14. Mary M. Petrinovich, "Abortion Taxpayers Suit: Unite with Sisters in a Joint Action for Our Constitutional Rights to a Free Choice and to Medical Care for All Women," *LAWLN*, October 1970, 5.

15. "Ideas for Stickers?," *VWCN*, May 1973, 3.

16. Julia Stein, "Emma Viser–Joanne Little Day," *Sister*, August 1975, 1. The front cover of this issue displayed a striking graphic in chiaroscuro style with Joanne Little's name in all capital letters and the phrase, in slightly smaller capital letters, "Free our sisters, free our selves!"

17. "Come to a Female Liberation Meeting," *FLN*, March 26, 1973, last page. This photograph, cropped differently, also appeared in *Womankind* [Louisville, Kentucky], April 20, 1971, 10.

18. "Christmas in Prison," *Distaff*, December 12, 1980, 2.

19. "The United Women's Contingent," *FLN*, March 1971, 6.

20. Ellen Lynch to *FLN*, December 16, 1971, 1.

21. *AIW*, July 10, 1970, 8.

22. *Distaff*, [January] 1973, 8.

23. Women's Counseling Service, "Reflections on Collectives," *AIW*, October 30, 1970, 9.

24. Priscilla J. Warner, "Some Thoughts of a Sister," *VWCN*, October 8, 1971, 4.

25. Sister Nina Anasa Harding to *FLN*, February 6, 1971, 1.

26. "So Far Our Analysis Labels Common to All Women," *AIW*, July 30, 1971, 8–11.

27. Ibid., 8.

28. Ibid., 9.

29. *VWCN*, August 1972, 7.

30. Havlin, "'To Live a Humanity,'" 91.

31. Cassell, *Group Called Women*, 19.

32. Lorde, *Sister Outsider*, 116; Polletta, *Freedom Is an Endless Meeting*, 154.

33. Morgan, "Introduction," xvii–xviii.

34. Ibid., xviii.

35. Uttal, "Nods That Silence," 318.

36. Lugones and Rozezelle, "Sisterhood and Friendship," 141.

37. Fox-Genovese, "Personal Is Not Political Enough." 109.

38. Lorde, *Sister Outsider*, 119; hooks, "Sisterhood," 296, 299, 304.

39. hooks, "Sisterhood," 295, 296.

40. Lugones and Rozezelle, "Sisterhood and Friendship," 141.

41. Carrillo, "And When You Leave," 63–64.

42. Polletta, *Freedom Is an Endless Meeting*, 154.

43. Lugones and Rozezelle, "Sisterhood and Friendship," 137.

44. hooks, "Sisterhood," 296.

45. Dill, "Race, Class, and Gender," 136.

46. Jakobsen, *Working Alliances*, 65; Wiegman, "Progress of Gender."

47. Alarcón, "Theoretical Subject(s)," 359. See also hooks, "Sisterhood," 303; Trinh, *Woman, Native, Other*, 86–88.

48. See also Zinn and Dill, "Theorizing Difference from Multiracial Feminism," 327.

49. "Goals and Objectives," *Triple Jeopardy*, September–October 1971, 8.

50. "Hijas de Cuauhtémoc," mission statement, [early 1970s], Oral History Collection: Los Angeles Women's Movement, (Chicana Student Publications), box 1, California State University, Long Beach, Special Collections and University Archives.

51. "PYS Sister's Group," *Asian Women's Center Newsletter*, Summer 1973, 4, Women's Center—CSU Dominguez Hills Collection, folder "Asian Women," SCL.

52. "Hitch-Hikers," *LAWLN*, January 1971, 2.

53. *VWCN*, December 1972, 1, February 1973, 1.

54. Rona Foster to *FLN*, June 14, 1971, 1.

55. This part of the movement's repertoire reflects a more general trend among what sociologists term "new social movements." See, for example, Melucci, *Nomads of the Present*; Johnston, Laraña, and Gusfield, "Identities, Grievances, and New Social Movements."

56. Young, *Changing the Wor(l)d*, 26.

57. Scott, "Deconstructing Equality-versus-Difference," 34.

58. Butler, *Excitable Speech*, 5.

59. Ibid., 133.

60. Ibid., 30.

61. Ibid., 25.

62. Campbell, "Rhetoric of Women's Liberation," 393.

63. Daily log entry, January 27, 1972, VWC Records, box 1, folder 9.

64. "Women's Slave Names," *FLN*, October 25, 1971, 3.

65. Glenys A. Waldman to *FLN*, April 10, 1972, 2.

66. "Use of Maiden Name Challenged," *Distaff*, October 1974, 5.

67. "News Flashes," *VWCN*, [July] 1974, 5.

68. "What's in a Name?," *Sister*, June 1974, 6.

69. Annis x to the Valley Women's Center, July 1971, VWC Records, box 3, folder 4.

70. "Ms., Where Are You?," *VWCN*, April 1972, 8.

71. Nancy, "The New Symbol to Represent Us!," *LAWLN*, July 1971, 1. A letter from Anna Syarse to *FLN*, August 28, 1972, 3, offers a similar critique, describing the standard woman symbol as a "sexist sign branded on women by men."

72. ERA Enterprises catalog, [November 1973], Women's Center—CSU Dominguez Hills Collection, SCL.

73. Martin and Miller, "Space and Contentious Politics," 143.

74. Melucci, *Nomads of the Present*; Melucci, "Process of Collective Identity"; James and Lobato, "Family Photos"; Kurzman, "Introduction"; Marquez, "Choosing Issues, Choosing Sides"; Polletta, *It Was Like a Fever*; Somers, "Narrative Construction of Identity."

75. On social movement frames as structures for meaning making, see Benford, "Insider's Critique," 413.

76. Snow et al., "Frame Alignment Processes," 464.

77. Hunt, Benford, and Snow, "Identity Fields," 185–86.

78. Tarrow, "Mentalities," 188; Melucci, *Nomads of the Present*, 349.

79. Benford and Snow, "Framing Processes," 619–20; Dobrowlsky, "Women's Movement in Flux," 170.

80. Robnett, "External Political Change," 279.

81. Reger, "More Than One Feminism."

82. The widespread citations of Freeman's "Tyranny of Structurelessness," which critiques the assumption that a lack of formal structure is equivalent to structurelessness, reflect the centrality of consensus and collectivity within U.S. feminism.

83. "Boston Area Women's Center Fund Raising Drive," *FLN*, April [1971], 4; "March on Washington against the War," *FLN*, April 19, [1971], [7].

84. Cassell, *Group Called Women*, 19.

85. Polletta, *Freedom Is an Endless Meeting*, 151.

86. Mary Anderson to VWC, September 5, 1972, VWC Records, box 3, folder 13.

87. Gerry Hill to *FLN*, February 19, 1971, 1.

88. Mary Drucher to *FLN*, March 4, 1971, 1.

89. Pamela Read to *FLN*, June 28, 1971, 1.

90. Gael Murphy Milan to *FLN*, September 6, 1971, 1.

91. Lucia Bequart to *FLN*, November 1, 1971, 1.

92. *FLN*, February 6, 1971, 5.

93. *LAWLN*, April 1971, 8.

94. *VWCN*, February 1973, 1.

95. Farrell, "Attentive to Difference," 56.

96. "Women's Center . . . Out of the Basement and Back into Business," *Distaff*, August 1973, 2.

97. Theo Kalikow to *FLN*, February 28, 1972, 2.

98. Pauline Collins to *AIW*, March 12, 1971, 3.

99. Althusser, "Ideology," 174.

100. Butler, *Excitable Speech*, 33.

101. Ibid., 36.

102. Ibid., 72. Specifically, Butler builds on J. L. Austin's taxonomy of speech acts as locutionary, illocutionary, and perlocutionary to make her argument about how words do or do not do what they say (*How to Do Things*).

103. Butler, *Excitable Speech*, 107.

104. Harper, "Nationalism and Social Division," 249.

105. Butler, *Excitable Speech*, 136. For how direct address acts as a rhetorical trope that animates that which addresses, see Johnson, "Apostrophe."

106. *Sister*, October 1973, 10.

107. Donna Swanson, editorial, *Distaff*, December 1974, 2.

108. "Strategy and Perspectives: Come Tell Us What You Think of Us," *FLN*, December 6, 1971, 2; A Sister to *FLN*, January 10, 1972, 4.

109. Sue Kirk to *Sister*, September 1977, 11.

110. Bobby Darwall to *FLN*, May 23, 1971, 1.

111. Sandi Warren to *Sister*, March 1973, 14.

112. Kathy to *AIW*, July 20, 1973, 11.

113. See also Rooney, "What's the Story?," 4.

114. Warner, "Publics," 81.

115. Jakobsen, *Working Alliances*, 137.

**CHAPTER 5. IMAGING AND IMAGINING REVOLUTION**

1. Women and the War Group, "Why Women and the War," *Sister*, January 1973, 1.

2. "Amerikan Way of Death," *Sister*, January 1973, 2.

3. "Start Now," *AIW*, July 24, 1970, 2.

4. "The Right to Choose," *Distaff*, January 1973, 9.

5. "Forum on Autonomy," *VWCN*, March–April 1976, 1.

6. "Speech by Pat Galligan of Female Liberation at NPAC Conference," *FLN*, July 12, 1971, 6.

7. Sherry Goldsmith and Robin Prentiss, "Women's Union, One More Time . . . ," *Sister*, June 1973, 11.

8. Rosa, editorial, *AIW*, May 1974, 2.

9. *FLN*, February 1971, 2.

10. Mary Gehman, "DISTAFF Marks Special Anniversary: One Year of Publication," *Distaff*, November 1980, 9. After Swanson and Gehman ceased coediting the paper,

*Distaff* experienced its four-year hiatus. This gap suggests that identity politics was not the primary or only reason for the partnership's end.

11. See Kennedy, "Socialist Feminism," 503–8.

12. "El Día Internacional de la Mujer/International Women's Day," *Triple Jeopardy*, March–April 1973, 8.

13. Kennedy, "Socialist Feminism," 504.

14. *VWCN*, May 1973, 1.

15. Moraga and Anzaldúa, introduction, xxiii.

16. davenport, "Pathology of Racism," 86; Smith and Smith, "Across the Kitchen Table"; Parker, "Revolution," 240; Moschkovich, "—But I Know You"; Lorde, *Sister Outsider*, 110.

17. See, for example, Fraser, "Feminism's Two Legacies."

18. Yamada, "Asian Pacific American Women," 75.

19. Although it evokes the era of French colonialism, the term *Indochina* was widely used in the 1970s to refer to the region that includes Vietnam, Laos, and Cambodia. Feminists and women from Vietnam, Laos, and Cambodia also used *Indochina* to refer to this geopolitical area, so I retain its usage here.

20. See, for example, Helfgott, "Art in *Life*"; Bohleke, "Americanizing French Fashion Plates."

21. Blackwell, *¡Chicana Power!*, 111.

22. On feminist hegemony, see Chela Sandoval, *Methodology of the Oppressed*, chapter 2. On discursive hegemony, see Gillies, "Excellence and Education," 21.

23. Hesford, *Feeling Women's Liberation*, 18.

24. Ibid., 210.

25. Codell, "Imperial Differences," 410; Thomas, *Pictorial Victorians*.

26. Spencer, *Visual Research Methods*, 32.

27. This cover is reproduced in Beins and Enszer, "'We Couldn't Get Them Printed,'" 191.

28. Wu, "Rethinking Global Sisterhood."

29. Bread and Roses Flyer, [May 1970], Wini Breines Papers, unnumbered box, folder "Bread and Roses Documents," AESL.

30. *It's Our Fight, Too!* [New England Free Press] n.d., 1, Fran Ansley Papers, box 1, folder 2, AESL.

31. "Mother Right: A New Feminist Theory," *AIW*, June 22, 1973, 5–8.

32. See, for example, "Don't Buy Farah Pants," *FLN*, October 23, 1972, 4; Maria Chardon, "¡Viva La Huelga!," *Sister*, September 1973, 4; "Not Everybody Loves an Oscar Mayer Weiner," *AIW*, August 21, 1970, 6–7. See also Movimiento de Liberación de la Mujer, "Mexican Feminists Denounce IWY," *Sister*, July 1975, 2; Robin, "Ligia Castro: From Rio to Bourbon Street," *Distaff*, March 1974, 7, 9–10.

33. *VWCN*, August 20, 1971, 1–2.

34. "Not Everybody Loves an Oscar Mayer Weiner," *AIW*, August 21, 1970, 6–7.

35. See, for example, Pomerleau, *Califia Women*; Blackwell, *¡Chicana Power!*; Valk, *Radical Sisters*; Hewitt, *No Permanent Waves*; Springer, *Living for the Revolution*; Roth, *Separate Roads*.

36. Wu, *Radicals on the Road*; Wu, "Rethinking Global Sisterhood."

37. Wu, "Rethinking Global Sisterhood," 194.

38. The barrel of gun with a bayonet may rise vertically behind her right shoulder, but the photograph is ambiguous. *It's Our Fight, Too!* [New England Free Press], n.d., 2, Fran Ansley Papers, box 1, folder 2, AESL.

39. *Sister*, March 1973, 8.

40. *Woman Worker* used this image and two others to illustrate an article, "Our Vietnamese Sisters" (*Woman Worker*, May 1970, 4). *Battle Acts* used it to illustrate a report on a Baltimore meeting that included women who had traveled to Budapest to work with Indochinese women to plan conferences in Canada (Naomi Cohen, "The Baltimore Conference," *Battle Acts*, November 1970, 12–13).

41. For a brief history of the LNS, see Glessing, *Underground Press in America*, 73–75.

42. *Liberation News Service*, September 6, 1969, P-2.

43. International Women's Day Publication, March 1973, 3, Rochelle Ruthchild Papers, box 1, folder 19, AESL.

44. *Sister*, January 1973, 2.

45. "Women Fight Back," *Sister*, January 1973, 5.

46. *LAWLN*, November 1971, front cover.

47. *AIW*, September 11, 1970, 11.

48. This image was likely cropped from a photograph of Nguyen Thi Hien, a leader in a North Vietnamese militia squad ("Behind the Image").

49. "Amerikan Way of Death," *Sister*, January 1973, 2.

50. This West/non-West opposition mirrors that in the scholarship Mohanty critiques in "Under Western Eyes." She describes the way that academic studies reify, homogenize, and dehistoricize Third World women, assuming "an ahistorical, universal unity between women based on a generalized notion of their subordination" (344). See also Ong, "Colonialism and Modernity."

51. Mother's Day flyer, Ann Hunter Popkin Papers, box 3, folder 47, AESL; Cathy Wilkerson, *Women: The Struggle for Liberation: An Introduction*, 19, Charlotte Bunch Papers, box 1, folder 2, "Early WLM Writing—1967–1969," AESL.

52. Beins, "Radical Others," 150–51.

53. See Nancy Grey Osterud Papers, box 1, folder 9, AESL; Fran Ansley Papers, box 1, folder 5, AESL; Chicago Women's Liberation Union Herstory Project online poster gallery, http://www.cwluherstory.org/wga-posters/wga-poster52-145.html; Atlanta Lesbian Feminist Alliance Archives, box 10, folder "Black Women and Women's Movement 10.1," Sallie Bingham Center for Women's History and Culture, David M. Rubenstein Rare Book and Manuscript Library, Duke University.

54. Harriet Spiegel and Arlynn Robertson, "Revolutionary Women," *Women's Liberation Special*, [Spring 1970], Fran Ansley Papers, box 1, folder 5, AESL.

55. Ibid.

56. On the popularity of these *cartes* among those with enough income to purchase them, see Grigsby, *Enduring Truths*, chapter 9.

57. Painter, *Sojourner Truth*, 189.

58. Carla L. Peterson, *"Doers of the Word"*; Zackodnik, "'Green-Backs of Civilization'"; Painter, "Representing Truth," 483–85.

59. See Grigsby, *Enduring Truths*, especially chapter 4.

60. Different accounts of her speech offer varying language and descriptions of Truth. For insightful analyses of these differences, see Painter, *Sojourner Truth*.

61. *Distaff*, November 1979, 8. According to an editorial preface, Pat Evans, a former contributor to *Distaff* and director of the bureau, sent them this article, but it is not clear whether Evans also authored the article.

62. *Distaff*, November 1979, 8. The 1853 date appears to be an error.

63. *AIW*, October 30, 1970, 14, May 19, 1972, 4.

64. Ethel H., "March 8th International Women's Day Celebration Rousing Success," *LAWLN*, April 1971, 3.

65. Patricia Hill Collins, *Fighting Words*, 231.

66. *AIW*, June 26, 1970.

67. Quoted in Painter, *Sojourner Truth*, 167–68.

68. Lorde, *Sister Outsider*, 41–42.

69. Patricia Hill Collins, *Fighting Words*, 244.

70. Painter, "Representing Truth," 481. See also Mandziuk, "Commemorating Sojourner Truth"; Haraway, "Ecce Homo," 95.

71. Ahmed, *Cultural Politics*, 91–92.

72. Weber, "Black Power in the 1960s"; Nachescu, "Radical Feminism and the Nation"; Lisa Gail Collins, "Activists Who Yearn."

73. Weber, "Black Power in the 1960s," 495–96. For an analysis of the media coverage of this event, see Jason Peterson, "'Race' for Equality."

74. Connie Dorval-Bernal, "Interview with a Sandinista," *Distaff*, May 1980, 9.

75. Though focusing on a different archive, Zackodnik shows the way that nineteenth-century advertisements to sell enslaved people relied on a generic and iconic mode of representation ("Memory, Illustration," 142–48).

76. *FLN*, April 19, [1971], 7.

77. Lee, "Notes from the (Non)Field," 95.

78. Many of these feminist groups shared a commitment to challenging mainstream media's copyright regulations. See Atton, *Alternative Media*, 42–44.

79. "Sister Staff Notes," *Sister*, August 1973, 2; *AIW*, November 19, 1971, 4.

80. Evans, *Tidal Wave*, n.p.; Dow, *Watching Women's Liberation*, 44; Jervis, "End of Feminism's Third Wave"; Berkinow, "September 1968." Extending this image's circulation—and thus its centrality to the women's liberation movement—I include it in Beins, "Radical Others," 173.

81. Welch, "'Up against the Wall,'" 80.

82. Rosen, *World Split Open*, 160–61.

83. Dow, "Feminism, Miss America, and Media Mythology," 131. See also Kreydatus, "Confronting the 'Bra-Burners.'"

84. Dow, *Watching Women's Liberation*, 42–43. For the Miss Black America Pageant, see Welch, "'Up against the Wall.'"

85. *FLN*, October 26–November 1, 1970, 4.

86. Cassell, *Group Called Women*, 25.

87. For a structural and material analysis of the relationship between women's liberation and the New Left, see Roth, *Separate Roads*, 52–67.

88. See ibid., 188–91.

89. Jeanne, "Lib or Liberation?," *FLN*, October 1, 1970, 1.

90. Celeste Newbrough, *Distaff*, March 1973, 9.

91. Nancy Robinson, untitled, *LAWLN*, Fall 1970, 3.

92. Cassell, *Group Called Women*, 25.

93. *AIW*, July 10, 1970, 8.

94. See also Breines, "What's Love Got to Do with It?," 1119.

95. Morgan, "Goodbye to All That," 6.

96. Evans, *Personal Politics*, 179–83.

97. Roth, *Separate Roads*, 54–55.

98. These instructions are excerpted in "Happiness Is a Warm Gun," *Old Mole*, May 19–22, 1969, 4, Nancy Grey Osterud Papers, box 1, folder 8, AESL.

99. Willis, "Sisters under the Skin?" 112.

100. Morgan, "Introduction," xxxiv.

101. Breines, *Trouble between Us*, 111–14.

102. Ibid., 84. See also Nachescu, "Radical Feminism and the Nation," 46.

103. Welch, "'Up against the Wall,'" 88–90.

104. See, for example, Dow's analysis of the 1970 documentary *Women's Liberation* (*Watching Women's Liberation*, chapter 4).

105. Wu, "Journeys for Peace and Liberation," 579–80.

106. Maeda, "Black Panthers," 1085.

107. Rhodes, *Framing the Black Panthers*, 109; see also Lumsden, "Good Mothers with Guns," 908–9

108. Zackodnik, "Memory, Illustration."

109. Rhodes, *Framing the Black Panthers*; Reed, *Art of Protest*, chapter 2.

110. Rhodes, *Framing the Black Panthers*, 88.

111. Gaiter, "Revolution Will Be Visualized."

112. However, the FBI was indeed interested in women's liberation activities. For Phyllis Parun's FBI file, see Phyllis Parun Papers, Newcomb Archives and Vorhoff Library Special Collections, Newcomb College Institute, Tulane University, New Orleans. See also Salper, "U.S. Government Surveillance"; Rosen, "When Women Spied on Women."

113. Wu, *Radicals on the Road*, chapter 7.

114. Pat Sumi, "Vietnam," *Triple Jeopardy*, July–August 1972, 8.

115. Wu, *Radicals on the Road*, 245.

116. Longeaux y Vasquez, "Soy Chicana Primero," 17.

117. Hall, "Encoding/Decoding," 129.

118. See, for example, Snow and Benford, "Ideology, Frame Resonance"; Benford and Snow, "Framing Processes." On the power of branding, see Vestergaard, "Humanitarian Branding"; on repetition as an activist method, see Stephenson-Abetz, "Everyday Activism."

## CONCLUSION. FEMINISM REDUX

1. The full statement reads, "*Breaking Ground* is a radical feminist journal produced by members of the Carleton community. The purpose of *Breaking Ground* is to

develop people's ideas about women, their cultural contributions, and their place in the world. In this journal, anti-sexist, anti-racist, anti-homophobic, and anti-classist perspectives are advanced, clarified, appreciated, applied, and celebrated" (1997; journal in possession of the author).

2. Walker, "Being Real," xxxiii.

3. Walker, "Becoming the Third Wave," 41.

4. Munro, "Feminism"; Phillips and Cree, "What Does the 'Fourth Wave' Mean?"; Garrison, "U.S. Feminism," 166; Benn, "After Post-Feminism."

5. See, for example, Dicker and Piepmeier, introduction; Dean, "Who's Afraid of Third Wave Feminism?," 339; Heywood and Drake, "What Is the Third Wave?"; Garrison, "U.S. Feminism"; Garrison, "Contests"; Gilley, "Writings of the Third Wave."

6. See Hewitt, *No Permanent Waves*, 1–12.

7. Hewitt, "From Seneca Falls to Suffrage?"

8. Kinser, "Negotiating Spaces," 124.

9. See also Fernandes, "Unsettling 'Third Wave Feminism'"; Townsend-Bell, "Writing the Way to Feminism," 128; Whittier, "Political Generations."

10. Piepmeier, *Girl Zines*, 33–34. See also Gilmore, "Bridging the Waves"; Zarnow, "From Sisterhood to Girlie Culture."

11. Peoples, "'Under Construction,'" 421.

12. Garrison, "U.S. Feminism."

13. Walker, "Becoming the Third Wave," 41.

14. Popkin, "Bread and Roses."

15. Yanney, "Practical Revolution," 8.

16. *Sister*, December [1976]–January [1977], 4. This editorial nonetheless notes that "the movement, or whatever one calls it, is not dead. In the sea of low spirits there are some good tidings," one of which is the recent growth of *Sister*'s staff, resources, and energy.

17. Cindy Frazier and Kate McDonough, "Statement from the Women's Center," *Sister*, February–March 1977, 10.

18. Ryan, *Feminism and the Women's Movement*, 69.

19. Cassell, *Group Called Women*, 177.

20. Curthoys, *Feminist Amnesia*, 53.

21. Echols, *Daring to Be Bad*, 5.

22. Evans, "Re-Viewing the Second Wave," 259.

23. Bradley, *Mass Media*, xi.

24. Kennedy, "Socialist Feminism," 510.

25. Baxandall and Gordon, introduction, 1.

26. Flannery, *Feminist Literacies*, 13.

27. Ibid., 14.

28. The 1977 formation of the National Women's Studies Association further institutionalized feminism in the academy. See also Boxer, *When Women Ask the Questions*.

29. Martha Allen, "Development of Communication Networks."

30. Enszer, "Whole Naked Truth," 20.

31. Densmore, "Cell 16," 5.

32. For an insightful study of the institutionalization of *Signs*, *Feminist Studies*, and *Frontiers*, see McDermott, *Politics and Scholarship*.

33. Whittier, "Political Generations," 770.

34. Ibid., 763.

35. Whittier, "Turning It Over," 188.

36. Isaac, "Movement of Movements."

37. Darnton, "What Is the History of Books?"

38. McDonald, "Implicit Structures," 111.

39. Wingfoot, "Different Generations, Different Issues."

# BIBLIOGRAPHY

**ARCHIVAL RESOURCES**

*Sallie Bingham Center for Women's History and Culture, David M. Rubenstein*
*Rare Book and Manuscript Library, Duke University, Durham, North Carolina*

Atlanta Lesbian Feminist Alliance Archives

*California State University, Long Beach, Special Collections and University Archives*

Oral History Collection: Los Angeles Women's Movement
Virtual Oral/Aural History Archive

*Iowa Women's Archives, University of Iowa, Iowa City*

*Ain't I a Woman?*
Dale McCormick Papers
Jo Rabenold Papers
Aaron Silander Papers
Women's Resource and Action Center Records

*Lesbian Herstory Archives, Brooklyn, N.Y.*

*Newcomb Archives and Vorhoff Library Special Collections,*
*Newcomb College Institute, Tulane University, New Orleans*

*Distaff*
Mary Elizabeth Gehman Papers
Phyllis Parun Papers
Voices from the Louisiana Women's Movement: First-Hand Accounts from People
    Who Made It Happen, March 24, 2001 (videotapes)

*Northeastern University Libraries, Archives and Special Collections Department, Boston*

Female Liberation: A Radical Feminist Organization Records

*Radcliffe Institute, Arthur and Elizabeth Schlesinger Library on the History of*
*Women in America, Harvard University, Cambridge, Massachusetts*

Fran Ansley Papers
Wini Breines Papers
Charlotte Bunch Papers
Nancy Grey Osterud Papers
Ann Hunter Popkin Papers
Rochelle Ruthchild Papers

*Sophia Smith Collection, Smith College, Northampton, Massachusetts*

*Female Liberation Newsletter*
Third World Women's Alliance Records
*Valley Women's Center Newsletter*
Valley Women's Center Records
Voices of Feminism Oral History Project
Women's Liberation Collection

*Southern California Library, Los Angeles*

Los Angeles Women's Liberation Movement Collection
Joan Robins Papers
*Sister*
Women's Center—CSU Dominguez Hills Collection

*University of Massachusetts, Amherst, W. E. B. Du Bois Library,*
*Special Collections and University Archives*

Valley Women's Union Records


### SECONDARY SOURCES

Abarca, Meredith E. 2006. *Voices in the Kitchen: Views of Food and the World from Working-Class Mexican American Women*. College Station: Texas A&M University Press.

Adams, Kate. 1998. "Built Out of Books: Lesbian Energy and Feminist Ideology in Alternative Publishing." *Journal of Homosexuality* 34 (3–4): 113–41.

Adams, Thomas R., and Nicolas Barker. 1993. "A New Model for the Study of the Book." In *A Potencie of Life: Books in Society: The Clark Lectures, 1986–1987*, ed. Nicolas Barker, 5–43. London: British Library.

Adamson, Nancy. 1995. "Feminists, Libbers, Lefties, and Radicals: The Emergence of the Women's Liberation Movement." In *A Diversity of Women: Ontario, 1945–1980*, ed. Joy Parr, 252–80. Toronto: University of Toronto Press.

Ahmed, Sara. 2004. *The Cultural Politics of Emotion*. New York: Routledge.

Alarcón, Norma. 1990. "The Theoretical Subject(s) of This Bridge Called My Back and Anglo-American Feminism." In *Making Face, Making Soul = Haciendo Caras: Creative and Critical Perspectives by Feminists of Color*, ed. Gloria Anzaldúa, 356–69. San Francisco: Aunt Lute.

Allen, Martha. 1988. "The Development of Communication Networks among Women, 1963–1983—A History of Women's Media in the U.S." PhD diss., Howard University.

——. 1990. "Women's Media: The Way to Revolution," *off our backs*, February 28, 14.

Allen, Pamela. 1970. *Free Space: A Perspective on the Small Group in Women's Liberation*. New York: Times Change.

Althusser, Louis. 1971. "Ideology and Ideological State Apparatuses (Notes toward an Investigation)." In *Lenin and Philosophy and Other Essays*, trans. Ben Brewster, 127–86. New York: Monthly Review.

Anderson, Benedict. 1991. *Imagined Communities: Reflections on the Origin and Spread of Nationalism*. Rev. ed. London: Verso.

Andres, Lauren. 2013. "Differential Spaces, Power Hierarchy, and Collaborative Planning: A Critique of the Role of Temporary Uses in Shaping and Making Places." *Urban Studies* 50 (4): 759–75.

Angus, Lis, Pam Dineen, and L. Robertson. 1972. "Toronto Women's Caucus: A Two-Year Experience in a Cross-City Women's Liberation Group." *League for Socialist Action/Ligue Socialiste Ouvrière Discussion Bulletin* 23 (December). http://www.socialisthistory.ca/Docs/1961-/WomensLib/LSA-TWC.htm.

Arnold, June. 1976. "Feminist Presses and Feminist Politics." *Quest: A Feminist Quarterly*, Summer, 17–26.

Atton, Chris. 2001. *Alternative Media*. London: Sage.

Austin, J. L. 1975. *How to Do Things with Words*. 2nd ed. Cambridge, Mass.: Harvard University Press.

Bakhtin, Mikhail. 1984. *Rabelais and His World*. Trans. Hélène Iswolsky. Bloomington: Indiana University Press.

Bambara, Toni Cade. 1970. *The Black Woman: An Anthology*. New York: New American Library.

Barale, Michèle Aina. 2000. "Queer Urbanities: A Walk on the Wild Side." In *Queer Diasporas*, ed. Cindy Patton and Benigno Sánchez-Eppler, 204–14. Durham, N.C.: Duke University Press.

Baxandall, Rosalyn, and Linda Gordon. 2000. Introduction to *Dear Sisters: Dispatches from the Women's Liberation Movement*, 1–18. New York: Basic Books.

Beins, Agatha. 2015. "Making a Place for Lesbian Life at the Lesbian Herstory Archives." In Stone and Cantrell, *Out of the Closet*, 25–49.

———. 2015. "Radical Others: Women of Color and Revolutionary Feminism." *Feminist Studies* 41 (1): 150–83.

———. 2016. "A Revolution in Ephemera: Feminist Newsletters and Newspapers of the 1970s." In Harker and Farr, *This Book Is an Action*, 46–65.

Beins, Agatha, and Julie R. Enszer. 2013. "'We Couldn't Get Them Printed,' So We Learned to Print: *Ain't I a Woman?* and the Iowa City Women's Press." *Frontiers: A Journal of Women's Studies* 34 (2): 186–221.

"Behind the Image: North Vietnam." 2014. *Military History*, October 14. http://www.military-history.org/articles/behind-the-image-north-vietnam.htm.

Benford, Robert D. 1997. "An Insider's Critique of the Social Movement Framing Perspective." *Sociological Inquiry* 67 (4): 409–30.

Benford, Robert D., and David A. Snow. 2000. "Framing Processes and Social Movements: An Overview and Assessment." *Annual Review of Sociology* 26: 611–39.

Benn, Melissa. 2013. "After Post-Feminism: Pursuing Material Equality in a Digital Age." *Juncture* 20 (3): 223–27.

Berezin, Mabel. 2001. "Emotions and Political Identity: Mobilizing Affect for the Polity." In *Passionate Politics: Emotions and Social Movements*, ed. Jeff Goodwin, James M. Jasper, and Francesca Polletta, 83–98. Chicago: University of Chicago Press.

Berkinow, Louise. 2005. "September 1968: Women Protest Miss America." *Women's*

*eNews*, September 1. http://www.womensenews.org/story/our-story/050901
/september-1968-women-protest-miss-america.

Bikman, Minda. 1970. "The Ladies' Invasion of Man's Home Journal." *Village Voice*,
March 26, 7–8, 24.

Blackwell, Maylei. 2011. *¡Chicana Power!: Contested Histories of Feminism in the Chicano Movement*. Austin: University of Texas Press.

Blanchard, Margaret. 1992. "Speaking the Plural: The Example of *Women: A Journal of
Liberation*." *NWSA Journal* 4 (1): 84–97.

Bohleke, Karin J. 2010. "Americanizing French Fashion Plates: *Godey's* and *Peterson's*
Cultural and Socio-Economic Translation of *Les Modes Parisiennes*." *American
Periodicals: A Journal of History and Criticism* 20 (2): 120–55.

Boxer, Marilyn Jacoby. 1998. *When Women Ask the Questions: Creating Women's Studies
in America*. Baltimore: Johns Hopkins University Press.

Bradley, Patricia. 2003. *Mass Media and the Shaping of American Feminism, 1963–75*.
Jackson: University Press of Mississippi.

Breines, Winifred. 2002. "What's Love Got to Do with It? White Women, Black
Women, and Feminism in the Movement Years." *Signs: Journal of Women in Culture and Society* 27 (4): 1095–1133.

———. 2006. *The Trouble between Us: An Uneasy History of White and Black Women in
the Feminist Movement*. New York: Oxford University Press.

Broude, Norma, and Mary D. Garrard, eds. 1994. *The Power of Feminist Art: The American Movement of the 1970s, History and Impact*. New York: Abrams.

Brown, Gavin, and Jenny Pickerill. 2009. "Space for Emotion in the Spaces of Activism." *Emotion, Space, and Society* 2 (1): 24–35.

Bunch, Charlotte. 1987. *Passionate Politics: Feminist Theory in Action*. New York: St.
Martin's.

Butler, Judith. 1993. *Bodies That Matter: On the Discursive Limits of "Sex."* New York:
Routledge.

———. 1997. *Excitable Speech: A Politics of the Performative*. New York: Routledge.

———. 1999. *Gender Trouble: Feminism and the Subversion of Identity*. New York:
Routledge.

Cadman, Eileen, Gail Chester, and Agnes Pivot. 1981. *Rolling Our Own: Women as
Printers, Distributors, and Publishers*. London: Minority.

Campbell, Karlyn Kohrs. 1990. "The Rhetoric of Women's Liberation: An Oxymoron."
In *Methods of Rhetorical Criticism: A Twentieth-Century Perspective*, 3rd ed., ed.
Bernard L. Brock, Robert L. Scott, and James W. Cheseboro, 388–402. Detroit:
Wayne State University Press.

Carden, Maren Lockwood. 1974. *The New Feminist Movement*. New York: Sage.

Carrillo, Jo. 1983. "And When You Leave, Take Your Pictures with You." In Moraga and
Anzaldúa, *This Bridge Called My Back*, 63–64.

Cassell, Joan. 1989. *A Group Called Women: Sisterhood and Symbolism in the Feminist
Movement*. New York: McKay.

Certeau, Michel de. 1984. *The Practice of Everyday Life*. Trans. Steven Rendall. Berkeley: University of California Press.

Chartier, Roger. 2007. "Introduction: Aesthetic Mystery and the Materialities of the Written." In *Inscription and Erasure: Literature and Written Culture from the Eleventh to Eighteenth Century*, trans. Arthur Goldhammer, vii–xiii. Philadelphia: University of Pennsylvania Press.

Chu, Judy. 1986. "Asian American Women's Studies Courses: A Look Back at Our Beginnings." *Frontiers: A Journal of Women's Studies* 8 (3): 96–101.

Cline, David P. 2006. *Creating Choice: A Community Responds to the Need for Birth Control, 1961–1973*. New York: Palgrave Macmillan.

Cobbs, Lisa. 1976. "State of the Press, 1976." *Feminist Bulletin*, July–August, 15.

Codell, Julie. 2006. "Imperial Differences and Culture Clashes in Victorian Periodicals' Visuals: The Case of *Punch*." *Victorian Periodicals Review* 39 (4): 410–28.

Colebrook, Claire. 2001. "Certeau and Foucault: Tactics and Strategic Essentialism." *South Atlantic Quarterly* 100 (2): 543–74.

Collins, Lisa Gail. 2006. "Activists Who Yearn for Art That Transforms: Parallels in the Black Arts and Feminist Art Movements in the United States." *Signs: Journal of Women in Culture and Society* 31 (3): 717–52.

Collins, Patricia Hill. 1998. *Fighting Words: Black Women and the Search for Justice*. Minneapolis: University of Minnesota Press.

Combahee River Collective. 1978. "A Black Feminist Statement." In *Capitalist Patriarchy and the Case for Revolution*, ed. Zillah Eisenstein, 362–72. New York: Monthly Review.

Cover, Rob. 2005. "Engaging Sexualities: Lesbian/Gay Print Journalism, Community Belonging, Social Space and Physical Place." *Pacific Journalism Review* 11 (1): 113–32.

Crampton, Jeremy W. 2009. "Cartography: Performative, Participatory, Political." *Progress in Human Geography* 33 (6): 840–48.

Curthoys, Jean. 1997. *Feminist Amnesia: The Wake of Women's Liberation*. New York: Routledge.

Darnton, Robert. 1982. "What Is the History of Books?" *Daedalus* 111 (3): 65–83.

davenport, doris. 1983. "The Pathology of Racism: A Conversation with Third World Wimmin." In Moraga and Anzaldúa, *This Bridge Called My Back*, 85–90.

Davis, Lydia. 2007. *The Making of "Our Bodies, Ourselves": How Feminism Travels across Borders*. Durham, N.C.: Duke University Press.

Dean, Jonathan. 2009. "Who's Afraid of Third Wave Feminism? On the Uses of the 'Third Wave' in British Feminist Politics." *International Feminist Journal of Politics* 11 (3): 334–52.

Densmore, Dana. 2014. "Cell 16: Gender and Agency with Digressions into Naming." Paper presented at A Revolutionary Moment: Women's Liberation in the Late 1960s and Early 1970s, Boston, March 27–29. http://www.bu.edu/wgs/files/2013/10/Densmore-Cell-16-Gender-and-Agency-with-Digressions-into-Naming.pdf.

Dicker, Rory, and Alison Piepmeier. 2003. Introduction to *Catching a Wave: Reclaiming Feminism for the Twenty-First Century*, 3–28. Boston: Northeastern University Press.

Dieter, Michael. 2011. "The Becoming Environmental of Power: Tactical Media after Control." *Fibreculture Journal* 18: 177–205.

Dill, Bonnie Thornton. 1983. "Race, Class, and Gender: Prospects for an All-Inclusive Sisterhood." *Feminist Studies* 19 (1): 131–50.

Dismore, David. 2010. "When Women Went on Strike: Remembering Equality Day, 1970." *Ms.*, August 26. http://msmagazine.com/blog/2010/08/26/when-women -went-on-strike-remembering-equality-day-1970/.

Dobrowlsky, Alexandra. 2008. "The Women's Movement in Flux: Feminism and Framing, Passion and Politics." In *Group Politics and Social Movements in Canada*, ed. Miriam Smith, 159–80. Peterborough, Ont.: Broadview.

Dow, Bonnie J. 2004. "Feminism, Miss America, and Media Mythology." *Rhetoric and Public Affairs* 6 (1): 127–60.

———. 2014. *Watching Women's Liberation, 1970: Feminism's Pivotal Year on the Network News*. Urbana: University of Illinois Press.

Dunbar, Roxanne. 1969. "Female Liberation as the Basis for Social Revolution." *No More Fun and Games*, February, 103–15.

DuPlessis, Rachel Blau, and Ann Snitow. 2007. "A Feminist Memoir Project." In *The Feminist Memoir Project: Voices from Women's Liberation*, ed. DuPlessis and Snitow, 3–24. New Brunswick, N.J.: Rutgers University Press.

———. 2007. "Preface to the 2007 Edition." In *The Feminist Memoir Project: Voices from Women's Liberation*, ed. DuPlessis and Snitow, xi–xxiv. New Brunswick, N.J.: Rutgers University Press.

Echols, Alice. 1989. *Daring to Be Bad: Radical Feminism in America, 1967–1975*. Minneapolis: University of Minnesota Press.

Enke, Anne. 2007. *Finding the Movement: Sexuality, Contested Space, and Feminist Activism*. Durham, N.C.: Duke University Press.

Enszer, Julie R. 2013. "The Whole Naked Truth of Our Lives: Lesbian-Feminist Print Culture from 1969 through 1980." PhD diss., University of Maryland.

———. 2016. "'What Made Us Think They'd Pay Us for Making a Revolution?' Women in Distribution (WinD), 1974–1979." In Harker and Farr, *This Book Is an Action*, 66–86.

Evans, Sara. 1980. *Personal Politics: The Roots of Women's Liberation in the Civil Rights Movement and the New Left*. New York: Vintage.

———. 2002. "Re-Viewing the Second Wave." *Feminist Studies* 28 (2): 259–67.

———. 2003. *Tidal Wave: How Women Changed America at Century's End*. New York: Free Press.

———. 2015. "Women's Liberation: Seeing the Revolution Clearly." *Feminist Studies* 41 (1): 138–49.

Ezekiel, Judith. 2002. *Feminism in the Heartland*. Columbus: Ohio State University Press.

Farrell, Amy. 1998. *Yours in Sisterhood: Ms. Magazine and the Promise of Popular Feminism*. Chapel Hill: University of North Carolina Press.

———. 2008. "Attentive to Difference: *Ms.* Magazine, Coalition Building, and Sisterhood." In *Feminist Coalitions: Historical Perspectives on Second-Wave Feminism in the United States*, ed. Stephanie Gilmore, 48–62. Urbana: University of Illinois Press.

"Feminist Chronicles—1973." 2014. *Feminist Majority Foundation*. http://www .feminist.org/research/chronicles/fc1973a.html.

Ferguson, Michaele L. 2007. "Sharing without Knowing: Collective Identity in Feminist and Democratic Theory." *Hypatia* 22 (4): 30–45.

Fernandes, Leela. 2010. "Unsettling 'Third Wave Feminism': Feminist Waves, Inter-sectionality, and Identity Politics in Retrospect." In Hewitt, *No Permanent Waves*, 98–118.

Firestone, Shulamith, and Anne Koedt. 1970. "Editorial." In *Notes from the Second Year: Women's Liberation: Major Writings of the Radical Feminists*, 2. New York: Radical Feminism.

Fish, Stanley. 1980. *Is There a Text in This Class? The Authority of Interpretive Communities*. Cambridge: Harvard University Press.

Flannery, Kathryn Thoms. 2005. *Feminist Literacies, 1968–1975*. Urbana: University of Illinois Press.

Fox-Genovese, Elizabeth. 1979. "The Personal Is Not Political Enough." *Marxist Perspectives* 2 (4): 94–113.

Fraser, Nancy. 2015. "Feminism's Two Legacies: A Tale of Ambivalence." *South Atlantic Quarterly* 114 (4): 699–712.

Freeman, Jo [pseud. Joreen]. 1972. "The Tyranny of Structurelessness." *The Second Wave* 2 (1): 20–25, 42.

———. 1975. *The Politics of Women's Liberation: A Case Study of an Emerging Social Movement and Its Relation to the Policy Process*. New York: McKay.

———. 1976. "Trashing." *Ms.*, April, 49–51, 92–98.

Friday, Julia. 2001. "Prague 1968: Spatiality and the Tactics of Resistance." *Texas Studies in Literature and Language* 53 (2): 159–78.

Frontani, Michael. 2008. "Alternative Press." In *Encyclopedia of American Journalism*, ed. Stephen L. Vaughn, 13–17. New York: Routledge.

Gaiter, Colette. 2004. "The Revolution Will Be Visualized: Emory Douglas in the *Black Panther*." 65 (January). http://bad.eserver.org/issues/2004/65/gaiter.html.

Garrison, Ednie Kaeh. 2000. "U.S. Feminism—Grrrl Style! Youth (Sub)Cultures and the Technologics of the Third Wave." *Feminist Studies* 26 (1): 141–70.

———. 2003. "Contests for the Meaning of Third Wave Feminism: The Logic of Late Feminism." In *Third Wave Feminism: A Critical Exploration*, ed. Stacy Gillis, Gillian Howie, and Rebecca Munford, 24–37. New York: Palgrave Macmillan.

Gayle, Curtis Anderson. 2006. "History in Multiplicity: Locating de Certeau's 'Strategy' and 'Tactics' in Early Postwar Japan." *Japan Forum* 18 (2): 207–28.

Genette, Gerard. 1997. *Paratexts: Thresholds of Interpretation*. Trans. Jane E. Lewin. Cambridge: Cambridge University Press.

Gerhard, Jane. 2013. *The Dinner Party: Judy Chicago and the Power of Popular Feminism, 1970–2007*. Athens: University of Georgia Press.

Giardina, Carol. 2010. *Freedom for Women: Forging the Women's Liberation Movement, 1953–1970*. Gainesville: University Press of Florida.

Gilley, Jennifer. 2005. "Writings of the Third Wave: Young Feminists in Conversation." *Reference and User Services Quarterly* 44 (3): 187–98.

———. 2016. "Feminist Publishing/Publishing Feminism: Experimentation in Second-Wave Book Publishing." In Harker and Farr, *This Book Is an Action*, 23–45.

Gillies, Donald. 1997. "Excellence and Education: Rhetoric and Reality." *Education, Knowledge, and Economy* 1 (1): 19–35.

Gilmore, Stephanie. 2005. "Bridging the Waves: Sex and Sexuality in a Second Wave

Organization." In *Different Wavelengths: Studies of the Contemporary Women's Movement*, ed. Jo Reger, 97–116. New York: Routledge.

——, ed. 2008. *Feminist Coalitions: Historical Perspectives on Second-Wave Feminism in the United States*. Urbana: University of Illinois Press.

——. 2013. *Groundswell: Grassroots Feminist Activism in Postwar America*. New York: Routledge.

Gilmore, Stephanie, and Elizabeth Kaminski. 2007. "A Part and Apart: Lesbian and Straight Feminist Activists Negotiate Identity in a Second-Wave Organization." *Journal of the History of Sexuality* 16 (1): 95–113.

Glenn, Cheryl. 2000. "Truth, Lies, and Method: Revisiting Feminist Historiography." *College English* 62 (3): 387–89.

Glessing, Robert J. 1970. *The Underground Press in America*. Bloomington: Indiana University Press.

Godard, Barbara. 2002. "Feminist Periodicals and the Production of Cultural Value: The Canadian Context." *Women's Studies International Forum* 25 (2): 209–23.

Gray, Jonathan. 2006. *Watching with the Simpsons: Television, Parody, and Intertextuality*. New York: Routledge.

Grigsby, Darcy Grimaldo. 2015. *Enduring Truths: Sojourner Truth's Shadow and Substance*. Chicago: University of Chicago Press.

Hall, Stuart. 1980. "Encoding/Decoding." In *Culture, Media, Language*, ed. Stuart Hall, Dorothy Hobson, Andrew Lowe, and Paul Willis, 128–38. London: Hutchinson.

Hanisch, Carol. 2001. "Struggles over Leadership in the Women's Liberation Movement." In *Leadership and Social Movements*, ed. Colin Barker, Alan Johnson, and Michael Lavalette, 77–95. Manchester: Manchester University Press.

Haraway, Donna. 1992. "Ecce Homo, Ain't (Aren't) I a Woman, and Inappropriate(d) Others: The Human in a Post-Humanist Landscape." In *Feminists Theorize the Political*, ed. Judith Butler and Joan Scott, 86–100. New York: Routledge.

Harker, Jaime, and Cecilia Konchar Farr, eds. 2016. *This Book Is an Action: Feminist Print Culture and Activist Aesthetics*. Urbana: University of Illinois Press.

Harper, Phillip Brian. 1993. "Nationalism and Social Division in the Black Arts Poetry of the 1960s." *Critical Inquiry* 19 (2): 234–55.

Havlin, Natalie. 2015. "'To Live a Humanity under the Skin': Revolutionary Love and Third World Praxis in 1970s Chicana Feminism." *Women's Studies Quarterly* 43 (3–4): 78–97.

Hebdige, Dick. 2002 [1979]. *Subculture: The Meaning of Style*. New York: Routledge.

Helfgott, Isadora A. 2010. "Art in *Life*: Fashioning Political Ideology through Visual Culture in Mid-Century America." *American Periodicals: A Journal of History, Criticism, and Bibliography* 20 (2): 269–94.

Hesford, Victoria. 2013. *Feeling Women's Liberation*. Durham, N.C.: Duke University Press.

Hewitt, Nancy. 2010. "From Seneca Falls to Suffrage? Reimagining a 'Master' Narrative in U.S. Women's History." In Hewitt, *No Permanent Waves*, 15–38.

——, ed. 2010. *No Permanent Waves: Recasting Histories of U.S. Feminism*. New Brunswick, N.J.: Rutgers University Press.

Heywood, Leslie, and Jennifer Drake. 1997. "What Is the Third Wave? Third Wave

Cultural Contexts." In *Third Wave Agenda: Being Feminist, Doing Feminism*, 25–39. Minneapolis: University of Minnesota Press.

Hogan, Kristen. 2008. "Women's Studies in Feminist Bookstores: 'All the Women's Studies Women Would Come In.'" *Signs: Journal of Women in Culture and Society* 33 (3): 595–621.

———. 2016. *The Feminist Bookstore Movement: Lesbian Antiracism and Feminist Accountability*. Durham, N.C.: Duke University Press.

Hole, Judith, and Ellen Levine. 1971. *Rebirth of Feminism*. New York: Quadrangle.

Holland, Dorothy, Gretchen Fox, and Vinci Daro. 2008. "Social Movements and Collective Identity: A Decentered, Dialogic View." *Anthropological Quarterly* 81 (1): 95–126.

hooks, bell. 1995. "Sisterhood: Political Solidarity between Women." In *Feminism and Community*, ed. Penny A. Weiss and Marilyn Friedman, 293–315. Philadelphia: Temple University Press.

Hubbard, Phil. 2005. "Place/Space." In *Cultural Geography: A Critical Dictionary of Ideas*, ed. David Sibley, David Atkinson, Peter Jackson, and Neil Washbourne, 41–48. London: Tauris.

Hunt, Scott A., Robert D. Benford, and David A. Snow. 1994. "Identity Fields: Framing Processes and the Social Construction of Movement Identities." In *New Social Movements: From Ideology to Identity*, ed. Enrique Laraña, Hank Johnston, and Joseph R. Gusfield, 185–208. Philadelphia: Temple University Press.

Isaac, Larry. 2008. "Movement of Movements: Culture Moves in the Long Civil Rights Struggle." *Social Forces* 87 (1): 33–63.

Jakobsen, Janet. 1998. *Working Alliances and the Politics of Difference: Diversity and Feminist Ethics*. Bloomington: Indiana University Press.

James, Daniel, and Mirta Zaida Lobato. 2004. "Family Photos, Oral Narratives, and Identity Formation: The Ukrainians of Berisso." *Hispanic American Historical Review* 84 (1): 5–36.

Jasper, James. 1998. "The Emotions of Protest: Affective and Reactive Emotions in and around Social Movements." *Sociological Forum* 13 (3): 397–424.

Jasper, James, and Jane D. Poulson. 1995. "Recruiting Strangers and Friends: Moral Shocks and Social Networks in Animal Rights and Anti-Nuclear Protests." *Social Problems* 42 (4): 493–512.

Jay, Karla. 2000. *Tales of the Lavender Menace: A Memoir of Liberation*. New York: Basic Books.

Jervis, Lisa. 2004. "The End of Feminism's Third Wave: The Cofounder of *Bitch* Magazine Says Goodbye to the Generational Divide." *Ms.*, Winter. http://www.msmagazine.com/winter2004/thirdwave.asp.

Johnson, Barbara. 1987. "Apostrophe, Animation, and Abortion." In *A World of Difference*, 184–99. Baltimore: Johns Hopkins University Press.

Johnston, Hank, Enrique Laraña, and Joseph R. Gusfield. 1994. "Identities, Grievances, and New Social Movements." In *New Social Movements: From Ideology to Identity*, ed. Enrique Laraña, Hank Johnston, and Joseph R. Gusfield, 3–35. Philadelphia: Temple University Press.

Kahn, Kim Fridkin, and Edie N. Goldenberg. 1991. "The Media: Obstacle or Ally of

Feminists?" *Annals of the American Academy of Political and Social Science* 515: 104–13.

Karlyn, Kathleen Rowe. 2003. "*Scream*, Popular Culture, and Feminism's Third Wave: 'I'm Not My Mother.'" *Genders* 38. http://www.genders.org/g38/g38_rowe_karlyn .html.

Kelly, Christine A. 2000. "Whatever Happened to Women's Liberation? Feminist Legacies of '68." *New Political Science* 22 (2): 161–75.

Kennedy, Elizabeth Lapovsky. 2008. "Socialist Feminism: What Difference Did It Make to the History of Women's Studies?" *Feminist Studies* 34 (3): 497–525.

Kesselman, Amy. 2001. "Women's Liberation and the Left in New Haven, Connecticut, 1968–1972." *Radical History Review* 51: 15–33.

Kinser, Amber E. 2004. "Negotiating Spaces for/through Third-Wave Feminism." *NWSA Journal* 16 (3): 124–53.

Kitchin, Rob, and Martin Dodge. 2007. "Rethinking Maps." *Progress in Human Geography* 31 (3): 331–44.

Kreydatus, Beth. 2008. "Confronting the 'Bra-Burners': Teaching Radical Feminism with a Case Study." *History Teacher* 41 (4): 489–504.

Kurzman, Charles. 2008. "Introduction: Meaning Making in Social Movements." *Anthropological Quarterly* 81 (1): 5–15.

Laflen, Angela, and Brittany Fiorenza. 2012. "'Okay, My Rant Is Over': The Language of Emotion in Computer-Mediated Communication." *Computers and Composition* 29 (4): 296–308.

Lear, Martha Weinman. 1968. "The Second Feminist Wave." *New York Times Magazine*, March 10, 24–25, 50, 53, 55–56, 58, 60–62.

Lee, Rachel. 2001. "Notes from the (Non)Field: Teaching and Theorizing Women of Color." In *Women's Studies on Its Own*, ed. Robyn Wiegman, 81–105. Durham, N.C.: Duke University Press.

Leffler, Ann, Dair L. Gillespie, and Elinor Lerner Ratner. 1973. "Academic Feminists and the Women's Movement." *Critical Sociology* 4 (1): 44–55.

Lichtenstein, Grace. 1970. "Feminists Demand 'Liberation' in *Ladies' Home Journal* Sit-In." *New York Times*, March 19, 51.

Liddle, Kathleen. 2005. "More Than a Bookstore: The Continuing Relevance of Feminist Bookstores for the Lesbian Community." *Journal of Lesbian Studies* 9 (1–2): 145–59.

Liebling, A. J. 1960. "The Wayward Press: Do You Belong in Journalism?" *New Yorker*, May 14, 105–9.

Longeaux y Vasquez, Enriqueta. 1971. "Soy Chicana Primero." *El Cuaderno* 1 (2): 17–20.

Longhurst, Robyn. 2003. "Introduction: Subjectivities, Spaces and Places." In *Handbook of Cultural Geography*, ed. Kay Anderson, Mona Domosh, Steve Pile, and Nigel Thrift, 283–89. London: Sage.

Lorde, Audre. 1984. "Poetry Is Not a Luxury." In *Sister Outsider*, 36–39.

———. 1984. *Sister Outsider: Essays and Speeches by Audre Lorde*. Freedom, Calif.: Crossing.

Lugones, María, and Pat Alake Rosezelle. 1995. "Sisterhood and Friendship as

Feminist Models." In *Feminism and Community*, ed. Penny A. Weiss and Marilyn Friedman, 135–46. Philadelphia: Temple University Press.

Lumsden, Linda. 2009. "Good Mothers with Guns: Framing Black Womanhood in the *Black Panther*, 1965–80." *Journal of Mass Communication Quarterly* 86 (4): 900–922.

Maeda, Daryl J. 2005. "Black Panthers, Red Guards, and Chinamen: Constructing Asian American Identity through Performing Blackness, 1969–72." *American Quarterly* 57 (4): 1079–1103.

Mandziuk, Roseann M. 2003. "Commemorating Sojourner Truth: Negotiating the Politics of Race and Gender in the Spaces of Public Memory." *Western Journal of Communication* 67 (3): 271–91.

Marquez, Benjamin. 2001. "Choosing Issues, Choosing Sides: Constructing Identities in Mexican-American Social Movement Organizations." *Ethnic and Racial Studies* 24 (2): 218–35.

Martin, Deborah G., and Byron Miller. 2001. "Space and Contentious Politics." *Mobilization: An International Journal* 8 (2): 143–56.

Martin, James. 2005. "Identity." In *Cultural Geography: A Critical Dictionary of Ideas*, ed. David Sibley, David Atkinson, Peter Jackson, and Neil Washbourne, 97–102. London: Tauris.

Massey, Doreen. 1995. "Places and Their Past." *History Workshop Journal* 39: 182–92.

———. 2005. *For Space*. London: Sage.

Mather, Anne. 1974. "History of Feminist Periodicals, Part 1." *Journalism History* 1 (3): 82–85.

McClellan, Anita D. 1989. "An 'Unpaid-for Education': A Feminist Labor Organizer in Boston Publishing." *Frontiers* 10 (3): 16–21.

McCoy, Beth A. 2006. "Race and the (Para)Textual Condition." *PMLA* 12 (1): 156–69.

McDermott, Patrice. 1994. *Politics and Scholarship: Feminist Academic Journals and the Production of Knowledge*. Urbana: University of Illinois Press.

McDonald, Peter. 1997. "Implicit Structures and Explicit Interactions: Pierre Bourdieu and the History of the Book." *The Library*, 6th ser., 19 (2): 105–21.

McMillan, John. 2009. "'Our Founder, the Mimeograph Machine': Participatory Democracy in Students for a Democratic Society's Print Culture." *Journal for the Study of Radicalism* 2 (2): 85–110.

Meeker, Martin. 2006. *Contacts Desired: Gay and Lesbian Communications and Community, 1940s–1970s*. Chicago: University of Chicago Press.

Melucci, Alberto. 1989. *Nomads of the Present: Social Movements and Individual Needs in Contemporary Society*. Philadelphia: Temple University Press.

———. 1996. *Challenging Codes: Collective Action in the Information Age*. Cambridge: Cambridge University Press.

———. 2003. "The Process of Collective Identity." In *Social Movement and Culture*, ed. Hank Johnston and Bert Klandermans, 41–63. Minneapolis: University of Minnesota Press.

Merrifield, Andrew. 1993. "Place and Space: A Lefebvrian Reconciliation." *Transactions of the Institute of British Geographers* 18 (4): 516–31.

Meyer, David S. 2002. "Opportunities and Identities: Bridge-Building in the Study of Social Movements." In Meyer, Whittier, and Robnett, *Social Movements*, 3–21.

Meyer, David S., Nancy Whittier, and Belinda Robnett, eds. 2002. *Social Movements: Identity, Culture, and the State*. New York: Oxford University Press.

Mohanty, Chandra Talpade. 1984. "Under Western Eyes: Feminist Scholarship and Colonial Discourses." *Boundary 2* 12 (3)/13 (1): 333–58.

Moraga, Cherríe, and Gloria Anzaldúa. 1983. Introduction to *This Bridge Called My Back*, xxiii–xxvi.

———, eds. 1983. *This Bridge Called My Back: Writings by Radical Women of Color*. 2nd ed. Latham, N.Y.: Kitchen Table, Women of Color Press.

Morgan, Robin. 1970. "Goodbye to All That." *Rat*, February 9–23, 6–7.

———. 1970. "Introduction: The Women's Revolution." In *Sisterhood Is Powerful: An Anthology of Writings from the Women's Liberation Movement*, xiii–xli. New York: Random House.

———. 2001. *Saturday's Child: A Memoir*. New York: Norton.

———, ed. 1984. *Sisterhood Is Global: The International Women's Movement Anthology*. Garden City, N.Y.: Anchor/Doubleday.

Moschkovich, Judit. 1983. "—But I Know You, American Woman." In Moraga and Anzaldúa, *This Bridge Called My Back*, 79–84.

Munro, Ealasaid. 2013. "Feminism: A Fourth Wave?" *Political Insight* 4 (2): 22–25.

Murray, Simone. 2004. *Mixed Media: Feminist Presses and Publishing Politics*. London: Pluto.

Nachescu, Voichita. 2008. "Radical Feminism and the Nation: History and Space in the Political Imagination of Second-Wave Feminism." *Journal for the Study of Radicalism* 3 (1): 29–59.

Newton, Huey P. 2002. "Intercommunalism: February 1971." In *The Huey P. Newton Reader*, ed. David Hilliard and Donald Weise, 181–99. New York: Seven Stories.

Nicholls, Walter. 2009. "Place, Networks, Space: Theorising the Geographies of Social Movements." *Transactions of the Institute of British Geographers* 34 (1): 78–93.

Norman, Brian. 2006. "The Consciousness-Raising Document, Feminist Anthologies, and Black Women in *Sisterhood Is Powerful*." *Frontiers* 27 (3): 38–64.

Ogbar, Jeffrey O. G. 2001. "Yellow Power: The Formation of Asian-American Nationalism in the Age of Black Power, 1966–1975." *Souls: A Critical Journal of Black Politics, Culture, and Society* 3 (3): 29–38.

Ong, Aihwa. 1988. "Colonialism and Modernity: Feminist Re-Presentations of Women in Non-Western Societies." *Inscriptions* 3–4: 79–93.

Onosaka, Junko R. 2006. *Feminist Revolution in Literacy: Women's Bookstores in the United States*. New York: Routledge.

Painter, Nell Irvin. 1994. "Representing Truth: Sojourner Truth's Knowing and Being Known." *Journal of American History* 81 (2): 461–92.

———. 1996. *Sojourner Truth: A Life, a Symbol*. New York: Norton.

Parker, Pat. 1983. "Revolution: It's Not Neat or Pretty or Quick." In Moraga and Anzaldúa, *This Bridge Called My Back*, 238–42.

Pearson, Kyra. 1999. "Mapping Rhetorical Interventions in 'National' Feminist Histories: Second Wave Feminism and *Ain't I a Woman.*" *Communication Studies* 50 (2): 158–73.

Peoples, Whitney A. 2010. "'Under Construction': Identifying Foundations of Hip-Hop Feminism and Exploring Bridges between Black Second Wave and Hip-Hop Feminisms." In Hewitt, *No Permanent Waves*, 403–30.

Petersen, Tasha. 1974. "Gimme Shelter." In *Class and Feminism: A Collection of Essays from THE FURIES*, ed. Charlotte Bunch and Nancy Myron, 24–34. Baltimore: Diana.

Peterson, Carla L. 1995. *"Doers of the Word": African-American Women Speakers and Writers in the North.* New Brunswick, N.J.: Rutgers University Press.

Peterson, Jason. 2009. "A 'Race' for Equality: Print Media Coverage of the 1968 Olympic Protest by Tommie Smith and John Carlos." *American Journalism* 26 (2): 99–121.

Phillips, Ruth, and Viviene E. Cree. 2014. "What Does the 'Fourth Wave' Mean for Teaching Feminism in the Twenty-First Century Social Work?" *Social Work Education* 33 (7): 930–43.

Piepmeier, Alison. 2009. *Girl Zines: Making Media, Doing Feminism.* New York: New York University Press.

Polletta, Francesca. 2002. *Freedom Is an Endless Meeting: Democracy in American Social Movements.* Chicago: University of Chicago Press.

———. 2009. *It Was Like a Fever: Storytelling in Protest and Politics.* Chicago: University of Chicago Press.

Polletta, Francesca, and James Jasper. 2001. "Collective Identity and Social Movements." *Annual Review of Sociology* 27: 283–305.

Pomerleau, Clark. 2013. *Califia Women: Feminist Education against Sexism, Classism, and Racism.* Austin: University of Texas Press.

Popkin, Anne. 1978. "Bread and Roses: An Early Moment in the Development of Socialist Feminism." PhD diss., Brandeis University.

Price, Charles, Donald Nonini, and Erich Fox Tree. 2008. "Grounded Utopian Movements." *Anthropological Quarterly* 81 (1): 127–59.

Reed, T. V. 2005. *The Art of Protest: Culture and Activism from the Civil Rights Movement to the Streets of Seattle.* Minneapolis: University of Minnesota Press.

Reger, Jo. 2002. "More Than One Feminism: Organizational Structure and the Construction of Collective Identity." In Meyer, Whittier, and Robnett, *Social Movements*, 171–84.

———. 2008. "Drawing Identity Boundaries: The Creation of Contemporary Feminism." In *Identity Work in Social Movements*, ed. Jo Reger, Daniel J. Meyers, and Rachel L. Einwohner, 101–20. Minneapolis: University of Minnesota Press.

Rhodes, Jane. 2007. *Framing the Black Panthers: The Spectacular Rise of a Black Power Icon.* New York: Norton, 2007.

Robnett, Belinda. 2002. "External Political Change, Collective Identities, and Participation in Social Movement Organizations." In Meyer, Whittier, and Robnett, *Social Movements*, 266–85.

Rodriguez, Elvia. 2013. "Covering the Chicano Movement: Examining Chicano

Activism through Chicano, American, African American, and Spanish Language Periodicals, 1965–1973." PhD diss., University of California, Riverside.

Rooney, Ellen. 1996. "What's the Story? Feminist Theory, Narrative, Address." *differences: A Journal of Feminist Cultural Studies* 8 (1): 1–30.

Rosen, Ruth. 2000. "When Women Spied on Women." *The Nation*, September 4–11, 19–25.

———. 2000. *The World Split Open: How the Modern Women's Movement Changed America*. New York: Viking.

Rossiter, Ned. 2006. *Organized Networks: Media Theory, Creative Labour, New Institutions*. Rotterdam: NAi.

Roth, Benita. 2004. *Separate Roads to Feminism: Black, Chicana, and White Feminist Movements in America's Second Wave*. Cambridge: Cambridge University Press.

———. 2008. "The Reconstruction of Collective Identity in the Emergence of U.S. White Women's Liberation." In *Identity Work in Social Movements*, ed. Jo Reger, Daniel J. Meyers, and Rachel L. Einwohner, 257–75. Minneapolis: University of Minnesota Press.

Ryan, Barbara. 1992. *Feminism and the Women's Movement: Dynamics of Change in Social Movement Ideology and Activism*. New York: Routledge.

Salper, Roberta. 2008. "U.S. Government Surveillance and the Women's Liberation Movement." *Feminist Studies* 34 (3): 431–55.

Sandoval, Chela. 2001. *Methodology of the Oppressed*. Minneapolis: University of Minnesota Press.

Sandoval, Marisol, and Christian Fuchs. 2010. "Towards a Critical Theory of Alternative Media." *Telematics and Informatics* 27 (2): 141–50.

Santana, Mario. 2000. *Foreigners in the Homeland: The Spanish American New Novel in Spain, 1962–1974*. Cranbury, N.J.: Associated University Presses.

Scott, Joan Wallach. 1988. "Deconstructing Equality-versus-Difference; or, The Uses of Poststructuralist Theory for Feminism." *Feminist Studies* 14 (1): 32–50.

———. 2011. *The Fantasy of Feminist History*. Durham, N.C.: Duke University Press.

Sewall, William H., Jr. 2001. "Space in Contentious Politics." In *Silence and Voice in the Study of Contentious Politics*, ed. Ronald R. Aminzade, Jack A. Goldstone, Doug McAdam, Elizabeth J. Perry, William H. Sewell Jr., Sidney Tarrow, and Charles Tilly, 51–88. Cambridge: Cambridge University Press.

Showden, Carisa R. 2009. "What's Political about New Feminisms?" *Frontiers* 3 (2): 166–98.

Silander, Aaron. 1996. "Emerging Women's Voices: The Story of the Iowa City Women's Press, 1972–1985." Honors thesis, University of Iowa.

Sjoholm, Barbara. 2012. "She Who Owns the Press." In *Make Your Own History: Documenting Feminist and Queer Activism in the Twenty-First Century*, ed. Lyz Bly and Kelly Wooten, 159–68. Los Angeles: Litwin.

Smith, Barbara, and Beverly Smith. 1983. "Across the Kitchen Table: A Sister-to-Sister Dialogue." In Moraga and Anzaldúa, *This Bridge Called My Back*, 113–27.

Snow, David A., and Robert D. Benford. 1988. "Ideology, Frame Resonance, and Participant Mobilization." *International Social Movement Research* 1: 197–218.

Snow, David A., E. Burke Rochford Jr., Steven K. Worden, and Robert D. Benford. 1986. "Frame Alignment Processes, Micromobilization, and Movement Participation." *American Sociological Review* 51 (4): 464–81.

Somers, Margaret R. 1994. "The Narrative Construction of Identity: A Relational and Network Approach." *Theory and Society* 23 (5): 605–49.

Spain, Daphne. 2011. "Women's Rights and Gendered Spaces in 1970s Boston." *Frontiers* 32 (1): 152–78.

———. 2016. *Constructive Feminism: Women's Spaces and Women's Rights in the American City.* Ithaca: Cornell University Press.

Spencer, Stephen. 2011. *Visual Research Methods in the Social Sciences: Awakening Visions.* New York: Routledge.

Springer, Kimberly. 2005. *Living for the Revolution: Black Feminist Organizations, 1968–1980.* Durham, N.C.: Duke University Press.

Staggenborg, Suzanne. 1998. "Social Movement Communities and Cycles of Protest: The Emergence and Maintenance of a Local Women's Movement." *Social Problems* 45 (2): 180–204.

Stephenson-Abetz, Jenna. 2012. "Everyday Activism as a Dialogic Practice: Narratives of Feminist Daughters." *Women's Studies in Communication* 35 (1): 96–117.

Steward, Gary A., Jr., Thomas E. Shriver, and Amy L. Chasteen. 2002. "Participant Narratives and Collective Identity in a Metaphysical Movement." *Sociological Spectrum* 22 (1): 107–35.

Stokes, Ashli Quesinberry. 2005. "Constituting Southern Feminists: Women's Liberation Newsletters in the South." *Southern Communication Journal* 70 (2): 91–108.

Stone, Amy L., and Jaime Cantrell, eds. 2015. *Out of the Closet, into the Archives: Researching Sexual Histories.* Albany: State University of New York Press.

Sturken, Marita, and Lisa Cartwright. 2001. *Practices of Looking: An Introduction to Visual Culture.* Oxford: Oxford University Press.

Sullivan, Elizabeth. n.d. "Carol Seajay, Old Wives Tales, and the Feminist Bookstore Network: Historical Essay," *FoundSF.* http://www.foundsf.org/index.php?title=Carol_Seajay,_Old_Wives_Tales_and_the_Feminist_Bookstore_Network.

Tanselle, G. Thomas. 1998. "The History of the Book as a Field of Study." In *Literature and Artifacts*, 41–55. Charlottesville: Bibliographical Society of the University of Virginia.

Tarrow, Sidney. 1992. "Mentalities, Political Cultures, and Collective Action Frames: Constructing Meanings through Action." In *Frontiers in Social Movement Theory*, ed. Aldon D. Morris and Carol McClurg Mueller, 174–202. New Haven: Yale University Press.

———. 1998. *Power in Movement: Social Movements and Contentious Politics.* 2nd ed. Cambridge: Cambridge University Press.

Taylor, Diana. 2003. *The Archive and the Repertoire: Performing Cultural Memory in the Americas.* Durham, N.C.: Duke University Press.

Taylor, Verta, and Nancy Whittier. 1999. "Collective Identity in Social Movement Communities: Lesbian Feminist Mobilization." In *Waves of Protest: Social Movements since the Sixties*, ed. Jo Freeman and Victoria Johnson, 169–94. Lanham, Md.: Rowman and Littlefield.

Third, Amanda. 2006. "'Shooting from the Hip': Valerie Solanas, SCUM, and the Apoc-
alyptic Politics of Radical Feminism." *Hecate* 32 (2): 104–32.

Thomas, Julie. 2004. *Pictorial Victorians: The Inscription of Values in Word and Image*.
Athens: Ohio University Press.

Tilly, Charles. 1977. "Getting It Together in Burgundy, 1675–1975." *Theory and Society* 4
(4): 479–504.

Townsend-Bell, Erica E. 2012. "Writing the Way to Feminism." *Signs* 38 (1): 127–52.

Travis, Trysh. 2008. "The Women in Print Movement: History and Implications." *Book
History* 11: 275–300.

Trinh T. Minh-ha. 1989. *Woman, Native, Other*. Bloomington: Indiana University
Press.

Uttal, Lynet. 1990. "Nods That Silence." In *Making Face, Making Soul = Haciendo
Caras: Creative and Critical Perspectives by Feminists of Color*, ed. Gloria Anzaldúa,
317–20. San Francisco: Aunt Lute.

Valk, Anne. 2002. "Living a Feminist Lifestyle: The Intersection of Theory and Action
in a Lesbian Feminist Collective." *Feminist Studies* 28 (2): 303–32.

———. 2008. *Radical Sisters: Second-Wave Feminism and Black Liberation in Washington, D.C.* Urbana: University of Illinois Press.

Veron, Eliseo. 1971. "Ideology and Social Sciences: A Communicational Approach."
*Semiotica* 3 (1): 59–76.

Vestergaard, Anne. 2008. "Humanitarian Branding and the Media: The Case of Am-
nesty International." *Journal of Language and Politics* 7 (3): 471–93.

Walker, Rebecca. 1992. "Becoming the Third Wave." *Ms.*, January, 39–41.

———. 1995. "Being Real: An Introduction." In *To Be Real: Telling the Truth and Changing the Face of Feminism*, xxix–xl. New York: Anchor.

Warner, Michael. 2002. "Publics and Counterpublics." *Public Culture* 14 (1): 49–90.

Warrior, Betsy. 1969. "Sex Roles and Their Consequences." *No More Fun and Games*,
February, 21–31.

Watkins, Rychetta. 2012. *Black Power, Yellow Power, and the Making of Revolutionary
Identities*. Jackson: University Press of Mississippi.

Weber, Shirley N. 1981. "Black Power in the 1960s: A Study of Its Impact on Women's
Liberation." *Journal of Black Studies* 11 (4): 483–97.

[Weiser], Barb, and Joan [Pinkvoss]. 1982. "The Invisible Lesbian/Feminist Printer."
*Feminist Bookstores Newsletter* 6 (1): 9–10.

Welch, Georgia Paige. 2015. "'Up against the Wall Miss America': Women's Liberation
and Miss Black America in Atlantic City, 1968." *Feminist Formations* 27 (2): 70–97.

Whittier, Nancy. 1995. "Turning It Over: Personnel Change in the Columbus, Ohio,
Women's Movement, 1969–84." In *Feminist Organizations: Harvest of the New
Women's Movement*, ed. Myra Marx Ferree and Patricia Yancey Martin, 180–98.
Philadelphia: Temple University Press.

———. 1997. "Political Generations, Micro-Cohorts, and the Transformation of Social
Movements." *American Sociological Review* 62 (5): 760–78.

———. 2002. "Meaning and Structure in Social Movements." In Meyer, Whittier, and
Robnett, *Social Movements*, 289–308.

Wiegman, Robyn. 2001. "The Progress of Gender: Whither 'Women'?" In *Women's Studies on Its Own*, 106–40. Durham, N.C.: Duke University Press.

Willis, Ellen. 1992. "Sisters under the Skin? Confronting Race and Sex." In *No More Nice Girls: Countercultural Essays*, 101–16. Middletown, Conn.: Wesleyan University Press.

Wingfoot, Alana. 1998. "Different Generations, Different Issues." *Feminist Ezine*. http://www.feministezine.com/feminist/historical/Third-Wave-Feminism.html.

Withers, Josephine. 1994. "Feminist Performance Art: Performing, Discovering, Transforming Ourselves." In *The Power of Feminist Art: The American Movement of the 1970s, History and Impact*, ed. Norma Broude and Mary D. Garrard, 158–73. New York: Abrams.

Wood, Bronwyn E. 2012. "Crafted within Liminal Spaces: Young People's Everyday Politics." *Political Geography* 31 (6): 337–46.

Wu, Judy Tzu-Chun. 2009. "Journeys for Peace and Liberation: Third World Internationalism and Radical Orientalism during the U.S. War in Vietnam." *Pacific Historical Review* 76 (4): 575–84.

———. 2010. "Rethinking Global Sisterhood: Peace Activism and Women's Orientalism." In Hewitt, *No Permanent Waves*, 193–220.

———. 2013. *Radicals on the Road: Internationalism, Orientalism, and Feminism during the Vietnam Era*. Ithaca: Cornell University Press.

Yamada, Mitsuye. 1983. "Asian Pacific American Women and Feminism." In Moraga and Anzaldúa, *This Bridge Called My Back*, 71–75.

Yanney, Linda J. 1991. "The Practical Revolution: An Oral History of the Iowa City Feminist Community, 1965–1975." PhD diss., University of Iowa.

Young, Stacey. 1997. *Changing the Wor(l)d: Discourse, Politics, and the Feminist Movement*. New York: Routledge.

Zackodnik, Teresa C. 2005. "The 'Green-Backs of Civilization': Sojourner Truth and Portrait Photography." *American Studies* 46 (2): 117–43.

———. 2015. "Memory, Illustration, and Black Periodicals: Recasting the Disappearing Act of the Fugitive Slave in the 'New Negro' Woman." *American Periodicals* 25 (2): 139–59.

Zajicek, Anna M., Allyn Lord, and Lori Holyfield. 2003. "The Emergence and First Years of a Grassroots Women's Movement in Northwest Arkansas, 1970–1980." *Arkansas Historical Quarterly* 62 (2): 153–81.

Zanoni, Amy E. 2013. "'Working on Many Levels': A History of Second Wave Feminism in Baltimore." Master's thesis, University of Maryland, Baltimore County.

Zarnow, Leandra. 2010. "From Sisterhood to Girlie Culture: Closing the Great Divide between Second and Third Wave Cultural Agendas." In Hewitt, *No Permanent Waves*, 273–302.

Zinn, Maxine Baca, and Bonnie Thornton Dill. 1996. "Theorizing Difference from Multiracial Feminism." *Feminist Studies* 22 (2): 321–31.

# INDEX

academic publishing, 150, 151, 179n28

activism: creating space and place for feminism, 55–58; impact of black activism on feminism, 120–22; scales of, 65–66; sisterhood and, 95–96; watershed year, 6–7

Adams, Thomas, 12, 152

affect (emotion): antiracist struggles and, 133; collective identity and, 12–13, 44, 106, 112; economies of emotion, 120; feminism and revolutionary movements, 138–39, 141; fit with environment, 53; meaning and, 5

Ahmed, Sara, 5, 45, 53, 144

*Ain't I a Woman?* (periodical): about, 25–28, 132, 149, 160n50, 160n55; distribution of labor for, 83; editorial practices and identity in, 68, 80–81, 169n67; emergence of, 20; image of Sojourner Truth, 2, 130–31, 132–33; importance of location in, 24–25; production struggles of, 75; publication schedule of, 71; regional focus of, 48, 49. *See also* feminist periodicals; Iowa City, Iowa

"Ain't I a Woman?" (speech by Sojourner Truth): accounts of, 177n60; at International Women's Day, 131; use by *Ain't I a Woman?*, 2, 129, 130, 132

Alarcón, Norma, 100

Aldrich, Ann, 63–64

Aldrich, Michele L., 53, 84

Allen, Martha, 8, 18, 20, 151

*All the Women Are Welcome to Read Their Poetry* (Iowa City Women's Press), 72

Alpert, Jane, 122

alternative and underground publications, 19, 95; New Left media, 17, 18–19

Althusser, Louis, 109, 112

amateur/expert binary, 86, 87, 170n95

amateurism in publishing, 66–67, 69, 72–75. *See also* professionalism

American Indians, 9, 122

Amherst Women's Liberation (AWL), 33–35

*Amherst Women's Liberation Newsletter*. See *Valley Women's Center Newsletter*

An, Mary, 62–63

Anderson, Benedict, 45

"And When You Leave, Take Your Pictures with You" (Carrillo), 99

*Angela Davis: Portrait of a Revolutionary* (film), 118

Anthony, Susan B., 19

antiobscenity ordinances, 77

antiprofessionalism, 76–77, 168n41

antiracist work, 118

antiwar discourse, 125–27, 134–35

Arnold, June, 43–44

Asian American activism, 10, 54, 141

Asian media, 20

Asian Women's Center, 10

*Asian Women's Center Newsletter*, 33, 100

*Asian Women's Journal*, 143

Atkinson, Ti-Grace, 92

authorship, 85–90, 113, 170n93. *See also* editorial practices; feminist periodicals; publication process; *and specific publications*

Aviles, Olga, 134, 141

Bambara, Toni Cade, 10

Barale, Michèle Aina, 64

Barker, Nicolas, 12, 152

*Battle Acts* (periodical), 39, 124, 176n40

Baxandall, Rosalyn, 149

*Beebo Brinker* (Ann Weldy novel), 64

Berkeley, Calif., 41

"Black Feminist Statement, A," 10

*Black Panther*, 20, 142

Black Panthers, 121–22, 139, 141, 142; Davis, Angela, 121, 131; Douglas, Emory, 128; Newton, Huey P., 19

Black Power: clenched fist, 134; media, 20; movement, 121–22; Truth, Sojourner, and, 131, 132, 133. *See also* race and racism; women of color

Blackwell, Maylei, 11, 119

*Black Woman, The* (Bambara), 10

black women, images of, 127–28. *See also* radical Other; Truth, Sojourner

Black Women Organized for Action, 9

Blanchard, Margaret, 79

*Boston Area Socialist Feminist Organization Newsletter*, 39

*Boston Globe*, 88

Boston Women's Health Book Collective, 39

bra burning, 137

Bradley, Patricia, 149

Bread and Roses, 122, 127, 148

*Bread and Roses Newsletter*, 39

*Breaking Ground* (periodical), 145, 178–79n1

Breines, Winifred, 140

Bunch, Charlotte, 8, 24, 68

Bureau for Women (La.), 129

Butler, Judith, 5, 6, 102, 109–10, 174n102

bylines, 73, 113

"cacophony of ideas," 10, 146

Cadman, Eileen, 8, 79

*Camera Obscura* (periodical), 150

captions, 124

Carlos, John, 134

Carrillo, Jo, 99

Cassell, Joan, 44, 61, 98, 138, 149

Cell 16 (feminist group), 38–39, 52–53

Certeau, Michel de, 56, 57, 61

"Certificate of Sisterhood," 134

Chartier, Roger, 12

Chester, Gail, 8, 79

Chicago Women's Graphics Collective, 91, 127

Chicana activism, 11, 122

Chicana/o publications, 10, 20, 33, 97, 143

Chicana Service Action Center, 10, 33, 48

Chicano liberation, 119

children in images, 125, 127, 128

Chrissos, Heidi, 62

civil rights movement, 67, 97–98, 121, 133, 151

Clarke, Cheryl, 10

class bias, 96–97, 98–99, 140. *See also* power and privilege; *and specific publications*

Clement, Carol, 77

clenched fist, 121, 132, 133–34

cohort model of feminism, 151

Colaneri, Marie, 62

collective identity: correlation with structure, 105–6, 173n82; demarcation of boundaries, 92–93; discourse and, 101–7; dynamism of, 64; frame analysis for, 104–5; identity formation, 5–6; identity politics, 123; importance of periodicals to, 67–69, 111–12; politics of inclusion and, 100; race and racism in, 118–19; role of place and space in, 44–45; seriality and repetition in, 61–62; theory of, 12–13. *See also* radical Other; sisterhood; social movement identity

collectivity: editors' shared housing, 27, 160n48; focus of *Ain't I a Woman?*, 27, 160n52; through letters to the editor, 3–4, 87; professionalism and, 29, 85, 160n64; as value and practice, 79–85. *See also* editorial practices; feminism; nonhierarchical structures; publication process; *and specific publications*

Collins, Patricia Hill, 131, 133

*Colored American Magazine*, 141

Combahee River Collective, 10

Comisión Femenil de Los Angeles, 10

communication networks, 7, 20, 84

communications circuit, 12, 70, 77–79, 152

conflicts and exclusion, 52–54

Connecticut River Valley, 46–47

corporate models, 29

corporatization of publishing, 18, 80

Cover, Rob, 52

cover images: clenched fist, 134; context for, 121; revolutionary images, 124, 127–28; self-representation of blacks, 141; sexist, 18, 139; *Sister*'s inaugural issue, 115; Truth, Sojourner, 2, 132, 133; *Valley Women's Center Newsletter*, 46, 64. *See also* images in periodicals

creative works, 50–51

Curthoys, Jean, 149

*Daring to Be Bad* (Echols), 149

Darnton, Robert, 12, 70, 78, 152

Daro, Vinci, 12–13

Darwall, Bobby, 111–12

Davillier, Brenda, 18

Davis, Angela, 121, 131, 141–42

intertextual reading and analysis, 10–11, 65, 72, 76, 120, 143

invisibility of feminist communities, 41–43, 163n9

Iowa City, Iowa, 21, 24–25, 148. See also *Ain't I a Woman?*

Iowa City Women's Liberation Front, 25, 159n45

Iowa City Women's Press, 25; *All the Women Are Welcome to Read Their Poetry*, 72

"I Saw a Woman Sleeping" (Schreiner), 50

Jakobsen, Janet, 114

Jasper, James, 12, 13

Jeannette Rankin Brigade March on Washington, D.C., 6

Jong, Erica, 120

journals, 21–22, 158n24

Kennedy, Elizabeth Lapovsky, 118, 149

King, Mary, 146

Kinser, Amber, 147

KNOW, Inc., 4, 123

labor, distribution of. *See* collectivity; publication process

*Ladder, The*, 131

*Ladies' Home Journal*, 19, 55, 137

"language acts," 102

"languages-of-power," 45

Las Hijas de Cuauhtémoc, 10, 100

last names, 103–4

*L.A. Women's Liberation Newsletter*: about, 30–33, 108; circulation of, 22; distribution problems, 78; emergence of, 20; ideas about leadership, 62–63; on International Women's Day celebration, 55, 58; regional focus of, 48; serial features of, 60–61; takeover of *Los Angeles Free Press*, 17. *See also* feminist periodicals; Los Angeles, Calif.; *Sister*

leadership, 62–63

Lee, Rachel, 135

Lesbian Herstory Archives, 3, 145

lesbian women, 63–64

letters to the editor, 3–4, 13, 41, 87, 107–9, 112

letters to the periodical, 59–60, 78, 95, 103

liberal/radical binary, 105

Liberation News Service (LNS), 123, 125, 135

*Liberator, The* (newspaper), 19

Liebling, A. J., 25

*Lilith* (periodical), 7

Lindsey, Karen, 59, 60

linguistic conventions, breaking from, 103–4

location: importance of, 23–25; transformation of, 48–49

Longeaux y Vasquez, Enriqueta, 98, 143

Longhurst, Robyn, 44

Lorde, Audre, 86, 133

Los Angeles, Calif., 21, 33, 54–55, 148. See also *L.A. Women's Liberation Newsletter*

*Los Angeles Free Press* women's issue (1971), 17

Los Angeles Women's Liberation Movement, 149

*Los Angeles Women's Newsletter*, 127–28

Louisiana Head and Master Laws, 161n67

Loyola University, 29–30

Lugones, María, 99–100

Luscomb, Florence, 88

mainstream media: Black Panthers' use of, 142; corporatization of, 18–19, 80; mastheads, 72; *Ms.* magazine and, 22; obstacles to publishing in, 25, 77, 86; representations of feminism, 42–43, 120, 136–39, 144; representations of gender and race, 140

*Making Face, Making Soul = Haciendo Caras* (Gloria Anzaldúa, ed.), 100

Male Chauvinist of the Month Award, 19

maps of women's liberation movement, 43, 46–48, 64

marches and demonstrations, 7, 18, 54–55, 58

marginalized populations, 63–64

Martin, James, 44

Martínez, Elizabeth Sutherland, 10

Mary of Brookline (Mass.), 58–60

mastheads, 72–75

McDermott, Mary, 59, 60

McDonald, Peter, 152

McMillan, John, 20

media industry in the 1960s and 1970s, 18–19

Meeker, Martin, 63–64

Melucci, Alberto, 12, 13

methodologies used. *See under* feminist periodicals

middle-class bias. *See* class bias

power and privilege, 11–12, 99, 116, 117–18. *See also* class bias

predictability, 58–64

premodern/modern binary, 126

Presidential Commission on the Status of Women (1961), 146

print culture: collective identity and, 45; constructing history through, 15; as evidence of U.S. feminism, 3–4, 51, 147–53

printing, constraints on, 136, 156n33

professionalism, 73–74, 76–77, 85, 158n24; amateurism in publishing, 66–67, 69, 72–75; antiprofessionalism, 76–77, 168n41

proper: space, 56, 57, 58, 60, 61, 148; text, 69, 120

*Psychology of Women Quarterly*, 150

publication process, 65–90; authorship, 85–90; description of, 69–70; distribution, 77–79; editorial reflections on, 70–71; feminist publications compared with mainstream publications, 72–73, 76–77; inconsistencies and typographical errors, 66–67, 70, 75, 157n48; juxtaposed with politics, 65–66; mastheads, 72–75; obstacles in, 83–84; paratextual disruptions, 75; participation in, 80–83; as reflection of feminist values, 67–69, 72–73, 76, 90; reprinting as practice, 4, 51, 95, 116, 136, 143; resistance to mainstream practices, 80; reuse of articles and images, 135–36; for scholarly journals, 150; structurelessness in, 84–85; volunteer labor in, 71–72, 80. *See also* authorship; collectivity; distribution process; editorial practices; feminist periodicals; nonhierarchical structures; *and specific publications*

publishers and presses: access to, 136, 159n28; examples of, 9, 24, 25, 29, 72; hiring practices, 68; Mother Jones Press, 81–82; New England Free Press, 39, 122, 123; radical, 80

publishing technologies, 8, 20, 67, 136. *See also* mimeograph machines

race and racism, 15, 96, 98–99, 114, 117–19. *See also* revolutionary feminism; *and specific publications*

racialization of feminism, 120–22

radical feminism, 9–10, 119–20, 145, 149

radical orientalism, 123

radical Other: images of, 123–29; U.S. feminism and, 134–35, 138, 140; Vietnamese women, 125–26; women of color and, 122–23. *See also Ain't I a Woman?*; collective identity; Indochinese women; transnational coverage in periodicals; Truth, Sojourner

radical whiteness, 122

radio and television, 46, 164n31

*Ramparts* (magazine), 19

*Rat* (newspaper), 17–18, 139

reader assistance: calls for, 71–72, 80, 82, 111, 159n33; calls for writers, 85, 170n93

reader/writer binary, 86, 87

Red Guards, 141

Reed, T. V., 67

Reger, Jo, 105

repetition: collectivity and sisterhood, 79, 80, 106, 114; identity formation and, 5–6, 14, 67; seriality and, 62, 66; solidification and limitation of meanings through, 119, 122, 131, 141, 143–44

reprinting. *See under* publication process

reproductive health, 9, 50, 58–60, 62, 116; Emma Goldman Clinic for Women, 25, 26; Feminist Women's Health Center, 18, 33, 161n74; *Our Bodies, Ourselves*, 39. *See also* self-help health movement

resistance and tactics, 57–58, 148

*Revolution, The* (Anthony), 19

revolutionary feminism, 115–44; as movement, 136–40; portrayals of revolutionary women, 123–36; semiotics of revolution, 140–44; women of color, 115–23. *See also* feminism; feminist periodicals; race and racism; *and specific publications*

Rhodes, Jane, 141

Robins, Joan, 33, 161n71

Robinson, Nancy, 33

Robnett, Belinda, 105

*Rolling Our Own* (Cadman, Chester, and Pivot), 8, 79

Rosen, Ruth, 137

Rosezelle, Pat Alake, 99

Roth, Benita, 44

Ryan, Barbara, 148

Sanders, Robin, 87

Sanger, Margaret, 19

Since 1970: Histories of Contemporary America